£3.50

THE LEICA BOOK

Theo Kisselbach

THE LEICA BOOK

English Translation:

F. Bradley, A. I. I. P., A. R. P. S.

Second Edition

HEERING-VERLAG
SEEBRUCK AM CHIEMSEE
1971

Title of the Original German Edition:

DAS LEICA-BUCH

Printed in Germany
© by Heering-Verlag GmbH, Seebruck am Chiemsee (Western Germany) 1971. Only authorised
translation. All rights including that of reproduction in whole or in part expressly reserved.
Printed by Wilh. Friedr. Mayr, Buchdruckerei, Miesbach/Obb.
ISBN 3 7763 2550 X

Only a beginning

Our world contracts day by day. Journeys between continents which used to take weeks only a century ago are today accomplished within a matter of hours. Science and technology advance in giant strides.

Nature's rhythm of the changing season, man's cycle of life and death remain the same.

The Leica is a universal chronicler and eyewitness. It records a mother's joy, the laughter of children, the life of animals and plants. It accompanies teachers and doctors, scientists and explorers wherever they go. It penetrates to the bottom of the sea and ascends the icy peaks of towering mountains. The Leica has become a part of modern life.

For thirty years, twenty-five as a member of the firm of Ernst Leitz, I have been privileged to watch this superb camera develop into what it is to-day. Leica photographers from the four corners of the globe tell me of their experiences. Often I have been able to give them help and advice.

This book initiates the beginner into the use of his Leica. To the advanced worker it offers valuable hints on the possibilities of the Leica system. Last, but not least, it is meant to be an encyclopaedia for all Leica enthusiasts. Those keen on processing their own material to the final enlargement will find useful advice for their darkroom work. The photographs in the text are intended as a guide and inspiration to better work.

At first an early end was predicted for 35 mm photography. The exact opposite has happened. Not only was the Leica perfected step by step, its uses, too, have expanded in a totally unexpected way. The film manufacturers meet the demands of Leica photography by a stream of steadily improved products. The Leica System is firmly established on decades of sound experience, absolute reliability, and continuing technical progress.

CONTENTS

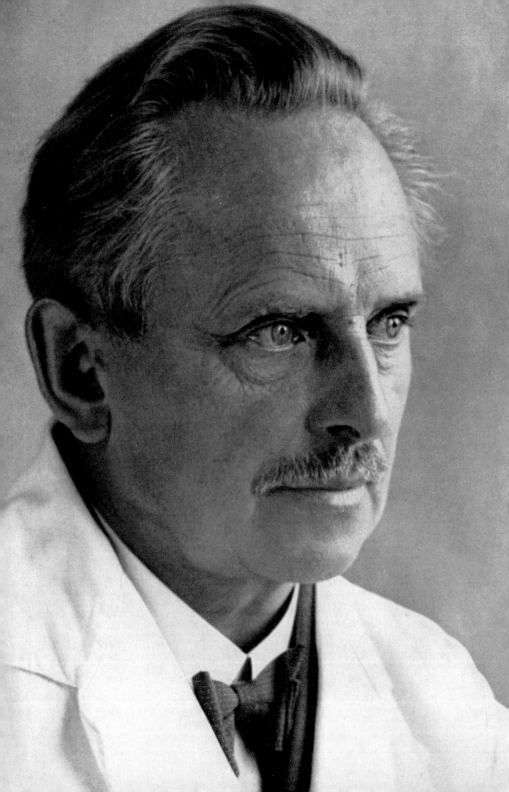

THE HISTORY OF THE LEICA

Oskar Barnack, to whom we owe the design of the Leica, had already been an enthusiastic amateur photographer in his younger years. He had observed, and confirmed mathematically, that only large-format pictures can have a plastic, natural, and life-like effect; they must be of sufficient size to be viewed from a distance at which the perspective is correct. Barnack would of course have liked best a camera of a format even larger than 18×24cm (10×8″). But even his 13×18cm (5×7″) "travelling camera" proved too much for him on his rambles in the Thuringian Forest, particularly since he had to carry the additional weight of 6 heavy double darkslides (for only 12 exposures) and a wooden tripod. "Something ought to be done about this" thought Barnack and tried to take 15 tiny pictures in rows on a single 13×18cm plate with the aid of a special contraption; but he found this a most tedious business. The enlargements did not satisfy him because of the coarse grain of the plate emulsion. Nevertheless, even then – in 1905 – Barnack had already conceived the basic idea of "small negative – large picture".

A few years later, in 1912, Barnack, who had by then become a master mechanic with Leitz, designed a cine camera; as an accessory for his exposure tests he built, as a mere by-product, as it were, a small camera for cine films. The fine grain of this type of film made him take up his earlier ideas again. Indeed an enlargement to postcard size was already quite presentable. After all, the camera format, i.e. the 18×24mm cine format, was very small. The length of his picture, however, was practically unrestricted. Barnack therefore combined two cine-frames into a single frame, which became the classical 24×36mm Leica size. It was as simple as that.

The cine film offered a number of advantages: it was readily available in large quantities at standard dimensions all over the world for the film industry; its perforations facilitated the exact film transport and ensured the plane position of the film in the picture gate.

But this work on the *prototype Leica* – the name "LEICA" of course did not yet exist then – was at that stage no more than a private hobby of Barnack's, whose duties did not include the design of a miniature camera. After all, Messrs. LEITZ were manufacturers of microscopes and optical precision instruments. This, of course, turned out to be a lucky coincidence, for Barnack was only too well aware that only the greatest possible precision in manufacture could ensure the success of his camera and of his principle "small negative – large picture" – if it ever came to be realized. Precision, however, has been writ large at LEITZ

Oskar Barnack, self-portrait with the 135 mm Hektor

Oskar Barnack at Bad Ems in 1913, with the cine-camera he constructed.

from the very beginning as the central feature on which their whole production programme is based.

Even then Barnack took many photographs with his private miniature camera which are still remarkable today. However, the outbreak of the 1914/18 War halted further progress in the design. Not until 1924 when an expansion of the production programme was considered did the question arise whether the risk of producing such an unconventional miniature camera should be taken. Barnack had developed his experimental model almost to the production stage. Prominent experts were discouraging; but at a memorable meeting Dr. Ernst Leitz decided to take the plunge: "Barnack's miniature camera will be built". It was given the name of "LEICA" (LEItz-CAmera).

At its very first appearance at the 1925 Leipzig Fair it caused a stir. The experience of the Leitz Works in the manufacture of microscopes benefited the Leica, which combined rigidity and handiness with the highest precision. Amateur photographers were the first to appreciate the potentialities of an integration of film

One of the early prototype Leica shots by Oskar Barnack, showing the "Eisenmarkt" at Wetzlar, the home of the Leica.

size, focal length, depth of field and instant readiness in a single camera; they obtained astonishing results. It was the beginning of a new kind of photographic vision and of photography altogether.

Old hands know the significance of this. And we ourselves cannot fail to recognize the pioneering achievement of the Leica when we browse in old volumes of photographic journals; they show us a world which seems strange to us today. What did people photograph in those days? Landscapes, genres, and still lives – beautiful photographs certainly, which we still enjoy looking at. But the human element, life itself, was lacking. The only form in which it appeared was that of "artistic" portraits or of stiff groups – people dressed up in their Sunday best rigidly posing before the camera.

The stage was now set for the debut of the handy and instantly ready LEICA! Many photo-fans realized at once the possibilities of a completely new photographic approach opened up by this revolutionary design. The Leica enabled them to capture life, action, quickly, unnoticed, and from the most surprising

Taken with the prototype Leica in 1917. Oskar Barnack on holiday with Ernst Leitz, the founder of the firm, in the Black Forest.

angles. Leica photographs revealed people as they really were instead of showing them in their conventional, assumed poses. Thousands of amateurs were delighted with the new and inexhaustible possibilities of effortlessly recording with their Leica whatever attracted their eye.

This immediate success of the Leica is not quite so easily explained as it would appear to us today. Before the First World War, cine films were relatively slow, and their grain sufficiently fine. The call of the film industry for higher speed brought faster, but also grainier films on the market. As a result, the situation was entirely changed when the LEICA first appeared. Only one emulsion was available which enabled it to prove its worth: a special aerial film made by Perutz. Its grain was fine and its contrast high, two properties which are essential to aerial photography. Good enlargements could be obtained from these negatives only after expert film development. This explains many a criticism heard in the early days. Nowadays many manufacturers produce high-quality films; top-class results are therefore within any Leica-owner's reach today.

The LEITZ designers meanwhile were busy improving the LEICA further and further. Prof. Max Berek, who had computed the classical standard 50 mm Elmar f/3.5 lens, was also generally responsible for the production of interchangeable lenses of various focal lengths and apertures. The LEICA was the first camera to be fitted with a coupled rangefinder for interchangeable lenses. The focal-plane shutter was developed to include slow speeds and covered exposure times from 1 to $^1/_{1000}$ sec.

The ice was broken, the success of the Leica assured. Press photographers began to realize the new possibilities, and the new, live-action style of pictorial journalism rapidly gained ground among them. Explorers and scientists worked with the LEICA, which soon took on the role of an "optical diary" on expeditions and research projects of all kinds. It became an indispensable recording tool for scientific establishments. Engineers, technologists, doctors, architects, all enjoyed the advantages derived from its compactness and precision.

The development proceeded from the simple LEICA to the Leica system with interchangeable lenses and accessories. These prepared the ground for progressively improved results in all photographic fields.

*Oskar Barnack's
prototype Leica.*

HOW A PICTURE IS BORN

This chapter contains a brief survey of the basic processes of producing a black-and-white photograph. It is intended for the benefit of the beginner – if you are an experienced Old Hand you may safely ignore it.

The optical part

Light is the first requirement if we want to "draw with light", i.e. to take a photograph. In a completely blacked-out room we see nothing at all, the darkness is absolute, and a person standing a few feet in front of us is simply invisible. Only after we have opened a door or a window will light reach him. Part of it is "swallowed up", absorbed (particularly by dark or black surfaces), but the rest is more or less "thrown back" (above all by bright, white surfaces) and reflected in all directions. Thus a large number of light rays enter our eyes, and the tiny eyelens projects them onto the light-sensitive back wall of our eye, where they produce an image of the object we see.

The design of a camera resembles that of the eye. In its simplest form the camera consists of a light-tight box with a collecting lens in its front panel. This lens projects the image of a portion of the scene in front of it onto the back of the camera. An image produced by a single-element lens is not very satisfactory. It may be acceptable in the centre, but towards the margins it will become gradually more unsharp and distorted. In order to eliminate these effects the single collecting lens has been replaced by several lens elements of different curvature and glass types, which together make up a lens system known simply as the camera lens. This camera lens retains the basic property of the collecting lens of *collecting* the light rays and of using them to form an image.

Demonstration of optical principles with a spider's web. All the photographer wanted to do was to take a picture of a spider's web hung with dewdrops. When she looked at the finished print through a magnifying glass she saw that a minute image of her helper who had held the background carton for her appeared upside-down on the dewdrops. On the following day she repeated the photograph of the spider's web, but this time only a small section of it at close range. Here you see the result. Each dewdrop demonstrates the property of a lens. The focal lengths differ with the diameters. The focal length determines the size of each "portrait".

Photograph Ingrid Leitz

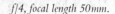

f/2, focal length 50mm. *f/4, focal length 50mm.*

The diagrams show the relationships between lens diameters and focal lengths (as multiples of a given lens aperture), and their individual images.

The photographs were obtained with lenses of the stated focal length and lens aperture or lens stop. The longer the focal length the larger the reproduction scale; stopping down increases the depth of field.

f/4, focal length 100mm. *The lens stop has been closed to f/8.*

The focal length

With a camera lens, as with a burning glass, we can form such a sharp image of the sun on a piece of paper that the concentrated rays set the paper alight. The distance between the lens and the paper at which this happens is called the *focal length of the lens*. It corresponds with the setting of the lens at which all objects at an infinite distance are in sharp focus. The size of a given image increases with the focal length of the lens. Obviously the image size also depends on the distance of the object from the camera. When the object distance is very large compared with the focal length of the lens it is called "infinity".

The focal length of a lens is engraved on its front mount behind the letter "f" (Latin = focus); it is stated in cm. For objects at distances shorter than infinity the distance between the lens and the film plane must be longer than its focal length. The lens must be *focused* on the correct distance. The closer the object distance, the longer this camera "extension".

The lens speed

The speed of a lens depends on the relationship between its diameter and its focal length.
The data engraved on the front mount of a lens refer to a lens aperture = 1. At a lens speed of 1:4 (f/4 in Anglo–American usage) the focal length is 4 times the free diameter of the lens at full aperture.

The lens stop

The lens aperture can be reduced by means of a built-in iris diaphragm; this decreases the speed of the lens; correspondingly, the image it forms on the film will be less bright, and a slower shutter speed must be used to allow for this.

To simplify matters only the denominator of the fraction is engraved on the lens mount; 8, for instance, really should be f/8. For practical reasons the stop values have been chosen so that each succeeding stop number represents half the speed of its predecessor, i.e. for a given exposure it requires half its shutter speed. The international aperture scale generally accepted today reads as follows: –

$$1 - 1.4 - 2 - 2.8 - 4 - 5.6 - 8 - 11 - 16 - 22 - 32$$

The depth of field

Strictly speaking a sharp image will be formed only of those objects situated at the distance on which the lens had been focused. Images of objects in front of or behind the "focusing plane" will be unsharp. Every photographic picture has, however, a certain "depth of field"; this means that the transition from critical sharpness to unsharpness will remain unnoticed within a certain range in front of and behind the focusing distance. This sharp zone decreases with the distance on which the lens is focused. Furthermore, the depth of field also depends on the lens stop. The smaller the stop, the larger the depth of field zone, so that small stops make it possible to obtain a sharp picture of objects at greatly varying distances on the same negative (fore- and background); with large stops, on the other hand, the distant background of near objects will be so blurred that it will cease to be a pictorially important feature.

The shutter

A shutter is necessary for the correct exposure of the highly sensitive film emulsion. In the earlier days, when lens speeds and film speeds were still slow, the lens cap was quite adequate for this purpose; it was simply removed from the lens by hand for the duration of the exposure. But as both photographic materials and lenses were progressively improved, exposure times became shorter and shorter, calling for shutters of great precision permitting high speeds – today speeds of $1/1000$ sec are quite common! Very high shutter speeds are necessary for the photography of fast-moving objects which would become blurred *("movement")* with slower shutter speeds. The design of the shutter depends on that of the camera: we distinguish between "between-lens" shutters built into the lens itself, and focal-plane shutters (Leica) where a slit moving across the film at a close distance exposes each portion of the picture for the correct time. This time can be adjusted mechanically.

Obviously, the exposure time required for a picture to have all the necessary detail depends on the brightness of the subject, the speed of the film and, last but not least, on the chosen lens stop. But since this, as we have already mentioned, also decisively affects the depth of field, the photographer is constantly faced with the choice between a considerable depth of field based on a small stop and a slow shutter speed, and the highest possible shutter speed, e.g. for quickly moving objects, when he will have to sacrifice some depth of field (hence critical focusing) by using a large stop.

Explanation of depth of field

These photographs of a little model will quickly explain the principle to you. In the first exposure (a) the lens, at full aperture, was focused on the house in the background. Sharpness decreases progressively towards the foreground; the dog is completely blurred. We now go to the other extreme, and focus on the dog. As picture (b) shows, sharpness disappears even more quickly towards the background; in neither case was the man pictured sharply.

a

b

In picture (c) we focused exactly on the obliging gentleman, still holding his pose, in the middle distance. The unsharpness of fore- and background is considerably reduced, but we are not yet satisfied. Leaving the focusing undisturbed, we stop the lens down and, lo and behold, we have succeeded at the fourth attempt to get the whole distance from the dog in the foreground to the house in the background sharp.

c

You may ask: "Would not less stopping down have been enough if we had focused on the traffic sign roughly half-ways between fore- and background?" The question shows that you have been thinking. However: At normal distances we obtain the best depth of field if we focus on the front third instead of the middle of the scene.

d

The chemical part

We use our lens to form an image of our object. We now must convert this image into a permanent picture on a film by chemical means.

Light is the active factor in our camera. We therefore require a substance which is altered under the influence of light (such substances are by no means rare. Wallpaper and curtains fade in the light, and our skin acquires a tan in strong sunlight). Our light-sensitive material, however, must react far more quickly, otherwise we would need exposure times lasting for hours.

Such a substance has been found in compounds of silver bromide. They form minute crystals which are mixed with a gelatine solution. Further treatment produces the various properties in the emulsion which are essential to the photographic purpose. The emulsion is coated on strips of celluloid, which are cut to film size.

The light-sensitive emulsion is "exposed" in our camera, although at first the picture is still invisible. The light has affected the silver bromide compound only physically. Where much of it entered the emulsion, many silver bromide crystals have become "activated"; where little light reached it, the effect has been only partial. No changes take place below the "threshold value". A certain minimum quantity of light is therefore required in order to produce a developable change.

Encounter across the fence. Such a simple picture has appeal, although why this should be so is not easy to explain. Is it the trust, tempered with a little timidity of the tiny adventurer? Is it the friendliness of the horse? The contrast between the sizes? The shy movement of the child, betrayed by the slight unsharpness of his left leg? – It is simply the unaffectedness of the live action recorded by an instantaneous exposure. It is this kind of action photography which makes the Leica so useful to us.   Photograph by Theo M. Scheerer

Portrait of a cat, negative

Developing – printing – enlarging

By immersing the film in a suitable chemical solution, the "developer", we separate the silver bromide *affected by the light* into bromine and metallic silver. Portions so affected appear black (silver) when viewed against the light; the bromine is absorbed by the developer. The unexposed silver bromide must be removed in the fixing bath following the developer. The photographic negative is ready! Holding up the film against the light we now see that the "tone values", i.e. the black-and-white values on the developed and fixed film, are exactly opposed to reality; we have obtained a "negative". After fixing, the film is washed and dried, when the picture will be permanent.

In order to produce a "true" positive picture we have to copy the negative by placing the film on a light-sensitive paper and exposing the latter through it.

24

Portrait of a cat, positive   *135 mm Hektor, flash photograph by Edi Sührer.*

Little light can pass through the dark (dense) portions of the negative; much through the light portions. After the exposure, the photographic paper, too, is developed, and a picture results whose black-and-white graduation is the opposite of that of the negative – i.e. it corresponds to reality (positive). Instead of "contact-printing" the film by placing it on a piece of photographic paper, we can "project" the negative film picture onto a larger sheet of bromide paper by means of an enlarger; this process is called *enlarging* (or projection printing).

The positive paper picture is the final photograph. Since the advent of colour photography we call it a black-and-white, or monochrome, photograph. Indeed it "translates" the actual colours into a black-grey-white scale. It is a pencil drawing rather than a painting from nature.

THE ADVANTAGES AND FACILITIES OF THE LEICA

The little Leica greatly simplifies the business of taking photographs. It relieves you of all the technical problems. Its operation is learned easily and quickly. A number of functions are coupled, ensuring rapid and reliable action. Winding the shutter also transports the film; and as the distance is measured during range-finding the lens is focused. After a few movements the Leica is ready for action. The viewfinder shows the object in direct vision; this allows the taking even of fast events in the correct field and at just the right moment – always! Easy to handle, quick to act, the LEICA is your perfect companion to record Life itself.

Poor light – no problem

The Leica format is ideal for the combined use of ultra-fast lenses and ultra-fast films. Larger formats are at a disadvantage here because of reduced film planeness and their shallow depth of field with large lens apertures.

A fast lens makes you independent of the existing illumination. You can freely take your photographs even in comparatively poor lighting conditions. Indeed, the light of a candle may be enough for recording the expression of a mood; it is much simpler than it is generally thought to be. Ultra-fast film – full aperture – accurate focusing, that is all. The decisive factor is to capture the natural atmosphere; flash light often drowns the existing normal illumination, which unfortunately changes the mood of the picture, too.

Free from "material cares"

A Leica cassette takes 36 exposures. Its weight is negligible and the film so cheap that you need have no inhibitions when you go into action. It does not matter if you choose two or three different exposure times for an important subject. When you take children at play you can make a whole series of pictures, choosing the best afterwards. How many trial exposures can we afford in order to explore the various forms of photographic representation? It will certainly not be the cost of the material that would discourage such studies. If the conventional cartridge seems too expensive, we can always fall back on the cheaper bulk film. A great deal of practice is necessary, for instance, when you photograph moving objects, to acquire the delicate flair for pressing the button at just the right moment!

All Souls' Night, Janitzio, Mexico, 50 mm Summicron f/2, $^1/_8$ sec.

Photograph by Ludwig Friedel

You cannot learn to drive a car merely by studying a textbook; you must sit behind the steering wheel; in photography, too, practical experience is the only way to improve your exposure technique. In time all manipulations will become instinctive, enabling you to concentrate completely on the picture.

No other format offers such a large selection of films of the most varied properties. A wide range from the ultra-fast film made for special scientific purposes to the document-copying film of maximum resolving power is available both in black and white and in colour.

Free choice of camera viewpoint

The interchangeability of the Leica lenses makes you completely free to choose your camera viewpoint. Furthermore, the various focal lengths reproduce a given object at various scales. This allows distant objects to be taken at sufficient size as through a field glass and to obtain pictorial effects which would be *impossible* even from a closer viewpoint.

Variation of the focal length also affords any desired change in the ratio between the fore- and background of a picture. Let us look closely at the two pictures on p.29. Strictly speaking the pictorial contents are identical. But the change in the pictorial treatment brought about by a change in both focal length and camera viewpoint is truly remarkable! This gives you the opportunity of influencing the general composition of your picture at will. The short focal length reduces the significance of the background opposite the object proper. Longer focal lengths on the other hand make the far distance a prominent feature of the subject. This freedom of choice of camera viewpoint is one of the most important advantages of the Leica system.

You must, however, not lose sight of the fact that the Leica is an instrument; it is a precious tool, not a robot. It would be wrong to say that it creates something of its own account. It merely provides the facilities. You must treat it with loving care. In the beginning it may prove a little awkward; but soon the relationship will become one of genuine affection. Perseverance will bring its own rewards. The simple motions of handling it will quickly become second nature to you. Your eye will find it easier from day to day to "see photographically". With every film your confidence will increase, results will become more reliable from exposure to exposure.

Gondolas in contre jour. 35 mm Summicron, f/11, $^1/_{250}$ sec.   *Photograph by Siegfried Hartig*

THE LEICA-M-SERIES

Leica Models with bayonet mount for the interchangeable lenses

The versatility of the *Leica System*, the vast choice of films, the large number of interchangeable lenses, the extensive range of accessories might lead the beginner to believe that photography with the Leica is difficult. Far from it. A simple Leica with a standard 50 mm lens represents a handy, first-class camera equal to many tasks even without accessories.

This basis can be extended at any time and according to inclination to cover the most varied special fields. It is this possibility of expansion and refinement of his photographic achievements which is of decisive importance to the discriminating and ambitious Leica enthusiast. Famous masters have been working with the Leica for years and owe their striking pictures to the adaptability and universality of the system. The characteristic features distinguishing the Leica M models from the older Leica models are mainly the measuring viewfinder, and the bayonet mount for the interchangeable lenses, which has replaced the earlier screw thread.

Over 800,000 of the "classical" screw-thread Leica models have gone out into the four corners of the globe. Robust in design, reliable in action, these Leicas will give good service for many years to come. You will find hints for their operation and a description of their accessories in the appendix.

The basic ideas underlying the Leica design have not changed – they have stood the rigid tests of 40 years' practice. Neither the negative nor the final enlargement indicates the model in which the exposure was made.

However, modern technological development never stands still, new knowledge leads to the improvement and simplification of existing features and products. The Leica-M models are no exception. The practical value and reliability in action of alterations and improvements have been tested during years of trials. The introduction of the Leica M4 gave a fresh impetus to the Leica system. This leading model satisfies the most exacting demands and is unsurpassed in action-readiness, simplicity of film loading, and quiet shutter function.

The main difference between the M4 and the earlier M3 and M2 models of the Leica consists in film loading and rewinding. The measuring viewfinder of the Leica M3, too, is different; it forms an almost same-size image, but has no field frame for 35 mm lenses. The Leica M1 has a viewfinder for 50 mm and

35 mm lenses with automatic parallax compensation, but no rangefinder. The model MD corresponds to model M1, but has no viewfinder. Both these models have been discontinued. The viewfinder of the Leica M2 is almost identical with that of the M4, but has no frame for the 135 mm focal length. In the following description the Leica M4 is given preference. The differences of the earlier models will be specially dealt with at the end of the various sections.

1 Automatic film counter

2 Release button

3 Rapid winding lever

4 Lever for unblocking the rewinding mechanism

5 Self-timer (delayed-action mechanism)

6 Shutter speed dial

7 Rangefinder window

8 Locking button for interchangeable lenses

9 Raised red dot on the interchangeable-lens mount

10 Accessory shoe

11 Depth-of-field scale

12 Focusing lever

13 Distance scale

14 Aperture scale

15 Field frame illuminating window

16 Field-of-view selector lever

17 Viewfinder window

18 Rewind crank handle

19 Eyelets for neckstrap

20 Viewfinder eyelens

21 Baseplate locking toggle

22 Electronic-flash contact bush

23 Flashbulb contact bush

24 Film type indicator

25 $^1/_4''$ tripod bush

Holding the Leica

How the Leica is held has a decisive influence on picture sharpness. A great many exposures are blurred if the camera is held carelessly. Normally it is the right eye which looks through the viewfinder. But by all means use your left eye if you can see better with it. Grip the Leica firmly, without applying pressure, with both hands. The rounded ends of the baseplate should rest in your palms during horizontal exposures. If possible place both hands against your head so that the Leica is supported by it. Move the eye close to the viewfinder, perhaps a little obliquely, yet looking through its centre. It is most important that the index finger of the right hand should move smoothly and steadily; the shutter should be released softly and with the right sense of touch, jerks must be avoided.

The shutter will be triggered before the button has been completely depressed.

Two positions are possible for vertical exposures: Grip the Leica so that the tip of your right thumb rests on the release button. At the moment of release press, as when gripping the camera, the thumb against one and the index or middle finger against the other side. Here, too, a particularly steady release

Wrong   *Right*

is possible if you prop the palms against the head. In the second position the index finger is used for pressing the button, as for horizontal pictures. This method is recommended if you see better with your left eye, as it enables you to place your right hand firmly against your forehead.

Please pay close attention to holding your camera and pressing the release button correctly, especially in the beginning. With the Leica held correctly, exposures of up to $1/_{15}$ sec without camera shake are not difficult; with a jerky release action this fault may occur even at $1/_{125}$ sec.

When your camera is in its ever-ready case, hold the flap back for upright pictures, to prevent it from partly blocking the lens.

A steady grip on the camera is particularly important with hand-held shots through lenses of long focal lengths such as 135 mm or 200 mm. Matters will be helped greatly on such occasions if you can support the lens hood on, or brace it against, some object; the Leica will be held more steadily, and there is less danger of camera shake than with a flimsy tripod.

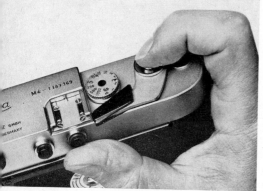

Pull the film transport lever to the right as far as possible. This transports the film and winds the shutter.

Depressing the *release button* actuates the shutter. A locking device prevents the release unless the shutter is wound fully. During the release the thumb should be removed from the film transport lever.

The *shutter speed dial* is set by turning it; it engages when the set speed faces the little index line. The speed dial does not rotate while the shutter is released.

The engraved number 1 indicates 1 sec, all the other numbers represent fractions of seconds. Intermediate speeds can be set between $^1/_{60}$ and $^1/_{1000}$ sec. In the "B" position the shutter remains open as long as the release button is depressed.

A *cable release* (with clamping screw) is used for time exposures. It has a standard thread and is screwed into the release button.

The *self-timer* is wound by means of a lever. It works with all shutter speeds from 1–$^1/_{1000}$ sec. When the lever is wound through 180° the shutter action is delayed for 10 seconds; and for 5 seconds when it is wound through 90°.

To release the delayed-action mechanism the small button above the self-timer instead of the shutter release button is pressed. Naturally, the shutter must first be wound.

38

Changing the lenses

The collapsible lenses are ready for action only after the barrel has been pulled out as far as possible and locked in position by a right turn. To exchange a lens the camera is gripped with the left hand; the thumb depresses the bayonet locking button. The right hand grasps the lens by the focusing ring, giving it a short turn to the left; it is now unlocked and can be easily removed.

Before the other lens is attached the red dots on lens mount and bayonet locking button must face each other. After a short turn to the right the lens will be heard to engage in the bayonet mount. A closed steel ring below the bayonet ensures both smooth locking action and a reliable fit. Do not change your lenses in direct, strong light, but in your own shadow.

39

Handling the lens

Looking at a Leica lens, e.g. the 50mm Summicron, you will find the following data engraved on its mount ring:

Summicron   (name of lens)

f = 50mm   (abbreviation for "focal length")

1:2   (abbreviation for the maximum lens aperture)

2 - 2.8 - 4 - 5.6 - 8 - 11 - 16 (possible stop values; international scale)

A knurled ring is rotated to obtain the desired stop value. The stop number indicates the ratio of the aperture diameter and the focal length of the lens. At each number – with some lenses also halfways between two numbers – the aperture ring engages with a click. The aperture scale has been calculated so that each succeeding stop number requires double the exposure time – half the shutter speed – as you stop down, $1/_{250}$ sec at f/4, for instance, becomes $1/_{125}$ sec at f/5.6.

The 50mm Elmar lenses as well as the first version of the 50mm Summicron have a collapsible mount. For use the lens is pulled out by the front ring as far as possible and locked by a right turn as far as it will go.

A number of lenses have an infinity lock. When the catch is depressed the focusing mount can be adjusted from infinity to 1m (40in). Rotation of the focusing lever also operates the rangefinder, with which the lever is coupled. The lens will produce maximum sharpness at the distance set on the mount. The transition to unsharpness towards the front and the rear is gradual, so that a perfectly acceptable sharpness is obtained within a certain range of depth. To enable you to read this useful range comfortably for all stops on the Leica, the aperture scale is engraved to the left and the right of the focusing index. You can now read the extent of the depth of field for each stop on your feet-metre scale. But the optimum sharpness within this range lies at the distance actually focused on. You will find details of the focusing range in the description of each lens.

50mm Summicron, f/11, $1/_{50}$ sec, electronic flash, Braun Hobby Automatic.
Photograph by Liesel Springmann

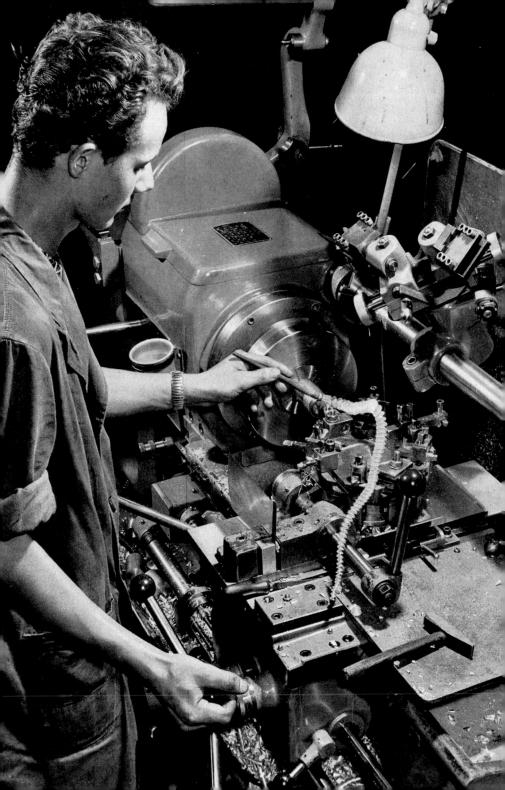

The depth-of-field ring engraved on every Leica lens gives the lens stop numbers to the left and the right of the index line. This is a more convenient way of obtaining the depth of field for any stop than looking it up in a table. The changes occurring at various focusing distances are shown on page 21.

Focusing on the model in the series below is always identical (traffic sign at 5m [17ft]). Only the lens stop varies.

Change of the depth of field at various stops

Here is a little model in order to demonstrate this effect more clearly. In the first picture at f/4 the depth of field extends from 4 to about 7m (13'4" to about 23'). The second picture was taken at f/8. The depth-of-field ring shows a useful range from 3.4 to about 10 m (11'4" to about 33'). In the third picture, at f/16, the depth of field extends from 2.4m (8') to infinity.

Although the large depth of field is very pleasant, it is not obtained without cost, because compared with f/8 you must expose 4×, and compared with f/4 16× longer at f/16. It is therefore normal practice to focus on a favourable point and to stop down just far enough to meet both needs – sufficient depth of field and short enough exposure time. The circle of confusion adopted as standard for the depth-of-field scale has a diameter of $^1/_{30}$ mm. The conventional depth-of-field

42

tables, too, are based on this value. In practical photography, however, it will soon become apparent that it is not necessary to adhere rigidly to such figures. In the close-up range, with a portrait for instance, a little less sharpness will in fact be welcome, whereas technical subjects or landscapes may demand even more sharpness.

In the latter case, for instance, you may stop down to f/8, but read the depth-of-field range for f/4, when you will obtain a circle of confusion of $1/60$ mm diameter for this narrower range. This means in practice that even in a $6\times$ enlargement the admissible unsharpness does not exceed $1/10$. In certain conditions this may be valuable in view of the high resolving power of our slow films which can still cope with this $1/60$ mm circle of confusion.

43

The bright-line frame and the field selector

The bright-line frame indicates the limits of the field. It is displaced diagonally as the lens is focused. This automatically compensates the viewfinder parallax (caused by the lateral difference between the positions of viewfinder and lens). If you want to find out how this compensation works, take out the lens. Slightly depress the roller of the rangefinder on top while you look through the viewfinder. In the Leica M4 and M2 the frames for the 35mm and 135mm fields will appear in the viewfinder if no lens is in the camera. When you insert a 50mm lens, these frames will disappear, and the frame for the 50mm lens will become visible. Likewise the outline for the 90mm field will be reflected in the viewfinder image when you insert a 90mm lens in your Leica.

The little lever below the viewfinder window is the field selector, with which the bright frames for the 50, 90 or 35, and 135mm focal lengths can be made visible independently of the lens in the camera. This provides an ideal subject finder which tells you immediately whether a change in the focal length is advisable.

The outline of the bright frame allows for the reduction of the image field, which is caused in close-up subjects by the increased extension of the camera lens. This reduced angle of view has been adapted as standard for the Leica; the field of subjects at infinity is therefore a little larger than that shown by the bright frame.

With the focal lengths from 21 to 50mm the minimum focusing distance of the rangefinder is 70cm (28in). Where the field-of-view frame is reflected into the viewfinder image, parallax will also be compensated down to this distance.

In the Leica M3

the field-of-view frames change according to a different system (see illustration p. 47). The bold frame for the 50mm focal length is permanently visible. 35mm lenses of various speeds are supplied with a viewfinder front attachment, which in the Leica M3 converts this 50mm frame into one for 35mm. When a 90mm lens is inserted, the frame for this focal length will appear, and with a 135mm lens in the camera you will see the 135mm field frame in the viewfinder. In the M3 the object is viewed at almost natural size (0.9×); a direct fading-in of the 35mm focal length is therefore not possible. In order to achieve this the reproduction scale has been reduced to 0.7× in the Leica M4 and the Leica M2. If you want to use a 135mm lens in long mount in a Leica M2, the rangefinder will be coupled, but you need an additional brilliant finder in the accessory shoe for observation.

Lever *away from the lens.
When a 35 mm lens is in-
serted the appropriate field-
of-view frame appears automatically. In addition 4 corners indicate the 135 mm
area in the central field.*

Lever *in middle position
indicates the field of the
50 mm focal length.*

Lever *towards the lens
shows the frame of the
90 mm focal length.*

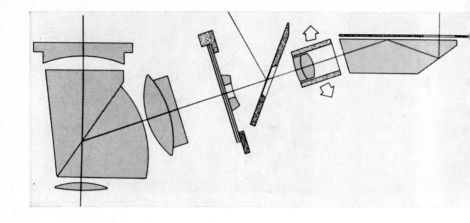

The measuring viewfinder

The diagram above illustrates the design of the measuring viewfinder of the Leica M2 and M4. The path of the measuring ray is indicated by lines; the reflection of the field-of-view frame into the viewfinder is also shown. The rangefinder ray on the right is projected into the image plane of a viewing system through a telescopic system coupled with the lens-focusing mechanism. The field frame illuminated by the centre window lies in the same plane. Field frame and rangefinder ray are together reflected by a beam splitter into the viewfinder eyepiece where they are joined by the ray coming from the view-finder, producing a double image of the sighted object. When the lens setting is changed the part-images move closer together or further apart. When the distance setting is correct the contours will coincide in this plane.

With focal lengths from 21 to 50mm the rangefinder of the Leica models M2 and M4 allows a minimum focusing distance of 70cm (28in) if the focusing mount of the lenses has been designed for this. In the Leica M3 the minimum focusing distance is 1m (40in).

The lines also show the path of the rays producing the bright frame. A masking plate controlled by the bayonet changing mount moves in front of this frame. When a 90mm lens is inserted the field frame for this focal length is automatically reflected into the viewfinder. In addition, the entire field frame is displaced as the lens is focused on various distances, automatically correcting the parallax between viewfinder and camera lens.

Viewfinder reflection of frames in the Leica M3. The bold frame outlines the field for the 50mm lens (lever in middle position).

The inner frame appears when a lens of 90mm focal length is inserted (lever points towards the lens).

The inner frame is changed automatically when a 135mm lens is inserted (lever points away from the lens).

A look through the viewfinder

The Leica is a dynamic camera, its strength lies in its instant readiness for any situation. It therefore includes a measuring viewfinder of outstanding performance. The following details are important:

1. The picture field is outlined by a bright line reflected into the viewfinder image. This frame participates in the focusing movement and automatically compensates the viewfinder parallax. A sufficiently large surrounding field allows ample reaction time for pressing the button just at the right moment during rapid movements and for sports subjects. The field-of-view selector enables you, even without changing the lens in the camera, to see whether a different focal length produces a more favourable picture area.

2. Observation through the viewfinder remains uninterrupted during the exposure, the moment at which the picture is taken is fully controlled by the photographer. An exposure taken at an unfavourable moment can be repeated within a second.

3. The measuring viewfinder is highly accurate. The focusing process is instantaneous. This is a decisive advantage in press photography. The base of the rangefinder and the reproduction scale of the viewfinder are important factors. In the Leica M3, the subject is observed at almost natural size (0.9), in the Leica M2 and M4 the viewfinder image is somewhat reduced (0.7).

4. The space-saving design of the measuring viewfinder is especially welcome with wide-angle lenses. Since it makes complicated back-focus constructions unnecessary, all efforts can be concentrated on lens speed and colour correction. Excellent wide-angle lenses such as the 35mm Summicron f/2 and 35mm Summilux f/1.4 are the result.

5. Measuring viewfinder or single-lens-reflex principle? Something can be said for both, but the Leica operates more silently because the moving mirror in a reflex camera makes more noise.

The rangefinder in the measuring viewfinder

In a measuring viewfinder the scale of reproduction is decisive for the focusing accuracy. It is therefore important for the viewfinder image not to be too much reduced, as this would make it impossible to produce coincidence in the most minute features.

The bright rectangle in the centre of the viewfinder image is the rangefinder field. When the lens is focused on infinity, objects at closer distances appear to have double contours. When the lens focusing ring is rotated, the two images approach each other until they merge into one. A little tip for beginners: – If you do not find the double image in the rangefinder field immediately, cover the outside window with a piece of cardboard. When you look through the viewfinder now you will see only the bright frame and the rangefinder field in the centre, which can easily be lined up with the object to be focused. If the viewfinder window is unblocked, double contours will appear in the range-finder field until the focusing is accurate.

For upright pictures within the near-focusing range below 2m (6ft 8in) the following method prepares you for rapid action: set the appropriate distance on the lens mount and, Leica in front of your eye, move towards and away from your subject until its contours coincide inside the rangefinder field. This requires some practice.

Looking obliquely into the measuring viewfinder has no effect on the focusing accuracy; furthermore, focusing is possible anywhere in the rangefinder field, e.g. along its long edges. Lines intersecting a long edge of the rangefinder field are therefore particularly suitable for rapid and accurate focusing.

(Illustration Doll: Knitting needle – split image, face – coincidence principle.) Correction lenses according to prescription can be fitted to the viewfinder for users with defective eyesight, when the viewfinder image will appear absolutely sharp to their naked eye. Most spectacle wearers are, however, able to manage with their normal glasses in position without difficulty.

The focal-plane shutter

The focal-plane shutter is a part of the Leica body. Two roller blinds traverse the width of the picture field closely in front of the film. The various shutter speeds are a function of varying the distances between the two blinds (width of slit). The spring tensions for the first and second blind are individually adjustable so that the shutter speeds can be set with great accuracy. Only a small proportion of the spring tension is used for the shutter action. This has the advantage of preventing fatigue in the springs so that it is practically immaterial whether or not the shutter is wound when the Leica is not in use.

In many respects the focal-plane shutter is more efficient than the between-lens shutter. This is clearly seen with fast lenses, high shutter speeds of $1/_{500}$ or $1/_{1000}$ sec, and long focal lengths. Since the shutter is located in the camera body instead of in the lens, changing the lenses is easy, although a little caution is necessary in bright light to avoid the entry of disturbing light; the light-masking strip does not make full contact with the blind as this would slow down its movement.

The rubber-cloth blind has proved to be a complete success; it resists both extremes of climate, and runs smoothly and almost silently. Because of its light weight, the ratio between the weight of moving parts and that of the whole camera is very favourable. The danger of damage to the rubberized cloth owing to the burning-glass effect of the camera lens is comparatively small, unless the Leica is left lying in the sun at full aperture for prolonged periods so that the rays can enter it vertically.

The shortest time at which the focal-plane shutter of the Leica can be synchronized with electronic flash is $1/_{50}$ sec (red flash symbol on the speed dial). With electronic flash the effective exposure time is the $1/_{1000}$ sec flash duration. The additional exposure of $1/_{50}$ sec to the existing room light is negligible, because the brightness of the flash in normal-sized rooms calls for medium and small stops.

In large rooms it is possible to replace the electronic flash with large flashbulbs, which can be synchronized up to $1/_{1000}$ sec. In normal conditions, however, the mixture of flash light and normal room lighting is often favourable.

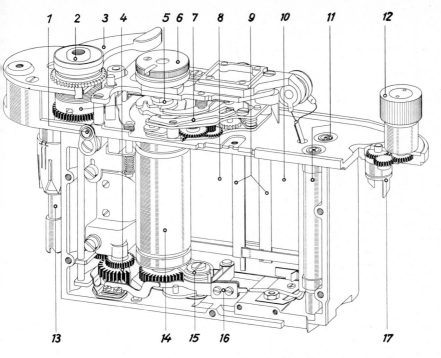

(1) *Reverse lever for rewinding film*
(2) *Release button*
(3) *Film transport lever*
(4) *Transport gears*
(5) *Timing cams*
(6) *Shutter speed dial*
(7) *Retarding mechanism for slow shutter speeds*
(8) *Second roller blind*
(9) *Edges of exposing slit*
(10) *First roller blind*
(11) *Spring-loaded rollers*
(12) *Pull-up rewind knob*
(13) *Film winding shaft*
(14) *Large roller*
(15) *Brake*
(16) *X-contact*
(17) *Film rewind fork*

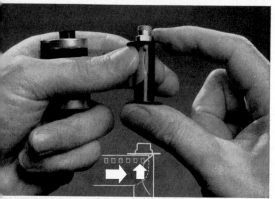

Inserting the film in the MD, M 1, M 2 and M 3 models

Never change the film in full sunlight; if possible, do it in the shade. Check with the rewind knob whether the camera is still loaded.

Turn the toggle in the baseplate towards "Open", and remove the baseplate. Open the back. Pull out the take-up spool. Pick up the film cassette in your left hand, knurled knob upwards. Push the film end under the clamping spring of the take-up spool. The perforated edge of the film must lie snugly against the upper spool flange.

Pull the film end out of the cassette sufficiently to be able to push both parts – cassette and spool – into the camera. The knurled knobs point upwards. The film enters the film guide slot.

The position of the film is as shown in the illustration. The emulsion side must face the focal-plane shutter. Check the position of the film through the open back: the teeth of the transport sprocket must engage the film perforation. Close the camera back, replace and secure the baseplate. Wind the film through one frame, pull out the rewind knob and turn it in the direction of the arrow engraved on it until the film is taut and you feel a slight resistance. During the next two film transports the rewind button must rotate

52

against the direction of the arrow; this is proof that the film is wound correctly.

In the Leica M3 the film counter is automatically zeroed; in the other Leica models the film counting disc must be returned to 0 by hand.

Rewinding the film

When the end of the film has been reached the transport lever becomes locked – a sign that the film has to be rewound: set the rewind lever★ on the camera front on "R", pull out the rewind knob and turn it in the direction of the arrow until you feel appreciable resistance. Overcome this by winding on through another turn, when you may open the camera and take the film out.

Always keep exposed and unexposed cartridges and cassettes in their wrappers etc.

★ Some M 1 and M 2 models have a button instead of a lever, see illustration on the right. This must be depressed for rewinding.

Loading and unloading the MD a and M 4 models

In these models film change has been considerably simplified and therefore speeded up. The removable take-up spool has been replaced by a fixed take-up shaft, with three prongs and slots to grip the film. The broken line shows how the film must be inserted. It does not matter if the beginning of the film protrudes a few mm beyond the second slot. The film must be trimmed as in the usual 35 mm cartridges.

Push the film in level. Close the camera back, hook the baseplate on to the right-hand lug, close it, and secure it with the toggle. Transport the film through one frame; now make it taut by turning the rewind crank handle. The film is correctly wound if the rewind crank handle rotates against the direction of the arrow when the film is again wound on.

Rewinding is considerably more convenient if you hold your M4 at an angle of 45° so that you can crank the handle vertically. Do not forget to move the little rewind lever on the front of the camera to "R" first, as with the other models.

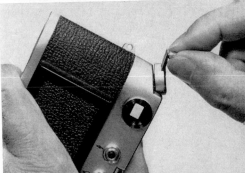

50 mm Summicron, f/5.6, $^{1}/_{250}$ sec.
Photograph by S. Hartig

Removing a partly exposed film

(Changing the type of film). After the shutter is wound the film counter shows the number of exposed frames. Rewind the film and note this number on the end of the film. When you reinsert this film keep the shutter released and transport the film to the noted number with the lens cap in position. This will bring the next unexposed frame into the picture gate. For good measure you may transport the film through an additional frame. Make certain to set the film counter of the Leica M1 or M2.

Marking a partly exposed film

Make a blank exposure, take out the lens, set the shutter at "B", press the release button to open the picture gate, and stick a self-adhesive label on the film.

Cutting off a partly exposed film for development

In the M models you can open the back in the darkroom and push the film out. But the following method is simpler: Make a note of the number indicated by the film counter and rewind the film. Mark the length of the exposed film with drawing pins in the darkroom.

You will have calculated this length as follows:

3.75 cm ($1^1/_2''$) is required for every exposure, and an additional 25 cm (10'') for both film ends. If your film counter points at 12, for instance, you obtain the following value: 12×3.75 cm $= 45$ cm $+ 25$ cm $= 70$ cm ($12 \times 1^1/_2 = 18'' + 10'' = 28''$).

Insufficient attachment of the film to the spool

If a film has not been attached firmly enough to the cassette it may become detached from the spool core, which will make rewinding impossible; to save the film it must be removed from the camera in complete darkness. With the Leica MDa and M4 models, which no longer have a take-up spool, the following procedure must be adopted:

Remove the baseplate and hold the camera with the open part downwards. Operate the film winding lever several times and tap the camera in the hand in between until the film slightly protrudes from it so that you can grip it. In order to avoid scratching it, pull the film out slowly, slightly turning it. Remember that the emulsion side faces outwards. If your hands are damp, dry them first by rubbing them with methylated spirits.

Rapid-loading spool for the Leica M 3, M 2, M 1, and MD models

The new spool is used in place of the earlier take-up spool. You can carry out the necessary modifications yourself. Screw a plastic spacer to the guide lug in the baseplate so that the plane face fits against the stop and parallel to the long side of the baseplate along the guide rail. The correct position is fixed by means of a screw (see illustration).

Films can be inserted more quickly with the new spool, since the spool need not be pulled out (exception: Leica M3; it is necessary briefly to lift the spool by pulling the movable inner pin in order to unwind the film counter). The beginning of the film is introduced into the Leica and attached to the spool as shown on the foil supplied; the foil should be stuck over of the existing diagram in the bottom of the Leica.

Correct insertion of the film is essential to perfect film transport. The aperture in the spool for the beginning of the film must face the transport drum. You can adjust it to this position by carefully moving the film winding lever. Pull just enough film out of the cartridge so that about $1^1/_2$ cm ($^5/_8$ in) of it enters the spool. The film need not have the complete trim usual with cartridges; a trim of 2–3 cm ($^7/_8$–$1^1/_8$ in) length is enough.

Do not omit the check usual during film insertion. Release the shutter after

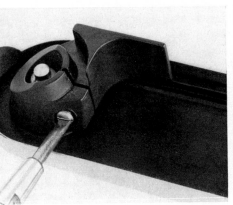
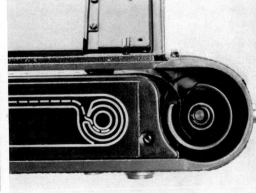

replacing the baseplate, and transport the film through one frame before you pull it taut by rotating the pulled-out rewind knob. When you wind the film on again, the rewind knob must rotate against the direction of the arrow.

Flash synchronization

Electronic flash units and most expendable flashbulbs can be easily synchronized with the Leica. "Synchronization" means making the shutter function and the duration of the flash coincide. The contact adjustment necessary to achieve this is built into the camera and works automatically.

There is a choice of two contact bushes in the back of the Leica. These bushes are specially shaped in the Leica M1–M3 and MD models. Use either the suitable special plug or the commercially available adapters. In the Leica M4 and MDa the contact bushes have been altered to accept standard plugs. See illustration bottom right.

The left-hand contact bush, marked with a flash symbol, is chosen for electronic-flash exposures; the shutter speed to be set must be $^1/_{50}$ sec or slower. This contact bush can be used also for short-peak flashbulbs, but the required shutter speed will now be $^1/_{30}$ sec. The first roller of the shutter is wound, exposes the film window, the flash is fired, and the second roller closes the film window again.

The right-hand contact bush, marked with a lamp symbol, is preferred for the synchronization of flashbulbs. This contact already fires when the first roller starts to move. This pre-firing time is necessary when you want to use higher shutter speeds. You can flash at up to $^1/_{500}$ sec with suitable types of flashbulb (GE5 and 25).

You will find detailed hints for exposure technique in the chapter on flash photography, p. 167.

Lens hoods

The use of a lens hood is always recommended. During rain, for instance, it protects the lens from raindrops, and generally from accidentally being touched. As far as possible the diameter of the lens hoods has been standardized at 42 mm for lenses with bayonet mount; this reduces the number of accessories required. Two versions of 42 mm lens hoods are available, the shorter one for 35 and 50 mm, and the longer one for 90 and 135 mm focal lengths.

The spring-loaded tongues of the lens hood are pushed inwards and engage in the groove of the lens mount. This position remains unchanged even when filters are used. Some of the lens hoods can be attached to the lenses back-to-front to take up less space in the ever-ready case. For lenses of other external diameters special lens hoods are available.

Filters

With the more recent lens versions series filters can be inserted (21 mm, 28 mm, 35 mm). Filters and their uses see pp. 140.

Bayonet adapters

Leica lenses with screw thread bought for earlier Leica models can be used on the M-models with a bayonet adapter. This is a ring of 1 mm depth with a bayonet fitting outside and a screw thread inside. Since it also changes the bright-line frame in the measuring viewfinder, it is available in 3 versions. The ring has the focal lengths with which it can be used engraved on it.

The rings fade the bright-line frames of the following focal lengths into the image of the measuring viewfinder:

50 mm – ring 14097, 90 mm – ring 14098, 135 mm – ring 14099.

In the Leica M2, ring 14099 fades in only the 35 mm frame, in the M4 additionally the 35 mm frame. If no frame has to be faded in, any ring can be used. The bayonet adapters are inserted into and removed from the camera like ordinary bayonet lenses. Lenses screwed into bayonet adapters can be removed as follows:

The bayonet lock is released and the adapter turned as far as possible; instead of removing the lens, use the stop as a lever for screwing the lens out of the bayonet adapter.

The Leicameter MR

Leica M models can be directly coupled with the Leicameter. The MR has a cadmium sulphide resistor; this both extends the measuring range and narrows the measuring angle. The instrument can be detached and used independently.

Attaching the Leicameter

Set the shutter speed dial of the Leica at "B" and the knurled knob of the exposure meter so that the triangular index points at "B". Now lift the knurled knob and secure it by a slight turn. Push the foot of the exposure meter fully into the accessory shoe of the camera and turn the knurled knob to the right until it engages. To remove the exposure meter set it at "B", lift the knurled knob and uncouple it by turning it in the direction of the arrow.

The film speed (3 to 3,200 ASA, 6 to 36 DIN) is set on the inner disc. The measuring range extends from 1.6 to 100,000 asb.

Measuring with the Leicameter

When you press the measuring button the measuring mechanism is switched on. Release the button after 2 sec; this switches the measuring mechanism off and arrests the pointer. At the same time push the field selector lever towards the lens;

60

this enables you to take an aimed reading, since the measuring field corresponds to the picture area covered by the 90mm lens in the viewfinder.

If the light is too weak to give you a pointer deflection turn the knurled disc in the top left-hand corner of the Leicameter so that its index mark faces the red dot; this increases its sensitivity 128 times. Measure as before, but take your reading off the red aperture numbers. When the knurled knob is turned, the shutter speed dial of the Leica is coupled from $1/1000$ sec to 1 sec. For the exposure range from 2 to 120 sec the knurled knob is lifted in the "B" position, i.e. uncoupled. Since the Leica shutter is set at "B", you expose the film by pressing the release button for the appropriate time.

The PX 13 or PX 625 mercuric-oxide battery used in the Leicameter MR is housed in the bottom of the instrument below a swivelling slide. With normal use the battery has a life of about 2 years. You can test its state with a switch next to the light-sensitive cell; it is satisfactory if the measuring pointer is deflected as far as the light dot.

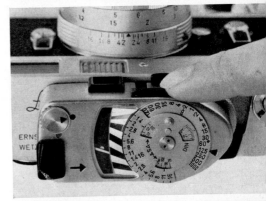

61

Leicameter MC

The Leicameter MC exposure meter is the earlier version with a selenium barrier layer cell, which does not need a special current source. The measuring angle is about 55°, its limiting sensitivity is considerably lower than that of the newer Leicameter MR.

Although attachment, removal, and speed setting are identical in both meters, the measuring process as such is different. The exposure meter measures directly; no measuring button is pressed. In good lighting conditions the small knurled disc in the top right-hand corner is rotated so that the triangular index faces the black dot. Now point the camera with the exposure meter at your subject, and with the ring above the shutter speed dial set a suitable shutter speed. The exposure meter pointer will indicate the appropriate lens aperture across a black or white channel of the scale. The pointer is not arrested. It is therefore necessary to point the camera in the direction of the subject while the meter is being read.

If the light is too weak to produce a pointer deflection, turn the knurled disc in the top left-hand corner so that the triangular index faces the red dot. The red aperture numbers opposite the channel scale are now valid.

By means of an attachable booster cell the sensitivity of the meter can be increased four times. Here the valid aperture numbers are read off the red scale, and the shutter speeds not against the triangular, but against the square symbol next to it.

Incident-light measurement, too, is possible. Insert the small opal screen into the guide grooves. It must not be used with the conventional direct (reflected-light) measurement as it will produce wrong results.

① Set lens stop   **③** Focus

② Set shutter speed   **④** Release shutter

Instructions in brief

Please do not turn over this page before you have committed the sequence of the numbers in the above illustration of the Leica firmly to your memory. You should observe these four stages during each Leica exposure. Their sequence is very important. From 1 to 3 it need not be rigidly followed, but practice has shown it to be preferable. To be able to concentrate your whole attention on the picture, undisturbed by any technical considerations, you must by repeated practice reach the stage when your fingers know what to do without conscious direction from the brain.

Pick up your empty camera and pretend to take photographs – of the lamp in the sitting room, of the window, of the garden gate, of the neighbour's house across the road; carry out each of the four operations in the correct sequence "as if you meant it". This wastes no film and makes you familiar with the basic rules of handling your Leica, so that in the end your subconscious mind will automatically take over many deliberations.

Leica MDa (adaptable for film marking)

The Leica MDa has no viewfinder. Otherwise it corresponds to the Leica M4. Film is therefore inserted and rewound as described there. The MDa is a special version for photographic recording for scientific and technical purposes. All accessories of the Leica-M system which are not based on the use of a viewfinder are suitable for this camera. This includes, among other items, the Reprovit IIa universal copying stand, the Visoflex mirror reflex attachment, the photomicrographic attachment, and the quarto-, octavo-, and postcard-size as well as the 1:1 to 1:3 copying gauges. The Leica MDa cannot be converted into another model. Its main applications are copying, close-up photography, and photomicrography.

The Leica MDa has a focal-plane shutter, speeds $1\text{-}1/_{1000}$ sec and B, flash synchronization as in the M4 with a contact bush each for flashbulbs and electronic flash. The film counter engages automatically when the base plate is being attached.

The Leica cassettes suitable for all M models as well as the conventional 35 mm cartridges can be used.

A special baseplate incorporating a recording device is available as an accessory; it allows the insertion of marking strips; the writing on the strip will be exposed together with the film, whose format will be reduced to 24×32.5 mm.

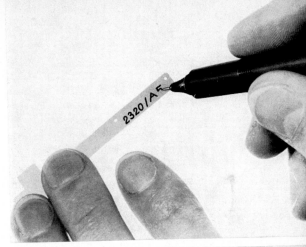

Top: It is best to enter the figures, letters, or symbols on the marking strips in India ink.

Centre: The strip is inserted in the camera; it covers an area of about 3.5 mm width along the narrow side of the film. The latest version of the groundglass screen in the Reprovit IIa makes allowance for the reduced picture field.

Bottom: Sufficient brightness of the negative area is essential if the marking is to stand out clearly.

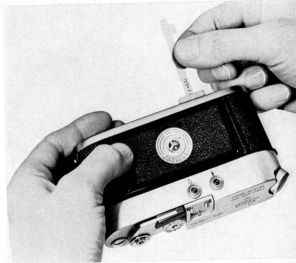

Tips and solace for beginners

You have watched your photo salesman insert the first film in your camera. Watching someone else do it, by the way, is the best method of learning the new, still unaccustomed manipulations. You leave the shop, eager to commit your first subjects to film. Perhaps your head is swimming with all the facts you have read in your operating instructions! Relax – you may just have bought the world's most versatile camera, but for the moment what you need to know for using it can be reduced to simple terms.

This is one of your lucky days. We may therefore take it for granted that the sun is shining. You have chosen a medium-speed film, an "all-purpose film". Its speed of 125 ASA is printed on its little cardboard box. Turning a corner you suddenly come upon a five-year old Tom Thumb straining to post a letter in a box. A woman passing by sets her shopping bag down and lifts the little boy up. A simple everyday scene which you want to capture on the spur of the moment. But your Leica was focused on infinity, the stop set at f/4 and the shutter at $^1/_{30}$sec. Before you have a chance to adjust your three settings, the whole incident has passed, and everything at the letterbox is back to normal. Please remember that there is such a thing as a "snapshot setting" for photographic strolls. On this sunny day, set your lens stop at f/11, and your shutter speed at $^1/_{125}$sec; all you have to watch during any photographic encounter is your distance setting, and you will be ready for action within seconds.

The first motif has escaped you. But it's market day today, and a good opportunity to get some practice. Markets all over the world abound with motifs. Life proceeds at a leisurely pace. You, too, can take your time. Practise range-finding on the "P" of the "Parking Prohibited" sign, which has the advantage of being stationary. Something else: guess your distance before you measure it. You would not believe how important it is to your photographic future to learn how to guess. Not only distances, but also light intensity. Because when it comes to the point, these things must be second nature to you.

Here is a little tip: do not guess the distance to the object at eyelevel, but trace it with the eye along the ground. Try to guess not only the distance, but also the intensity of the light.

It is only natural that in the beginning your Leica should claim much of your attention, little of which will be left for your motifs. But after a short while you will master everything in your sleep. At the moment you still wonder each time whether to hold your camera vertically or horizontally, whether to squat on your haunches, assume a broad stance, or stand on tip-toe. Later all this will be automatic, and you will be "all eye" for your subject-matter.

From the very beginning pay attention to your background – and the correct picture area. Do not rely on your photo salesman to find it for you. It is much more fun to look for it yourself. A bad background spoils the picture, a single step to the left or right will often transform the situation. The Leica makes it easy for you – it is so versatile.

Do not hesitate to play around and experiment with your first film; in fact this is what you ought to do. Try to find out the effect of opening your stop to values at the same shutter speed – you will receive $4\times$ as much light on the film as before, yet your negative will still be satisfactory. Or, conversely, leave your stop setting untouched and use $1/_{30}$sec instead of $1/_{125}$sec. You should, however, adopt $1/_{125}$sec as your standard shutter speed, allowing for dark subjects by opening the lens stop. Only if the light at your disposal is so poor that even with a large stop $1/_{125}$sec will no longer be enough should you use slower shutter speeds. Note on your developed film the change in the negative density. And then you should sacrifice a few more exposures for the remaining shutter speed scale up to $1/_{1000}$sec. The film costs little, experience is everything! Naturally, these trial exposures need not all be enlarged, except the "hits" which even your first film will be certain to contain. To reassure you we must confess that not every shot by even the most experienced worker is a success.

A very warmly recommended method can be used to assess the quality of theses trial exposures. Cut the individual negatives to be examined from the film, and glass-mount them in a 5×5cm (2×2in) changing frame. If you project them with your PRADOVIT-COLOR or some other 35mm projector at a width of more than 1m (40in), their technical quality will be clearly apparent on the image screen. Even the slightest blur, minor deviations from correct focusing, too little or too much exposure can be much better investigated than on the usual 7×10cm ($3^1/_4\times4^1/_4$in) enlargements.

THE LEICA SYSTEM

Every Leica with a standard lens of 50mm focal length is a fully efficient piece of photographic equipment. But since its lens is interchangeable it at once provides the basis for many possibilities of expansion: for what is known as the Leica System. This includes the interchangeable Leica lenses – from the wide-angle to the telephoto lens, from the standard to the ultra-fast lens – and the ingeniously matched accessories. You may well ask the question whether such a system is at all necessary. Does not a larger format provide so much reserve that you can do without additional lenses? It is worth while to go into this question a little further, because the really great advantages of the Leica can be appreciated and used to the full only when the background is known.

The picture of the turning skiers was taken with the 135mm Hektor. The speed of the skier demands $^1/_{500}$sec, the back-lighting a comparatively large stop, f/4.5 here, and the rapid event a camera which is able to record just the right moment. Only the long focal length makes this exposure from the opposite slope possible, at a distance of more than 80ft. If we approach the subject more closely, all conditions change, and the risk of being knocked down in the process is only one of the minor hazards. After all, are we not all prepared to take risks for a good picture?

135mm is a focal length which is also used with the 9×12cm format. We should therefore be in a position to enlarge the Leica field from this large camera format. In theory it should be possible. In practice conditions are different.

1. The precision with which such a large film lies in the focal plane of the large camera is not as high as that with which the film lies in your Leica. The necessary large part-enlargement will therefore never be as sharp as the enlargement from a Leica negative.

2. In order to ensure complete success with such rapidly moving subjects, a number of lucky coincidences are essential. I am giving away no secret when I tell you that the skiers had to do several turns before a satisfactory shot was obtained. But whether you take 5 or more repeats is unimportant with the Leica, as the exposure material is so inexpensive.

Photograph by Stefan Kruckenhauser

Nike temple, Acropolis, Athens. All three photographs were taken from the same point of view with a 21mm, a 35mm, and a 135mm lens. A total view is obtained with the 21mm Super-Angulon in spite of the short distance. The other two focal lengths produce partial views at larger scales. – Isopan FF film, f/8, ¹/₃₀ sec, orange filter.   *Photograph by Theo Kisselbach*

3. A further advantage is the handiness of the Leica which allows you to operate it reliably and quickly even at low temperatures. The larger and heavier the apparatus, the more cumbersome and complicated the equipment. For the 6×9cm format, for instance, the corresponding focal length would be 330mm, and for the 9×12cm format, as much as 480mm. With the 9×12cm cameras this would mean the need for a lens of almost 20″ focal length, and its weight alone would make its use for such a sports subject rather problematical.

Many more examples could be quoted of turning the Leica into *some specialized instrument* with little effort, simply by a change in the focal length or introduction of an accessory. This is the very fact responsible for the extraordinary popularity of this camera among notable explorers, scientists and amateurs: – every Leica can be adapted to cope with even the most difficult tasks.

One or two additional focal lengths may already enlarge the photographic possibilities considerably.

1. Interchangeable lenses allow the most favourable picture of a given subject from a given camera viewpoint; the Leica format is fully utilized, which is important for obtaining perfect enlargements.

"Am Plönlein, Rothenburg o.d. Tauber." – Here, too, the same subject was taken three times, this time with a 35mm, a 90mm and a 135mm lens. But here the camera viewpoint was progressively further removed from the scene. This produced radical changes in the perspective, clearly shown in the ratio between house and tower.   Photograph by Theo Kisselbach

2. But the advantage offered by the change in the pictorial perspective is even more decisive, if you can alter your viewpoint at will.

Eleven matched, interchangeable focal lengths for the Leica present you with innumerable possibilities of mastering even difficult new photographic territory. This, of course, does not mean that you should buy the complete series from the 21mm Super-Angulon to the 560mm Telyt straight away. Often a single additional lens is enough to enlarge the photographic possibilities to a surprising extent. If you want to take hand-held pictures as you have done for years choose a longer-focal-length lens with rangefinder coupling as a supplement, such as the 90mm or the 135mm lens. It is difficult to decide which of the two to give preference. The 90mm Elmarit is lighter, handier, and therefore easier to use. Its range is very universal, and since it is rangefinder-coupled down to 1m (40″), even hand-held close-ups are possible. At a distance of 1m (40″) a lens of 90mm focal length covers an area of about 20×30cm (8×12″).

The 135mm Tele-Elmar has a typical telephoto lens effect. At 18° its angle of view is appreciably narrower. It calls above all for a steady hand to avoid camera shake during the exposure. It has the very material advantage that its lens head can be unscrewed from its mount to be used in connection with a

Skier – The skier has been taken from the same point of view with the 50mm standard Elmar and the 200mm Telyt lens. Here, a third effect is added to the two principal results of a focal length, which are the pulling in of the pictorially important feature and the compression of fore-and background: The shallow depth of field enables the photographer to reproduce the essentials of his picture sharp in the focal plane, to suppress unimportant features in the background. Had he

universal focusing mount in the Visoflex or with a focusing bellows covering the near-focusing range. Especially the nature lover will appreciate this facility. My personal preference for touring is the 90mm Elmarit because of its light weight. Furthermore, the difference between the two focal lengths is already large enough for the two lenses to be used side by side each in their own right. The next acquisition will without doubt be a wide-angle lens of 35mm focal length. Have you never found yourself in a narrow street where the standard focal length was completely useless? Here the wide-angle lens is the only solution. You may want to know why I have not recommended this lens as a first addition; here is the reason why: The features on your film are reduced in size as the focal length decreases. In order to obtain a realistic pictorial impression,

wanted to show the skier as large with the 50mm lens as he did with the Telyt on the right, his point of view would have had to be closer to the subject (see diagram). It would have been possible but the perspective would have been changed for the worse.

Both photographs: Stefan Kruckenhauser

such pictures should therefore be more strongly enlarged. For your pictorial composition you can draw these positive conclusions: this lens will place strong emphasis on the foreground; the background will recede owing to rapidly converging vanishing lines, and the depth-of-field range will be large.

Pages 74 and 75:

The Temple of Apollo at Delphi, where Pythia sat on her tripod, was taken from the same point of view with 6 different focal lengths. The picture taken with the 21mm Super-Angulon shows the impressive mountain scenery surrounding the temple. The angle of view narrows as the focal length is increased, but details are reproduced correspondingly larger.

Photographs by Theo Kisselbach

73

21 mm

35 mm

50 mm

74

90 mm

135 mm

200 mm

75

Technical data of the Leica lenses

Name	Speed	Focal length (mm)	Angle of field			Number of elements	Filter diameter	Weight (g)	
			Diagonal	Horizontal long side	Vertical short side				
Elmar	f/2.8	50	45°	38°	26°	4	E39	220	Removable lens head
Summicron	f/2	50	45°	38°	26°	6	E39	285	Double helical mount
Summicron near	f/2	50	45°	38°	26°	7	E39	{345 {400	near-focusing range with viewfinder attachment
Summilux	f/1.4	50	45°	38°	26°	7	E43	325	
Noctilux	f/1.2	50	45°	38°	26°	6	VIII	515	
Super-Angulon	f/3.4	21	92°	81°	50°	8	E48	300}	To be used with brilliant finder
Elmarit	f/2.8	28	76°	65°	46°	9	E48	225}	
Summaron	f/2.8	35	64°	54°	38°	6	E39	{210 {135	With finder attachment / without finder attachment
Summicron	f/2	35	64°	54°	38°	8	E39	{225 {150	With finder attachment / without finder attachment
Summilux	f/1.4	35	64°	54°	38°	7	E41★	{325 {245	With finder attachment / without finder attachment
Elmar	f/3.5	65	36°	31°	21°	4	E41	125	Only with universal focusing mount for Visoflex II or III
Elmar	f/4	90	27°	23°	15°	3	E39	305	Removable lens head
Elmar collapsible	f/4	90	27°	23°	15°	4	E39	340	Collapsible, lens head not removable
Elmarit	f/2.8	90	27°	23°	15°	5	E39	320	Lens head removable
Tele-Elmarit	f/2.8	90	27°	23°	15°	5	E39	355	Lens head not removable
Summicron	f/2	90	27°	23°	15°	6	E48	{685 {540	Long mount / short mount
Elmar	f/4	135	18°	15°	10°	4	E39	440	Lens head removable usable also in short mount
Tele-Elmar	f/4	135	18°	15°	10°	4	E39	510	Lens head removable for Visoflex II/III
Elmarit	f/2.8	135	18°	15°	10°	5	VII	730	Lens head removable
Telyt	f/4	200	12°	10°	7°	4	E58	625}	Automatic diaphragm
Telyt	f/4.8	280	8.5°	7°	5°	4	E58	830}	Only Visoflex I–III
Telyt f/5.6 and 6.8		400	6°	5°	3.5°	2	VII	630	Usable in connection
Telyt	f/5.6	560	4°	3.5°	2.5°	2	VII	1835	with Televit

★ From No. 2166701 VII

50mm Elmar
f/2.8

50mm Summi-
cron f/2

50mm Summilux
f/1.4

50mm Noctilux
f/1.2

21mm Super-
Angulon f/3.4

28mm Elmarit
f/2.8

35mm Summa-
ron f/2.8

35mm Summi-
cron f/2

35mm Summilux
f/1.4

65mm Elmar
f/3.5

90mm Elmarit
f/2.8

90mm Tele-
Elmarit f/2.8

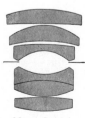
90mm Summi-
cron f/2

135mm Tele-
Elmar f/4

135mm Elmarit
f/2.8

200mm Telyt
f/4

77

In many situations it is either impossible or inadvisable to compensate poor lighting conditions by artificial light or flash, often because this would completely change existing or characteristic lighting. This is also the reason why a large American journal expressly asks its reporters to work in conditions of available light. But in order to achieve satisfactory negatives the highest lens speed is essential. For colour film, too, it is often necessary if supplementary lighting is not available.

Working with ultra-fast lenses has attractions of its own. When they are used together with ultra-fast films, lighting restrictions are almost a matter of the past, any match gives enough light to be used as a light source. How many situations with atmosphere can thus be captured with the Leica! On page 155 you will find important hints for determining the correct exposure time, which is particularly difficult in such unfavourable lighting conditions.

Here we have reached the limits of photographic possibilities, and there is no doubt at all that especially the Leica and the 35 mm Leica size offer considerable advantages over other formats. Since large formats also demand lenses of long focal lengths, weight and price of the equipment increase, and the depth of field decreases.

The Leica size represents the ideal solution; smaller sizes have their disadvantages with ultra-fast films, which have the coarsest grain and least resolving power; with the excessive enlargement which would be required by such ultra-small formats these would be two disturbing factors.

Wedding ceremony in the Russian Church at Wiesbaden. The picture of a young couple in front of the altar may be a personal or, as in this case, a historical document. On solemn occasions like this tact rules out the use of flash. By falling back on an ultra-fast lens the photographer makes a virtue out of necessity. A flash picture would hardly have reproduced the atmosphere in the subdued light of the church so naturally. The slight unsharpness in the background, a result of the large aperture, is rather an advantage. The technical data reveal that even in the twilight of the church the photographer did not have to make full use of his speed reserve. f/2, $^1/_{20}$ sec.

Photograph by Hermann Wagner

STANDARD FOCAL LENGTHS

In 35mm photography 50mm or thereabouts is considered the "normal" or "standard" focal length. Such lenses have an angle of view of about 45°. This value is measured diagonally. But in actual practice the angle for the short or the long side interests us more. The table on page 76 therefore contains all angles of view.

50mm Elmar f/2.8

The 50mm Elmar f/2.8 is a further development of the earlier 50mm Elmar f/3.5, a lens of great popularity because of its excellent performance.

The use of new types of glass has made an increase of its speed to f/2.8 possible. It is supplied in a collapsible mount. Since the performance of the Elmar is excellent also in the close-up range this lens can be used universally. It is also suitable as an enlarging lens provided the stops conventional in enlarging (e.g. f/5.6 or f/8) are used.

Black-and-white. Winner of the 1st Award, Leica Jubilee competition. 50mm Elmar, f/5.6,
$^1/_{125}$ sec. *Photograph by Theo M. Scheerer*

At the circus. — In the attractive field of action shots in the circus or theatre the fast Leica lenses used with ultra-fast films really come into their own. Here the speed potential of such lenses will be fully realized. 50 mm Summicron, f/2, ¹/₁₀₀ sec.   *Photograph by Bert Rupp*

Its speed of f/2.8 is completely adequate for the majority of subjects since, in any case, as a rule the depth of field required by the subject calls for stopping down.

50 mm Summicron f/2

The Summicron is one of the most important and universal Leica lenses. Its excellent correction and high brilliance make it especially suitable for colour photography. It can be used at full aperture for hand-held exposures even in poor lighting conditions in dull weather or dark thoroughfares and in ordinary artificial room lighting without difficulty.

The most recent version (Lens No. 2269251) is supplied in a black light-alloy mount. This has led to an appreciable reduction of weight without loss of

The 50 mm lenses: Summicron f/2, Summilux f/1.4, Noctilux f/1.2, Elmar f/2.8.

stability. The use of a new type of glass made it possible to reduce the number of elements from 7 to 6, with an improvement of the optical performance. The range of the focusing mount has been extended down to 0.7 m (28 in) but the rangefinder coupling of the Leica M3 ranges only from ∞ to 1 m (40 in). The little catch for the infinity setting has been omitted in the interest of quicker focusing. But you now have to get hold of the lens mount a little closer to the bayonet when you want to remove the lens from the Leica. The diaphragm clicks at half stops. The Summicron need be stopped down to no more than f/4 to reach its highest possible resolving power: but since the actual resolving power of high-quality lenses is in practice never fully utilized by normal films, no loss of sharpness is to be feared even with considerable stopping down (f/11).

For a long time the Summicron was available both in a simple rigid mount and as the near-focusing version. In the rigid version the lens head can be unscrewed from the focusing mount. It can be used with the copying gauge 16526 by means of the ring 16508. The lens heads of standard rigid Summicrons also fit the near-focusing device 16507 by means of ring 16508 when the focusing range of the dual-range Summicron is desired for close-up shooting; for use with Leitz enlargers, ring 17672 is required.

The version with a dual focusing mount is particularly practical. The lens can be switched from the normal ∞–1 m (40″) range to the near-focusing 88–48 cm (35–19″) range. Automatic focusing and parallax compensation, controlled by a viewfinder attachment, also extend to this range. At the shortest distance of 48 cm (19″) the reproduction scale is 1:7, i.e. $^1/_7$ natural size; it corresponds to an object field of about 16×24 cm (6×10″ approx.). The extension factor is 1.3, an increase which need be considered with colour film only. It is advisable to use small stops in the near-focusing range, since there is little depth of field here.

It is impossible to confuse the near- and distant ranges during focusing. An ingenious locking device prevents the use of the near-focusing range without the viewfinder attachment; this can be attached only when the focusing ring is in a certain position (see illustration). At the 1 m (40″) setting the focusing ring is lifted across the locking lug by a slight forward pull; it returns to its previous level at 88 cm (35″). The viewfinder attachment is now pushed on its holder as far as possible. This releases the lock, and the focusing ring can be operated in the near-focusing range. The attachment is locked on the lens at any setting of less than 88 cm (35″), which is the only position in which it can be removed. It is simply pulled off, and the focusing ring returned to the 1 m (40″) position by pulling it forward and lifting it across the locking lug; the normal range from 1 m (40″) to ∞ is now again operative. The attachment must be removed before the lens is changed.

ocusing ring on 1 m (40″)	*Pull and turn to 88 cm (35″)*	*Push-on finder attachment*

50mm Summilux f/1.4

The Summilux is a Gauss-type lens, consisting of 7 elements like the earlier 50mm Summarit f/1.5. New glasses produced by the addition of "rare earths" are largely responsible for the improvement in its performance; the glasses used are free from thorium, i.e. they are not radioactive.

The design of the Summilux was altered a few years ago; the new version (from Serial No. 1844001 onwards) is practically without coma, a fault which distorts point-shaped lights in the corners of the picture.

The new highly-refracting glasses are considerably heavier. Since, moreover, the diameter of a lens increases with its speed, the increase in weight is quite appreciable. The introduction of new light-alloy mounts has counteracted this effect without reducing the sturdiness of the construction. All parts subject to heavy mechanical wear, such as the focusing mount, rangefinder cam, changing bayonet or -thread, continue to be made of brass.

In spite of its high speed the Summilux is a universal lens which is easy to handle. Its use in darkness is facilitated by a positive click-stop aperture ring and a non-rotating focusing mount. The lens mount is not collapsible. At large apertures accurate rangefinder focusing is essential to ensure sharpness in the subject plane. When you look at the depth-of-field ring the taking of pictures at close distances would appear almost impossible. In practice it is very successful, because the conspicuous transition from unsharpness to sharpness and back to unsharpness often has great pictorial appeal. It is best to try out this effect on a practice film.

We can work with $^1/_{30}-^1/_{60}$ sec in normal room lighting with ultra-fast films (400–500 ASA) and suitable development (p. 215). With candle light at 1 m (40") the shutter speed decreases to about $^1/_8$ sec. Some practice is required to take pictures at this speed without camera shake. Propping your arms on the table or leaning your head against the wall are effective aids. If you are unable to release your shutter steadily at $^1/_8$ sec you will find the little table tripod, which you can take anywhere, an invaluable support.

Rubens, The Last Judgement, Alte Pinakothek, Munich. 50mm Summilux f/1.4.

Photograph by Kisselbach

50 mm Noctilux f/1.2

The Noctilux is a most unusual lens. Its high speed is combined with excellent correction, and even at full aperture its contrast rendering is outstanding. This makes it particularly suitable for use in poor lighting conditions and with very fast films. It owes its optical performance to its special design; it is the world's first production lens with aspherical elements, a feature which made it possible to confine the number of elements to 6 in spite of its high speed.

The mathematician, aided by modern computers, does not find it difficult to compute lenses of apertures larger than f/1.4. In practice, however, this increased speed makes sense only if the sum total of the residual optical aberrations is small enough not to impose photographic restrictions on the user. But the problem remains that the film may deviate from its flat position through 0.02 or 0.03 mm, to which these light giants are very sensitive at full aperture.

Vignetting by camera lenses

The following details are of a general nature and not confined to any one make of lens. We distinguish between natural and artificial vignetting, which means a decrease in the lighting intensity towards the margin of the image. Light rays passing through a lens obliquely instead of vertically also enter the film obliquely; they therefore act with less energy than in the centre. This loss is negligible with normal and long focal lengths, because a 15–20% reduction of light intensity can be ignored. But in wide-angle lenses with their larger angles of field the energy loss is correspondingly larger, and the fall-off of light is appreciable. Incidentally, this natural vignetting cannot be reduced by stopping down.

Artificial vignetting is caused by the lens mount. All efficient lens systems consist of several elements held in a mount. If we point a fast lens at full aperture against a bright surface and look vertically at the front lens from a distance we see a circle. If we tilt the lens slightly so that we look obliquely at the front surface the circle turns into a smaller, biconvex shape. The light loss of the marginal portions of the negative corresponds with this loss of area.

If we stop the lens down (e.g. from f/2 to f/4) and repeat the experiment we will notice that the area of the full circle remains visible much longer. Thus, stopping down reduces artificial vignetting. If uniformly bright areas are to be photographed, stopping down is strongly recommended, since such a subject reveals the falling off of light most clearly.

WIDE-ANGLE LENSES

As their name implies, these lenses cover a wide angle of field. Their focal length is relatively short compared with the photographic format. Since they produce a very large image circle, all details in the picture naturally appear smaller. Interiors and churches, in fact architectural subjects of all descriptions can often be taken only with a wide-angle lens. But landscapes under a high sky or deep gorges also call for a large angle of field. In advertising and technical photography, the increased three-dimensionality effect of the wide-angle lens is frequently used to obtain striking, even exaggerated perspectives. A typical feature of such views is the "large" reproduction of objects in the foreground, and their "small" rendering in the background.

The shorter the focal length the easier it is to obtain the simultaneous sharpness of near fore- and distant background when the lens is stopped down, because with a 35mm wide-angle lens the depth of field is greater than with a 50mm standard lens (at the same camera viewpoint and with the same stop),

> e.g. focusing on 2.5m (8′4″) f/8
> 35mm focal length: depth of field from 1.6 to 5.3m (5′4″ to 17′8″)
> 50mm focal length: depth of field from 2.0 to 3.3m (6′8″ to 11″)

Since the object field covered by the wide-angle lens is also larger, an exposure can often be risked without a look through the viewfinder.

In Eastern countries you are often faced with situations in which the taking of photographs is undesirable, or in which the "victims" immediately "jump to attention" as it were. Here is a method of taking your photographs almost unnoticed: carry your Leica openly round your neck (horizontal picture) by its neckstrap; line it up with your subject by turning your body; the right hand lies along the camera so that the thumb rests on the release button. The shutter speed, if possible, is set at $^1/_{250}$ or $^1/_{500}$ sec. In order to be able to take photographs by this method even while walking, practise first without, then with film. Release the shutter only when the weight of your body rests firmly on one leg, not when you are setting down the other leg; otherwise camera shake will be unavoidable. You can consider your exposure successful if you manage to utilize half the Leica format for your motif.

The next step in this technique, after some practice, is the "walking snapshot", but with the Leica vertical, and held with the hand extended (Fig.). A few films must be sacrificed in order to acquire the necessary skill and some feeling for distance and picture area.

21 mm Super-Angulon f/3.4

This lens is a further development of the 21 mm Super-Angulon f/4. The increase in the maximum aperture benefits mainly the light distribution. The lens mount calls for larger filters (E 48). Series VII filters, too, can be inserted into the new (oblong) lens hood.

To reduce vignetting to a minimum, short-focal-length wide-angle lenses demand front- and rear elements of large diameter, larger, for instance, than those of the 35 mm Summicron f/2.

Interiors and exteriors which for reasons of space require an extremely short object distance are the chief domain of this lens. It represents a considerable extension of the Leica System since it opens up a completely new perspective, especially in creative photography. In spite of the large angle of view the Super-Angulon is eminently suitable for colour work, as disturbing vignetting and distortion have been completely eliminated.

Distortion and converging verticals are often confused with each other. Converging verticals are caused when the camera is tilted i.e. when the camera back was not aligned vertically during the exposure. This phenomenon becomes more pronounced as the field angle of the lens increases. It is unavoidable according to the laws of central projection, just as lenses of extreme angles of field reproduce spheres as ellipsoids in the marginal regions of the picture area. Converging verticals can be corrected during the enlarging process (picture and diagram see page 236).

We speak of distortion when the reproduction of verticals or horizontals along the picture margin is imperfect, showing an inward or outward curvature. Inward curvature is described as "pin-cushion", outward curvature as "barrel" distortion. It is not affected by stopping down. All Leica lenses have been computed with special attention to freedom from distortion.

The correction of converging verticals presents some difficulties during enlarging. If at all possible, the Leica should be accurately lined up in the vertical and the horizontal when pictures are taken with the Super-Angulon. Converging verticals need, however, not be corrected if the Leica has been tilted so strongly that it can be taken as a deliberate measure.

The depth of field of the Super-Angulon is extraordinary. Nevertheless, the lens should be stopped down more than the depth-of-field scale recommends. For critical demands of sharpness the $^1/_{30}$ mm circle of confusion on which the scale is based is not enough. $^1/_{60}$ mm is better; this value is obtained if we stop down two steps further than the reading (depth-of-field scale reading f/5.6, stop down to f/11). On ultra-fine grain films this method ensures optimum sharpness, even with strong enlargements.

Coupled with the rangefinder the Super-Angulon can be focused down to 1 m (40″) on the Leica M 3, and down to 70 cm (28″) on the Leica M 2. Without rangefinder coupling focusing extends down to 40 cm (16″). At this distance a reproduction scale of 1:17 is obtained, covering an object field of 40×60 cm (16×24″). Pictures of architect's models taken at such a short distance are strikingly realistic. The emphasis on perspective is just what the subject demands. For model railways, geographical reliefs, etc., too, this short distance is very suitable, but portraits unfailingly become caricatures.

An attachable brilliant viewfinder indicates the field area. It shows a slight degree of barrel distortion, which, however, is completely absent from the camera lens. Before you mount the 21 mm lens on the Leica check the rear surface for

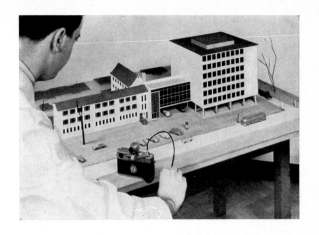

The perspective used by architects in their drawings can be obtained in pictures of models only with lenses of extremely short focal lengths. In order to secure sufficient depth of field at a focusing distance of 40 cm (16"), the 21 mm Super-Angulon had to be stopped down to f/22.

Photograph by R. Seck

perfect cleanness. A single fingermark is quite enough to reduce the optical performance of any lens considerably. Images of bits of fluff or foreign bodies appear, causing disturbing blemishes. Owing to the extreme depth of field of the Super-Angulon, particles of dirt on the filter, too, will spoil the picture at small stops. The use of a polarizing filter is not recommended here since with the large angle of field the extinction of polarized light is incomplete.

Pictures taken with the Super-Angulon can be recognized on the Leica film by their larger size exceeding that of normal pictures by a few tenths of a mm. The gaps between the negatives are therefore narrower.

The centre of Frankfurt am Main. This sweeping townscape was taken with the 28 mm Elmarit f/2.8 stopped down to f/5.6, $^1/_{125}$ sec.

28 mm Elmarit f/2.8

The focal length of this lens is intermediate between 21 and 35 mm. It combines high speed with a wide angle of field; its correction is excellent. The large number of elements is necessary to ensure freedom from vignetting in addition to these properties. The longitudinal section through this lens shows clearly that both the front- and the rear element are much larger than the lens aperture demands. This prevents the disturbing falling off of light towards the corners of the field in colour film.

The 28 mm Elmarit is practically free from distortion, which makes it eminently suitable for both internal and external architectural subjects. If you want to avoid converging verticals you must take great care to line up your Leica vertically as well as horizontally. If for some reason or other you have to tilt the camera you can correct this convergence in black-and-white photography at the enlarging stage.

92

The very great depth of field of the 28 mm Elmarit allows simultaneous sharp rendering of the near foreground as well as the distant background even at medium lens stops.

The brilliant viewfinder for the 28 mm focal length is used. In the Leica M3 the rangefinder is coupled down to 1 m (40″), in the M2 and M4 to 0.7 m (28″).

I find the 28 mm Elmarit f/2.8 a versatile wide-angle lens to supplement my 50 mm Summilux f/1.4 if I have to select a light-weight, yet useful photographic outfit for a journey. I would choose the 90 mm Tele-Elmarit f/2.8 as a third focal length.

Reception hall in the Leitz administrative building. 28 mm Elmarit f/2.8, f/8, 2 sec. With work from the tripod check the vertical and horizontal line-up of your Leica by moving two steps back and to one side respectively and aligning the camera.

THE 35 mm WIDE-ANGLE LENSES

There is a choice of three different lens speeds in the 35 mm focal length group: the Summaron f/2.8, the Summicron f/2, and the ultra-fast wide-angle lens, the Summilux f/1.4. At 64° the angle of field is the same for all speeds. Each of these lenses is available in two versions: the first has a viewfinder attachment, which converts the field of view of the 50 mm viewfinder into 35 mm, and is designed for the M3, but can also be used on the M2 and M4. Since the M2 and M4 already have the 35 mm bright frame in its viewfinder, the 35 mm lenses are available in a second version without finder attachment. With range-finder coupling the focusing range on the M2 and M4 extends from ∞ to 0.70 m (28″), and on the M3 with finder attachment from ∞ to 0.65 m (26″). This finder attachment is a permanent fixture on the lens, i.e. unlike the attachment of the near-focusing 50 mm Summicron it cannot be removed.

Swabian Jura. 55 mm Summicron f/2, f/8, $^1/_{15}$ sec, Agfa Agepe FF, Neofin developer. Photograph by Hans Steinhorst. Document copying film is a most unusual material for landscape photography. Development has a very important influence – Neofin and Rodinal 1:100 are suitable. No grain will appear even at maximum enlargement. The contrast of the delicate landscape can be increased without difficulty.

35 mm Summaron f/2.8

This is a six-element Gauss type. The introduction of new types of glass has made it possible to increase the speed of the well-tried 35 mm Summaron to f/2.8. Its colour correction has also been improved.

35 mm Summicron f/2

This is an eight-element Gauss-type of excellent performance. Even in bad lighting conditions instantaneous exposures can now be taken on colour film. The 35 mm Summicron is a lens for all purposes. Colour correction and resolving power are comparable with those of the top-quality 50 mm Summicron. Maximum resolving power is achieved already between f/4 and f/5.6. Further stopping down merely increases the depth of field.

35 mm Summilux f/1.4

This special, ultra-fast lens has been designed to meet the demands of modern press photographers for work in "available light".
Snapshots in extremely poor lighting conditions are particularly striking because of the greater depth and the larger angle of field than those taken with the 50 mm lens. The diameters of the front and rear lens are so large that at full aperture there is far less vignetting than would normally be expected with such a fast lens (vignetting see p.87). The large front lens diameter requires screw-in filters E41.

65 mm Elmar f/3.5

This lens has been designed for use on the Visoflex II and III. It has no helical focusing mount, but is used with the universal focusing mount (16,464). This produces continuous focusing from ∞ to 33 cm (13″). At the minimum focusing distance this means a reproduction scale of 1:2.5 and an object field of 6×9 cm (2$^1/_4$×3$^3/_4$″). With the aid of the ring 16,471 this reproduction scale can be further extended to 1:1.25, when the size of the object field will be 30×45 mm (1$^1/_4$×1$^3/_4$″). This very large focusing range enables the user of the 65 mm Elmar to change over from a landscape directly to a frame-filling close-up of a flower harbouring an insect. Half stop values can be set on the automatic diaphragm, whose minimum aperture is f/22. Combined with the universal focusing bellows II the 65 mm Elmar can be used from ∞ to a reproduction scale 1.4:1 (object field 15×23 mm, approx. $^3/_4$×1″). The design of the lens mount makes a special lens hood unnecessary. E 41 screw-in filters are required.

Section of a painting, Altar of The Presentation of Our Lady, Alte Pinakothek, Munich. 65 mm Elmar f/3.5, f/4, $^1/_{30}$ sec, 400 ASA film. Photograph by Kisselbach. Many museums permit photography provided no tripod and no flash is used.

THE 90 mm LENSES

One fine day, before setting out on a tough mountain walk, I had to make a decision on technical points alone – the cost made no difference – because for reasons of weight I could take only two lenses with me. After thorough consideration I chose the 35 mm Summicron f/2 and the 90 mm Elmarit f/2.8. Obviously such a decision must always be personal, but I would never have left the 90 mm lens at home, because to me this focal length has almost become standard, I use it so often.

The arguments in favour of this focal length are most varied. It represents an ideal compromise, it forces the photographer to condense the pictorial content, it has less depth of field, hence the various features do not appear to "stick together" in the picture.

97

A 90mm lens can be used for a variety of reasons. In the first subject shown here, disturbance of the scene by the presence of the photographer had to be prevented. He had to avoid getting too close. The longer focal length gave him the chance to make his subject fill his frame without attracting attention. Whenever it is essential to take live action shots quickly and without being seen, the "discretion" of such a lens will help you. Children's pictures taken with a standard 50mm lens must be taken from a kneeling or squatting position, because standing up the photographer would have to tilt his camera too much. The longer camera distance made possible by the 90mm Elmar allows more convenient operation. At the same time, disturbing background features are eliminated.

Photograph by S. Hartig

The Leica amateur who took the ghats at Benares from the steamer was confined to his standpoint, i.e. the railings. What he wanted was to combine all the characteristic features in his picture "Sadhus Bathing in the Ganges." Although he shows only a small section, as so often the part is more significant than the whole.

Photograph by Dr. Sprado

It was this same reason which made the photographer of the Romanesque relief use the 90 mm Elmar. The relief is a figure from the richly-ornamented church door of St. Trophime at Arles. The welter of detail would have appeared too small on a total view. Here, too, the large reproduction of a typical feature is more eloquent than a general representation. The layer of dust on the almost black stone conveniently softens the contrast of the harsh lighting of the southern sun.   *Photograph by Theo M. Scheerer*

This noonday scene of Santa Cruz, too, owes its charm to the unnoticed and rapid action at the right moment. It is a typical example of the simple means with which a striking picture can be composed. A narrow strip of sunlight makes the lamp and the figure stand out in contre jour. A splash of reflected sunlight on the wall of the building – an almost essential counterpoint – even picks out the group in the background. The long camera distance alone made this unnoticed snapshot possible.
          Photograph by H. Wildenhain

These examples, taken by four different photographers in the most different conditions, give an idea of the various uses of the very popular 90 mm focal length.

90mm lenses are available in various speeds and models.

90mm lenses are handy, every bit as much as the 50mm standard ones, and their weight, too, is light enough. The focusing mount allows focusing down to 1m (40″) which means a reproduction scale of 1:9 (about the size of a sheet of note paper 20×30cm [8×12″]). But focusing must be very accurate in the close-up range, rough guesswork is not enough.

The following method of focusing in the close-up range is much quicker than that of rotating the focusing mount of the lens; focus on the estimated distance and move backwards or forwards until the double images in the rangefinder merge into one. Only a little practice is necessary to master this technique. The following hint is useful for snapshots at some distance: Set lens stop and shutter speed. In order to preserve the moment of surprise do not focus directly on your subject but on an object the same distance away. If you work with a comparison distance your estimate will be excellent. You can easily make minor adjustments in order to make the distance from both points identical. Your standpoint represents, as it were, the apex of an isosceles triangle; one side is the focusing distance, the other the distance of your subject. Watch the scene up to

100

the suitable moment, swing round and press the button. After short practice you will be familiar with this technique, which can be used equally well with other focal lengths.

90 mm Elmarit f/2.8

The introduction of highly-refracting lanthanum glasses has made both an improvement of optical performance and an increase in speed possible. Compared with the four elements of the Elmar design, the Elmarit consists of five elements. In spite of a twofold increase in speed, it weighs only 30 g (1 oz) more. It lies in the hand as snugly as the Elmar. The lens head can be unscrewed and used in combination with a universal focusing mount on the Visoflex II from ∞ to 50 cm (20"). The object field at the minimum focusing distance is 80 × 120 mm ($3^1/_4 \times 4^3/_4$").

90 mm Tele-Elmarit f/2.8

This is a lens of true telephoto construction, i.e. it is 27 mm shorter than a long-focal-length 90 mm Elmarit f/2.8. The optical quality is excellent. The lens head of the Tele-Elmarit *cannot* be unscrewed; it is not intended for use on the Visoflex II or III, or on the focusing bellows. The optical quality is excellent. It has a non-rotating focusing mount and is rangefinder-coupled from ∞ to 1 m (40"). It is very popular on journeys because of its small volume.

90 mm Summicron f/2

An increase of the speed to f/2 in a lens of this focal length involves a considerable increase in volume and weight (685 g [$19^1/_2$ oz]) compared with the 235 g (120 oz) of the Elmarit. But if you are forced to work in difficult lighting conditions and cannot use shorter focal lengths because of the distance of your subjects you will be happy to have a lens like the Summicron. Owing to the liberal use of light alloy it is comparatively handy and its weight reasonable. The lens hood is a permanent fixture and collapsible. The click stops engage at half stops. A special version of this lens is available with pre-set diaphragm and short mount for use in the Visoflex II and III.

In modern colour photography, the use of long-focal-length, fast lenses with their very narrow depth of field has led to a new creative approach to pictorialism.

Photography with 135 mm lenses

The terms "short" or "long" focal length are always relative to the camera format. The diagonal of the film size is considered "normal" for the focal length of the camera lens; in the 24×36mm format this is approximately 45mm. Anything appreciably below this figure is "wide-angle". Long-focal-length lenses are not defined by their field angles, but by their optical design. Terms here are not defined as accurately as one would wish them to be. A long-focal-length lens of normal dimensions is a *long-distance*, not a telephoto, lens. In a *telephoto* system the distance between the front lens and the film plane is shorter than the focal length.

The 135mm focal length in the Leica format provides a 2.7× magnified image on the film compared with that by the 50mm standard lens. Our visual impression, by the way, does not correspond to the effect of the 50mm lens, because there is too little subsequent enlargement in practice. "Seeing" and "taking a photograph" are different processes, and we speak of natural perspective when we view a photograph only when

viewing distance = focal length of taking lens × enlarging factor.

Hence the 135mm focal length conveys the impression of a concentrated section of a picture better than an enlarged picture.

Only a few typical uses are chosen here from the vast range of applications of long-focal-length lenses. Many subjects can be photographed unnoticed because of the long-focal-length and the correspondingly long camera distance. Sports and street scenes, architectural details, commercial subjects, portraits, and above all the innumerable nature records are fields which are competently covered by the 135mm Tele-Elmar.

Such a long-focal-length lens can be used for many more subjects than is commonly assumed. Originally designed for the purpose of bridging an irreducible distance, of reproducing the subject at sufficient size to fill the frame, and of avoiding the need for strong part-enlargements, long-focal-length lenses are today increasingly used at any camera distance because we are beginning to realize the advantages of the more concentrated pictorial approach they engender – more concentrated than that of the standard focal length.

Young marmot. 135 mm Tele-Elmar f/4, f/5.6, $^1/_{125}$ sec.   *Photograph by Kisselbach*

In addition to their many advantages, the long focal lengths present their own difficulties. Above all they are far more sensitive to camera shake during hand-held exposures. In order to obtain sharp pictures it is essential to hold your camera steady, to focus accurately, to assume a rigid stance (whenever you can with support of the lens hood), and to release the shutter smoothly. If possible use a robust tripod.

The pictorial effect of a 135 mm lens is more easily judged on the groundglass screen of the Visoflex than by a look through the viewfinder. Nevertheless, the latter method is more reliable in rapid sports and press photography. Although it is often impossible to measure the distance of a moving subject, the place of an action is usually known beforehand, and the lens can be focused on it in good time. The viewfinder with excess field prepares the photographer better for the situation he may expect. The subject can be observed as it enters the picture area of the Leica from outside the 135 mm frame. Compared with the mirror reflex principle, the measuring viewfinder method involves no disturbing blackout at the vital moment of exposure. No time lapse occurs when the release button is pressed.

As the distance increases, guessing it becomes more difficult. My method for sports pictures, which often call for long-focal-length lenses is as follows: – A suitable distance is set on the lens and the size of a person appropriate at this distance determined in the viewfinder. At first this should be tried out with persons standing still to see what area they take up in the viewfinder; later with persons walking and running; in spite of the longer focal length the depth of field is almost the same. At the third stage of your practice watch the movement of the legs and count "left, right". After a few trial films, pressing the button at just the right moment has ceased to be a problem.

135 mm Tele-Elmar f/4

This lens is available in black finish only. It consists of five elements, two of which are cemented. It is of very short construction and of excellent optical quality.

The rangefinder-coupled focusing range is from ∞ to 1.5 m (60″); the focusing action is quicker than usual because the helical mount is closer to the camera body and has a coarse thread. The lens head can be used on the Visoflex II or III in the universal mount 16464 (without adapter ring), or, with adapter ring 16558, in the Bellows II. The Tele-Elmar cannot be used with the Visoflex I, because the intercept distance of this telephoto lens is too short.

104

*135 mm Elmarit f/2.8
with magnifying viewfinder attachment.
The telescopic lens hood is permanently
mounted on the lens.*

135 mm Elmarit f/2.8 with magnifying viewfinder attachment

The viewfinder attachment has been designed to magnify the 90 mm frame 1.5× in the measuring viewfinder of the Leicas M2 and M3. This affords several advantages: – The owner of a Leica M2 now also has a 135 mm lens available which he can couple directly with his measuring viewfinder. Owing to the magnifying attachment details can be recognized more clearly, with the result of increased focusing accuracy.

The design of the lens is very short. It is a telephoto system computed for the use of new, highly-refracting types of glass. Its correction is excellent. Even at full aperture resolution and marginal definition are outstanding.

The lens hood is permanently mounted on the lens, and is collapsible. Series VII filters should be used. After the retaining ring is unscrewed the filters are inserted and secured with the ring.

It is advisable to grip the retaining ring on one side only, as you would grip a child's hoop, to avoid deformation.

The iris diaphragm engages at full and half stops. The focusing movement is non-rotating and has a range from ∞ to 1.5 m (5'). The lens head can be unscrewed; it can be used up to ∞ on the Visoflex II or III with a special focusing mount. Owing to the telephoto design of the Elmarit, its rear lens is mounted so far to the rear that only a limited focusing range (not to ∞) is possible with the focusing bellows I or II.

105

Wooden-tiled roofs in Vorarlberg, Austria. – Left: 50mm Summicron f/2. Right: 200mm Telyt f/4.5. The view from above demands a long camera distance and a long-focal-length lens in order to arrange the well-spaced roofs pictorially. The 50mm picture, taken from the same spot, shows the same perspective. But the corresponding area on the negative is so small that it would have to be enlarged four times compared with the picture taken with the 200mm lens. A closer approach is not possible, as this would change the perspective and therefore the outlines at once.

Photograph by Prof. Stefan Kruckenhauser

The telephoto lenses of 200, 280, 400 and 560mm focal lengths

They are shorter than one would expect from their focal lengths, which classifies them as "telephoto systems". Their reduced length makes them easier to handle. Their optical design is identical, but the increased focal length has already a very marked effect in reportage. In other respects, too, the compression of space and the unusual perspective it provides is an effective means of pictorial composition.

In order to be able to judge even without setting up the camera whether an exposure is worth the effort I use the following simplified formula: $100 \times f$ (focal length) $= 100 \times$ upright or horizontal dimension. The distance must be at least $100 \times$ the focal length, the maximum error is below 2%. With a 35 mm wide-angle lens, for instance, I obtain an object field of 2.4×3.6 m $(8 \times 12')$ at a distance of 3.5 m (11'8''). The same area is covered by the 200 mm Telyt from a distance of 20 m (66'). Naturally we must allow for the fact that we normally photograph three-dimensional objects rather than planes.

Many users of a 200 mm lens expect it to have the effect of a strong fieldglass. They believe it to be possible to photograph a roebuck from 60 m (200') so that it fills the frame. At this distance the camera produces an image of the animal at $1/300$ its natural size. i.e. measuring no more than a few mm across.

$$\left(\frac{\text{focal length}}{\text{object distance}} = \text{reproduction scale} = \frac{200\,\text{mm}}{60{,}000\,\text{mm}} = \frac{1}{300} \right)$$

Nevertheless, the difference from the standard 50 mm focal length is already very considerable, as the next example will show. At the same camera position, our image with the 200 mm lens will be $4 \times$ as large as that with the 50 mm lens. The pictures opposite illustrate the effect in practice.

Hand-held shots are still possible with the 200 mm and the 280 mm Telyts. I most strongly recommend the technique of supporting the lens on the elbow of the angled left arm at shoulder level. Propping the camera on its lens hood is also very effective. Even when I am able to set up a tripod, for moving subjects I prefer this propping up of the lens hood to the rigid tripod fixture.

Modern metal tripods with adjustable centre column and high ball-and-socket heads may be very convenient for focusing, but used with long-focal-length lenses they tend to vibrate. Exposure times from $1/60$ to $1/8$ sec are particularly risky. Vibrations may be caused by the action of the shutter (law of inertia) and, outdoors, by wind pressure on the open lens hood.

The weight and the mechanical stability of a tripod play an important part in our efforts to avoid camera shake. Often a tripod is too light. With the conventional attachment of the camera approximately in the centre of gravity small forces are already sufficient to affect the rigidity of the setup. Long focal lengths have narrow angles of field, and the narrower the angle, the more disturbing the effect of any vibrations. Two points of support, i.e., if possible two tripods, are an excellent help, but they must be so arranged that the equipment can rest on both. By tapping the tripod legs you can make certain that everything is firmly supported.

The lens is always focused with a magnifier on the groundglass screen of a Visoflex attachment. Rangefinder coupling has been dispensed with, because with very long focal lengths the groundglass screen is superior. Not only is it possible to focus on it; the image on the groundglass screen is exactly proportional to the focal length, and it most accurately coincides with what will eventually appear on the film, even in the close-up range. The Visoflex III will be dealt with in a special chapter (pp. 118).

Even your first glance at the groundglass screen of the Visoflex attachment will convince you of the attraction, indeed fascination of photography with such an extraordinary focal length. It will take you some time to become used to having so little on your film. But you will very quickly realize the enormous advantage of this "limitation to essentials". The large angle of field of the standard focal length usually includes much too restless a background. Not so your Telyt with its narrow angle of field. Almost no disturbing feature is left, inessentials such as the background will be suppressed in well-balanced unsharpness; but important items stand out clearly and plastically.

Experience shows that often the most striking pictures are the result of full aperture and shallow depth of field.

The longer the focal length the more unusual will you find the perspective. Some subjects will show a stage-prop effect, even objects spaced in great depth will appear flat. A certain amount of practice is quite indispensable, and what

Leica M3 with Visoflex II and 200mm Telyt f/4.

Facing page: Venice, 200mm Telyt, f/4.5, $^{1}/_{250}$ sec. Photograph by Prof. Eugen Funk

108

is still simple with a 200 mm lens may already produce difficulties with the 400 mm lens.

In long-distance shots the subject contrast is characteristically poor. If possible, exposure should be less than that indicated by the meter (1–2 stops) and development extended. The best results are obtained on document-copying films, but their very narrow exposure latitude and slow speed requires some practice on a few trial films (p. 136).

200 mm Telyt f/4★

This lens is focused with the Visoflex attachment, has a non-rotating focusing movement, and a focusing range from ∞ to 3 m (10′). An adapter ring of 15 mm (0.6″) depth (14020) increases the range from 3 m to 1.7 m (10′ to 5′8″), and two adapter rings from 1.7 m to 1.3 m (5′8″ to 4′4″). Shorter distances can be focused with the universal focusing bellows (p. 186). The lens has an automatic diaphragm; its minimum aperture is f/22. The automatic diaphragm allows the selected stop to be pre-set on a ring. The normal stop ring can be opened as desired up to the moment of focusing, but it cannot be shut beyond the preselected value. Half-stops can also be set. The permanently fixed lens hood is collapsible.

280 mm Telyt f/4.8★

The new 280 mm Telyt fills a long-felt gap, as the difference between the 200 mm and the 400 mm lenses is very considerable. Its speed has been limited to f/4.8 in the interest of handiness. It is only half a stop less than f/4, but the difference in weight (1490 g, 3 lb, 50 oz), is enormous. The front lens diameter could also be kept small enough for E 58 filters, the same as for the 200 mm Telyt, to be used on it.

The lens has a non-rotating focusing mount, and a focusing range from ∞ to 5.6 m (18′8″). One adapter ring (14020) increases the range from 5.6 to 3.1 m (18′8″ to 10′4″), two rings increase it from 3.1 to 2.3 m (10′4″ to 7′8″). It includes an automatic diaphragm, and clickstops with half-stop settings; its minimum aperture is f/22. The lens hood is permanently fixed and collapsible.

★ Can be directly attached to the Visoflex I. For Visoflex II and III adapter ring 16 466 is required.

Photograph by Wilhelm Schack, 400 mm Telyt.

400 and 560 mm Telyt f/5.6

These long focal lengths are preferred for the photography of animals in their natural surroundings; they are finding increasing use in press photography, too, because the distances from which press cameramen have to operate are often very long. The art historian also greatly appreciates these lenses because they enable him to obtain close-ups of architectural details without the need to erect large scaffoldings.

These lenses must be very carefully focused because of their shallow depth of field. If instant readiness is essential, you can focus in the Visoflex with the lens stopped down – e. g. to f/8 or f/11 – and release the shutter directly. Do not stop down further than the sharp rendering of the main subject calls for. Unsharpness in the fore- or background enhances the pictorial impact and reduces the impression of flatness. We would urgently advise you to familiarize yourself with the handling of these lenses and their technical refinements by using up several trial films. In the beginning, record all the data such as lens stop and shutter speed. Here, too, it is a good idea to insert the negatives in 5×5 cm changing frames and to assess their quality on the projection screen.

Picture contrast is a very important feature to watch with long-distance shots, because the intervening atmosphere has the effect of reducing it. The contrast rendering of these new achromats, which consist of two cemented elements each, is quite outstanding. Reproduction quality as a whole has been considerably improved by the introduction of new optical glasses.

Both lenses have a permanently attached, extensible lens hood, leather covered to protect it from scratches when the lens is placed on a support or propped up during the exposure. Never forget the lens cap and -cover during transport, in order to prevent dust from entering the inside of the lenses. These Telyts form part of the Televit assembly described below.

Televit rapid focusing device for the 280, 400, and 560 mm Telyts

Depending on the focal length of the lens used in it the composition of the rapid focusing device varies. The 400 mm and the 560 mm Telyts use the same diaphragm tube. The components are assembled in the following sequence:

Leica – Visoflex III – Televit – Diaphragm tube – lens head.

Photograph by J. Behnke, 400 mm Telyt

The lens head of the 280mm Telyt is inserted by means of a bayonet adapter (14138). The lens head of the earlier 400mm Telyt f/5 can be attached with the same adapter.

The rapid focusing device proper consists of a sturdy tube with an inner part running on steel rails and extensible trough about 70mm, and a handgrip for holding and focusing. The Leica with the Visoflex is attached by means of a bayonet catch.

Handling the Televit calls for a certain amount of experience. Take the handgrip in your left hand, place your thumb on the rubber-covered rotating knob, and depress the bolt at the top of the handgrip with your index finger. This releases the arresting device of the coarse adjustment, and you can move the Leica with Visoflex freely backwards and forwards. Hold the Leica in your right hand as usual, the index finger covering the release button of the Visoflex. The coarse adjustment is arrested as soon as the left index finger releases the bolt. Now carry out fine focusing with your thumb on the large, rubber-covered rotating knob. Two distances can be set by means of two knurled screws on the left of the rapid focusing device. ∞ can be set with the screw nearer the camera.

Series VII filters are used, and inserted in a holder in the tube between the hand-grip and the bayonet for the Visoflex attachment. Since the filter is in the optical path behind the lens, the object must be focused with the filter in position. A special carrying strap for the outfit (14130) has tripod screws which fit the various tripod bushes in the Televit.

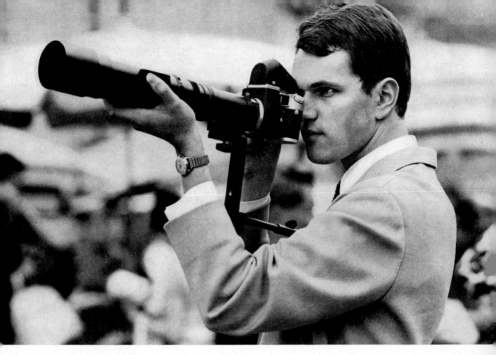

The new 400 mm rapid-action lens Telyt f/6.8

Rapid-action lens 400 mm Telyt f/6.8
for reportage, sports, and wild-life photography

Light weight and simple operation combined with excellent optical performance are the outstanding characteristics of this rapid-action lens. The detachable, adjustable shoulder stock provides firm support during instant levelling and aiming.

The front part of the lens mount is adjusted in a precision parallel guide for rapid and at the same time exact focusing. The focusing mechanism can be released with a push button and clamped in the desired setting.

The optical system is a highly corrected achromat with anti-reflection coating providing high image contrast. This is of particular importance in long-distance photography because the atmosphere always has the effect of reducing object contrast. Contrasty rendering, however, not only is of importance to the image quality, but also has a positive effect on focusing.

The long focusing range from ∞ to 3.60 m is a considerable advantage. It offers a minimum object field of 16×24 cm. This makes it possible to photograph small animals outside their critical distance at which they take flight, or frame-filling portraits from distances of more than 5 m (17 feet). A tube adapter, length 6 cm (14 182) extends the focusing range down to 2.30 m, when the minimum object field will measure 8 × 12 cm.

For convenient transport the lens can be dismantled into two parts and stored in a minimum of space.

Weight: lens 1,300 g, shoulder stock 500 g.

A filter pocket for series filters VII is built into the lens tube.

THE COATING OF THE LEICA LENSES

Not all the light entering a lens passes through it. According to the laws of refraction part of the light rays is reflected by both interfaces of the lens, i. e. on its front and rear.

In a modern, fast lens, the light may often have to pass no fewer than 12 such interfaces; it would therefore be weakened 12 times through losses owing to reflection, amounting to up to 50% of the total before it reaches the film if a method had not been found of reducing them to a minimum by a special treatment of the glass surfaces. But this is not all. Reflected light is not only lost to the exposure. It goes its own way, strays inside the camera and causes veiling, reduction of contrast, or even disturbing reflection images. These dangers, too, are eliminated by "anti-reflection coating".

All Leitz lenses have been coated for many years. This involves application of a film of a characteristic coloured sheen; it is called "B-(brilliant)film" and causes the potentially reflected light otherwise lost to the exposure or even detrimental to the picture to remain within the bundle of rays as it passes the interfaces. Hence, "blooming" a lens brings an appreciable gain in effective speed and an increase in brilliance. It is therefore obvious that coating is of particular importance in top-class lenses made up of many elements. Its benefits are even stronger in colour than in black-and-white photography. The two outside surfaces of any lens are hard-coated. Gentle wiping with a soft piece of chamois leather or a sable brush does not do any damage. Specially prepared tissue, offered by some manufacturers for the cleaning of camera lenses (not spectacles), can also be used.

The picture on the left was taken with an uncoated lens. Because of reflections inside the lens system reflected images of the lamp, and of the diaphragm, as well as stray light become noticeable. In order to make these effects more prominent this picture was strongly overexposed (f/4 – 1 sec. Normally $^1/_{1000}$ sec would have been enough).

Picture on the right: The same conditions with a coated lens. Diaphragm images and stray light have disappeared, reflections are much weaker.

116

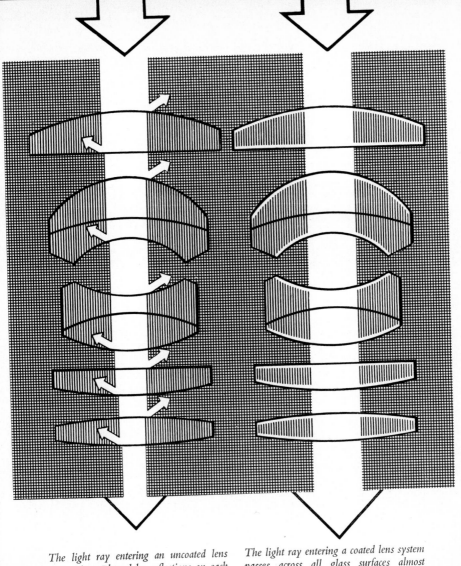

The light ray entering an uncoated lens system is weakened by reflections on each glass surface.

The light ray entering a coated lens system passes across all glass surfaces almost without loss owing to reflection.

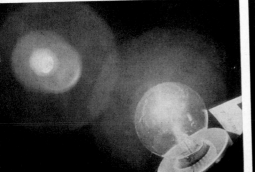

The Visoflex III mirror reflex attachment

The Visoflex III is one of the most important accessories in the Leica System. Groundglass screen observation offers advantages with longer-focal-length lenses and in the near-focusing range. The attachable Visoflex device converts any Leica into a single-lens-reflex camera. It also provides for different ways of swinging the mirror out of the optical path, e. g. almost silently.

The height of the Visoflex III is only 41mm, the release is directly coupled with the Leica, which makes hand-held exposures very convenient. The shortest focal length permitting infinity focusing is 65mm. The dimensions of some lenses are matched for the Visoflex I. The difference is compensated by means of an adapter (16466), which has a height of 22.5mm.

A 4× prism magnifier with horizontal eyepiece tube allows right-way-round observation of upright and horizontal pictures. The simple 5× magnifier presents the picture at right angles and side-reversed, and, with vertical subjects, also upside-down. This magnifier has been designed for special uses such as copying and photomicrography, where the lateral position of the eyepiece makes work easier.

The focusing screen is a genuine groundglass screen; in the centre it has a small focusing ring of 1mm diameter. Seen through the magnifier, this ring must

118

The wide range of possibilities with the Visoflex III

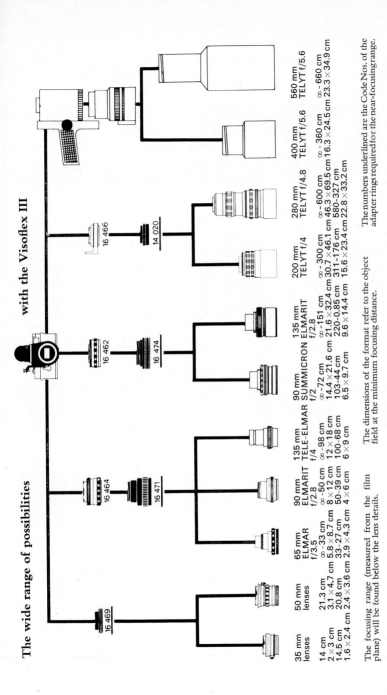

Lens	35 mm lenses	50 mm lenses	65 mm ELMAR f/3.5	90 mm ELMARIT f/2.8	135 mm TELE-ELMAR f/4	90 mm SUMMICRON f/2	135 mm ELMARIT f/2.8	200 mm TELYT f/4	280 mm TELYT f/4.8	400 mm TELYT f/5.6	560 mm TELYT f/5.6
	∞ - 4 cm	21.3 cm	∞ - 33 cm	∞ - 50 cm	∞ - 98 cm	∞ - 72 cm	∞ - 151 cm	∞ - 300 cm	∞ - 600 cm	∞ - 360 cm	∞ - 660 cm
	2 × 3 cm	3.1 × 4.7 cm	5.8 × 8.7 cm	8 × 12 cm	12 × 18 cm	14.4 × 21.6 cm	21.6 × 32.4 cm	30.7 × 46.1 cm	46.3 × 69.5 cm	16.3 × 24.5 cm	23.3 × 34.9 cm
	14.5 cm	20.8 cm	33 - 27 cm	50 - 39 cm	100 - 68 cm	103 - 44 cm	220 - 0.85 cm	311 - 176 cm	580 - 327 cm		
	1.6 × 2.4 cm	2.4 × 3.6 cm	2.9 × 4.3 cm	4 × 6 cm	6 × 9 cm	6.5 × 9.7 cm	9.6 × 14.4 cm	15.6 × 23.4 cm	22.8 × 33.2 cm		

Code Nos.: 16 469 · 16 464 · 16 471 · 16 462 · 16 474 · 16 466 · 14 020

The focusing range (measured from the film plane) will be found below the lens details.

The dimensions of the format refer to the object field at the minimum focusing distance.

The numbers underlined are the Code Nos. of the adapter rings required for the near-focusing range.

These possibilities are further extended when the Visoflex III is combined with the universal focusing bellows, see p. 186.

(1) Simple magnifier, 5× (side-reversed image), focusing eyelens

(2) Right-way-round observation magnifier, 4×

(3) Release button, adjustment screw below

(4) Release lever

(5) Bayonet changer

(6) Bayonet locking lever

(7) Groundglass screen with focusing ring, 1 mm dia.

(8) Thread for cable release

(9) Setting knob for mirror movement

(10) Button for locking and unlocking the lens

appear pinsharp. A correction lens (14118) for users with faulty vision is pushed on to the magnifier mount. The dioptres should be those of the distant glasses. The weight of the Visoflex assembly with long-focal-length lenses is such that it is not recommended to carry it on the simple neck strap for hooking into the eyelets on the Leica body. For this purpose a heavy-duty neck strap with 2 tripod screws (14130) is available.

In normal lighting conditions the image on the groundglass screen is bright enough to permit focusing at f/8. In the near-focusing range you can also set the suitable reproduction scale first, and move the camera backwards and forwards until the subject appears sharp on the screen.

Attaching the Visoflex III

The locking lever of the Visoflex is swung down – red dot facing red dot. The Visoflex bayonet is introduced into the Leica body. Check by very slight movement to the left and right whether the bayonet fittings are in the correct position, before pushing the lever up.

In the Visoflex III the mirror movement can be adjusted according to need. A rotating dial with coloured dots is located below the shaft of the release lever.

120

Yellow dot: The mirror quickly moves out of the beam path shortly before the shutter is released. Suitable for all rapid movements, with pressure point on the release lever.

Black dot: The mirror moves very slowly and silently out of the beam path. Suitable for animal photography.
The release lever returns to its original position without being wound.

Red dot: The mirror remains swung out. The camera must therefore first be focused. Pictures can be taken without mirror movement (copying, macrophotography, photomicrography).

Adjusting the release lever

The distance to the release button of the Leica is also adjusted in the red-dot position of the mirror movement setting knob. This adjustment is necessary so that the mirror is removed from the beam path in time for a rapid release. The small knurled screw on the release lever is turned until the distance to the release button of the Leica is about 1 mm (0.04″). With insufficient adjustment the mirror is moved too late out of the optical path during rapid release, blocking one corner of the film.

Yellow dot:
ick return of mirror

Black dot:
Mirror swings out

Red dot: Mirror is held
in top position

Red dot:
Adjust release

The Leica motor

In combination with all Leica M models (except the M3) the Leica motor permits serial exposures and single exposures with automatic film transport and shutter wind. For serial exposures there is a choice between the H (high speed) setting for about 3 frames per second and the L (low speed) setting for 1 frame per second. All shutter speeds from 1 to $^1/_{1000}$ sec can be set.

The electric motor is powered by 8 1.5v standard batteries (in Germany size R 6, in U.S.A. and in the U.K. size AA). A set of batteries is generally sufficient for about 40 films. The battery housing is attached to the underside of the motor without a cable.

Leica M, motor, and battery housing form a neat unit. The general uses of the Leica remain unrestricted, since the camera is fully operative without the motor. The function of the motor ist controlled by the two roller blinds of the focal-plane shutter of the Leica. At the instant the movement of the focal-plane shutter is unblocked the motor is switched off until the shutter movement is complete. This control by the shutter itself prevents premature film transport as well as functional disturbances through accidental setting of excessively slow shutter speeds with serial exposures of 3 frames per second.

The Leica motor has a second connection for current supply without battery housing, so that all sources delivering d. c. between 6 and 14v can be used. Since batteries are sensitive to cold, a second battery housing can be carried in the inside jacket pocket where it is kept warm.

Remote control via cable or by radio is possible via a two-pole, standard connection for both methods. Ordinary electric cables of up to 1,500m (1,650yd) length can be used. Induction coils on both sides of the circuit prevent accidental tripping through outside impulses during radio release.

The Leica motor is manufactured by E. Leitz, Inc., Rockleigh, New Jersey, U.S.A.

Leica cases

The wish to protect your valuable Leica equipment during transport is very reasonable; it is met by various cases. The ever-ready case is the most common. It is less popular among press photographers and professionals using the Leica, because "readiness" is not as instant as its name would suggest. But in the latest version (14534) the front part is detachable after the press stud in the rear has been pushed up to unlock it.

If you want to be instantly ready for action, you will prefer to carry the Leica by its carrying strap, keeping it in an amateur case or a universal holdall case for transport only. The amateur case accepts a 90 mm lens in addition to the Leica-M, the Leicameter, and a 50 mm lens. A special coupler, into which two Leica lenses can be locked on either side, allows the attachment of an additional lens of up to 50 mm focal length to the 90 mm lens for storage. The 90 mm lens can be replaced by a 135 mm lens. The amateur case also has space for lens hoods, 3 filters, and a few films.

The universal holdall case has been designed for more extensive outfits still; it has interchangeable inserts. Insert I accommodates a large Leica outfit with 2 M-bodies and various lenses of up to 135 mm focal length, but without Viso-flex. Insert II is suitable for one Leica M-body with Visoflex III and lenses of up to 280 mm focal length.

Since Leica outfits can be assembled to suit the most individual requirements it is very difficult to provide every user with precisely the case he needs. For some time cases of various sizes completely filled with foam rubber have been available; with a special knife foam rubber can be cut out to make room for whatever equipment needs to go in for shock-proof storage during transport.

If you want to spend long periods in the tropics you will buy a metal case to protect your Leica outfit; it closes hermetically. If you keep a little bag of silica gel inside, the danger of excessive humidity will be strongly reduced. After some time the silica gel must be reactivated by heating it.

THE PROPERTIES OF LEICA FILMS

The efficiency of the Leica depends to a large extent on the film. But no one film on the market today combines all the top qualities, and the demands vary according to the task in hand. If you expect the highest speed, you must accept a somewhat coarser grain. Such a film is thus used mainly where photography would otherwise be impossible because of insufficient light. Generally medium-speed films (50–200 ASA) are the most suitable for your purpose. Their properties as a whole, i. e. general speed, colour sensitivity, resolving power, grain size, freedom from halation, and gradation are the best balanced.

Manufactures have to go to great lengths to keep the sum total of these qualities as uniform as possible. When you buy a film you must be able to rely on their product.

The various properties of a film are described in some detail on the following pages so that you will know what to look for when you have to choose your own exposure material.

1. General speed

A comparison table of various speed ratings will be found on page 314. Films in the Anglo-American countries are rated in ASA/BSI (American Standards Association/British Standards of Industry) values, which for practical purposes are identical. They double with the film speed, i. e. a 50 ASA film is twice as fast as a 25 ASA film. Normal exposure meters have for years been calibrated so that they indicate values which are suitable for colour reversal films. For black-and-white films this means a reserve of 1–2 stop values depending on the developer, the developing time, and the temperature.

Some special developers of a high speed utilization make use of this reserve for their "magic effect". It is possible to set twice or even four times the rated speed on the exposure, meter, and yet to produce a well-exposed negative. The latest revision of the ASA scale, however, has led to a cutting down of this reserve to 1 stop-value for black-and-white films. These films are therefore rated higher, without having actually been altered; the higher rating should merely be set on the exposure meter. A further shortening of the exposure time is recommended only after accurate tests.

The Matterhorn. Photograph by J. Behnke

Soft

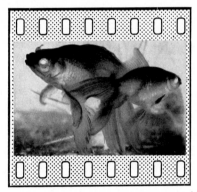
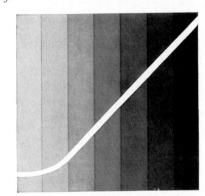

Normal

Hard

2. Gradation

The tone values of our photographic objects are very delicately graded according to their brightness and colour. Depending on the subject and on the lighting the total range of these tone values extends from the brightest white to the deepest black (contre-jour scenes) or is limited to slight differences in brightness (misty scenes). A film of normal gradation (tone rendering) represents, within certain limits, the various brightness values of the object as they would appear to the human eye. A film of soft gradation reduces the differences between the various tone values, and can therefore accommodate stronger lighting contrast. A hard-gradation film on the other hand emphasizes slight brightness contrast; it renders subjects which are poor in contrast brilliant; it is, however, unable to reproduce strong contrast at correct tone values.

The gradation depends on the type of film but can also be modified considerably by the type and duration of development. Accordingly we speak, e. g., of compensating development; this is a developing method which makes normal to contrasty films suitable for subjects of strong contrast. Very finegrain films have very often a brilliant gradation, which has to be influenced by such compensating development.

In order to indicate the gradation of individual films the densities are expressed in curves according to a certain system. Such "characteristic" curves can also be used for the evaluation of developer properties. The steeper the curve the more contrasty the film. The angle between the straight-line portion of the curve and the abscissa is expressed in gamma values. Since the average worker has no access to sensitometric instruments to measure the densities himself, the gamma values cannot be checked. It is therefore a useful practice to photograph a step wedge which can be obtained from the process departments of the film manufacturers. Comparison of the negative gradation of this "standard object" will quickly teach you whether a given emulsion is "soft", "normal", or "hard".

3. Colour sensitivity

Originally, the silver bromide crystals of the photographic emulsion are not sensitive to all colours. The range of colour sensitivity can be extended by the addition of suitable dyes to the emulsion during manufacture (sensitization). Nonsensitized films are sensitive to blue and ultra-violet only. A film which is sensitive also to green and yellow is called orthochromatic, and panchromatic if it is sensitive to all colours, including red.

In ordinary 35 mm photography panchromatic films are used almost exclusively. The terms "panchromatic" and "orthopanchromatic" mean practically the same. The red sensitivity of the first panchromatic films was satisfactory, but there was a gap in the sensitivity to green. When this gap was at last closed the manufacturers called the new film "orthopanchromatic". No panchromatic film on the market today has this gap in the green part of the spectrum any longer, so that this differentation has become unnecessary.

Non-sensitized film (ordinary positive film), used for special purposes, should be developed in Rodinal (1:50–7 minutes). Orthochromatic Leica films are today used for copying only, but even here they are gradually being replaced by panchromatic emulsions.

The films discussed here are black-and-white films which translate colour values into grey steps of various brightnesses. It is not easy for the novice to envisage this translation, particularly as it does not correspond with our visual impressions, from which it diverges appreciably. Even with a sensitized emulsion this translation is not exact. In daylight the film is too sensitive to blue and ultra-violet. If, for instance, we want to photograph a beautiful blue sky dappled with white clouds, we must first eliminate the excess sensitivity for blue. We can do this by using filters. Depending on the colour and the density of such filters we can lighten or darken certain colours and reproduce them as appropriate grey values.

The illustrations show the effect of this translation of the colour with grey values.

Colour-blind film, available as positive film, is practically no longer used for ordinary subjects and the only purpose of our illustration is to show how this emulsion falsifies the tone values of the various colours in reproduction.

Colour rendering with various photographic emulsions: White light is not colourless, but a summation of the entire spectrum. We can easily prove this by inserting a prism into the light beam and splitting up the light into its spectral colours (see diagram). The neighbouring, no longer visible, wave ranges act directly or can be activated by special sensitizers (infra-red).

The following points should be watched in photographic practice: – Colours reflected by objects are almost never pure spectral colours. Other colours are reflected along with them to a greater or lesser extent. The effect can vary greatly from our visual impression even on panchromatic films. This is what makes it so difficult to assess the translation into grey tones beforehand with any accuracy. In this respect, "colour pictures" are simpler to take than black-and-white ones.

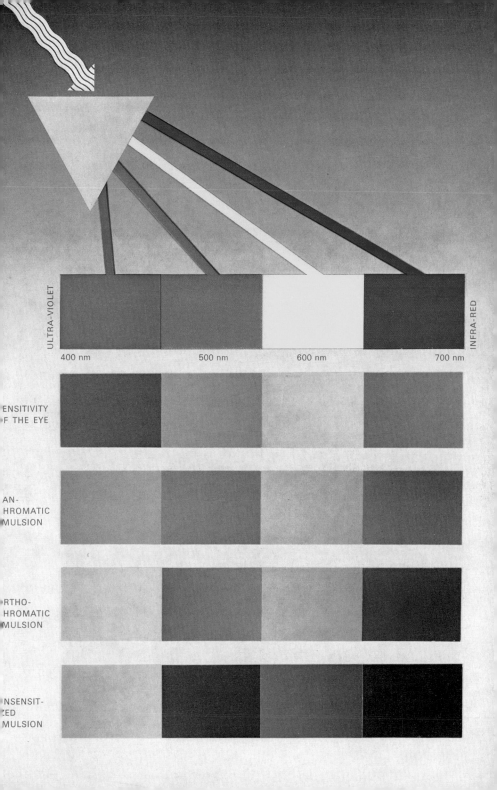

ULTRA-VIOLET

INFRA-RED

400 nm   500 nm   600 nm   700 nm

SENSITIVITY
OF THE EYE

PAN-
CHROMATIC
EMULSION

ORTHO-
CHROMATIC
EMULSION

UNSENSIT-
IZED
EMULSION

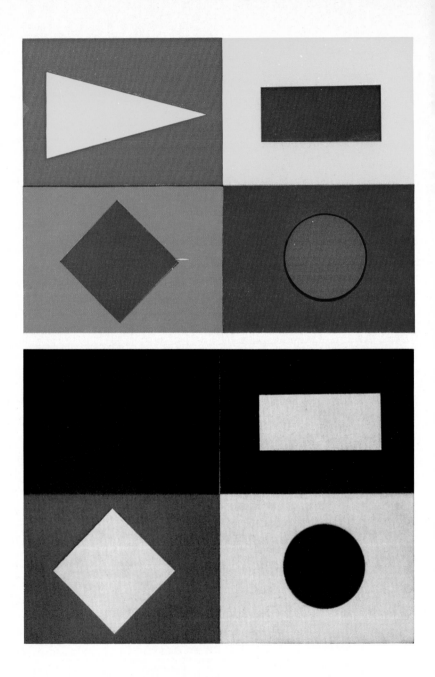

Top left: Original subject (complementary colours after Ostwald). – Bottom left: Exposure in daylight on non-sensitized, colour-blind material. – Top right: Exposure in daylight on panchromatic material.

This colour-blind film is, however, still popular for copying black and white originals.

Even modern panchromatic films do not reproduce all tone values correctly without a filter. It will be seen clearly that red is a little too dark, whereas blue is considerably lighter than the original. In order to obtain a reproduction corresponding to the tone values, this excessive sensitivity to blue in daylight has to be eliminated through the use of a filter. This "faithful" reproduction is, however, frequently lacking in contrast, and filtering must be exaggerated so that the desired effect is produced.

4. Grain and graininess

If the grain of the negative is not sufficiently fine a granular texture will often become apparent in medium-bright areas with little detail. During the development of the negative the silver bromide is reduced to metallic silver. In the course of this process the originally much smaller silver bromide crystal changes and forms irregular groups clumping together with neighbouring crystals. Whereas the term "grain" is used for the undeveloped silver halide, "graininess" refers to the developed emulsion.

The last 25 years have seen immense progress in film manufacture. Above all, the grain has become finer, the speed has been increased and the gradation improved. Previously, very fine-grain emulsions had steep gradation; today it is possible to produce such emulsions in any desired gradation.

Naturally, the rule that slow films have the finest grain is still valid. Grain size increases with the speed of the film. The thickness of the emulsion, and over-exposure, too, affect the grain structure because they determine the grain distribution. Thin-emulsion films are more favourable for our purposes.

By using fine-grain or ultra-fine-grain developers we attempt to prevent this clumping together in large groups of grains during the developing process. But nothing is gained if this can be achieved only by a generous exposure. The problem of graininess should therefore be attacked by the choice of a suitable film. This is easier and more reliable than trying to tackle it by means of a special developer.

It is possible that varying degrees of graininess are exhibited even by one and the same film. Since the subject contrast may vary greatly in our scenes, the negatives will turn out correspondingly soft or hard. This is compensated during enlargement. In uniformly light-grey areas graininess is more noticeable on hard than on soft paper.

If the finest possible grain is required for a maximum degree of enlargement, very fine-grain document-copying films should be used for the exposure. Their gradation is, however, very steep, and compensating development is important (p.213). This opens up a very interesting if somewhat difficult field of Leica photography for professionals and advanced amateurs.

5. Resolving power and contour sharpness

The term "resolving power" occurs in several contexts in photography. We speak of the resolving power of the eye, of the lenses, and also of the film. It always refers to differentiation of the most minute detail at a certain distance. What and how sharply we see depends on our eye. The resolving power of the human eye is limited to about 1 minute of arc by the light-sensitive cells which form the surface of the retina. Expressed in a practically measurable value this means that at a distance of 3.5 m (10′8″) we can still discern details 1 mm (0,04 in) across. In poor contrast or light this performance deteriorates to more than 3 minutes of arc.

In order to test the resolving power of photographic emulsions we use line gratings, radial grids or mires. The result is expressed in lines per mm. The value is not constant because the resolving power of a negative emulsion depends not only on its graininess, but also on the contrast of the photographic object, on the diffusion halo, on its gradation, on the wave length of the light, and on the quality of the camera lens.

All this requires critical focusing, exposure and development. It is true that a close relationship exists between resolving power and graininess, but the two concepts are quite distinct. A very thin-emulsion film may have a higher resolving power than a much thicker one of finer grain. Since the light-sensitive emulsion is a turbid medium, it tends to diffuse the light like a piece of opal glass. Very generous exposure, so-called over-exposure, therefore reduces the resolving power.

The developer, too, has some effect on resolution. Surface developers which do not act in the depth of the emulsion (such as Rodinal) produce good resolving power. They do not, however, act as fine-grain developers.

Contour sharpness is a concept which has been used in photography only within the last few years. It is an objective measure of the sharpness of a film independent of its graininess and gradation. The diffusion halo has a decisive effect on it. Contour sharpness is determined with the aid of a slit of $^{15}/_{1000}$ mm width which is contact-printed on the film without the use of a lens; the increase in slit width is measured on the film after development.

6. Freedom from halation

Halos will be formed only if the lighting is very contrasty during the exposure. A halo – or flare – will be caused around the light source in the picture. We distinguish between a diffusion and a reflection halo. The first is due to diffusion of the light inside the emulsion layer, the second due to light reflected by the acetate base behind the emulsion. Usually both forms occur combined. Diffusion halation is reduced in thin-emulsion films. Reflection halation is countered during the manufacturing process by means of dyeing the base, or introducing an intermediate layer, or a colour backing. These are so-called "anti-halation layers".

These comparison pictures of the church of Altenburg Monastery near Wetzlar demonstrate the extent to which effective anti-halation measures influence the result in difficult photographic conditions. Both films are made by the same manufacturer. The film of the top picture has an ordinary grey base, and has been available until recently. It has now been superseded by the film on which the lower picture was taken, with additional anti-halation protection. Although pictures with such great lighting contrast are rare, they are of great interest photographically.

134

The most suitable film

Speed is considered the dominant quality of a film – sometimes wrongly. But we, too, classify a film according to its speed. When you use a film for the first time, follow the hints of the manufacturer and compare the values of your own exposure meter with relevant figures of the instruction leaflet usually enclosed with the film. If the differences are considerable, caution is always indicated; several exposures should be made, and the data recorded and assessed after development.

1. Fast films (above 200 ASA)

Special film for poor lighting conditions. Latest types up to 1600 ASA (33 DIN). Every increase in speed expands the range of uses in poor light. If possible utilize the entire Leica frame. Ultra-fast films are grainier than slow ones, and you will obtain good results only with accurate exposure (better little than too generous). Overexposure considerably increases the grain and reduces resolving power.

Today the gradation is normal to contrasty, whereas in the past ultra-fast films were almost always soft. Finegrain developers are recommended. If possible develop in complete darkness by time.

Especially suitable for: photography in the home without flash, indoor reportage, theatre, circus, variety shows, street scenes at night, bad weather, rain, blizzard.

2. Normal or medium-speed films (50–200 ASA)

Universal films, which have the most favourably balanced properties. Speed almost always sufficient for normal daylight. Considerably higher resolving power than ultra-fast films. Little graininess, so that part-enlargements are possible. Keep well inside the wide exposure latitude of such films – correctly exposed negatives are much easier to enlarge. Please remember that different brands of film may differ in their properties in spite of the same speed rating. Above all, developing times may vary greatly.

3. Slow films (up to 40 ASA)

Special films for extreme enlargements. Very thin emulsion layer and high resolving power reproduce the finest detail without any disturbing grain structure. Thin-film emulsions demand accurate exposure. When in doubt, take a series of exposures until you are familiar with your film. Exposure times are longer owing to the low sensitivity; this increases the danger of camera shake. When the highest sharpness is essential a tripod is often indispensable.

4. 35 mm black-and-white panchromatic reversal film

Special film for the direct production of transparencies. A positive ready for projection is obtained immediately by the reversal development of the camera film. This process is unsurpassed in tone range, freedom from halation, and fine grain. Exposure latitude is narrow as in colour reversal film, and calls for accurate exposure. This material is eminently suitable for learning to expose correctly, and most of the experience gained can be usefully applied to work with colour reversal film. This film is particularly convenient for the photography of book reproductions to be projected; you will produce a first-class transparency directly with a minimum of effort; it is also cleaner than any transparency obtained from a negative. Standard reversal processing is included in the retail price.

Negatives can be produced without difficulty by contact-printing them on positive film, or, for superior quality, by enlarging them on sheet film. The exposure should be generous and development short to keep the contrast down. Reversal stations are listed in the leaflets accompanying the film, which is made by Eastman Kodak (Direct Positive Panchromatic) and Agfa-Gevaert. In urgent cases the user can carry out the reversal process himself if he is familiar with darkroom work.

5. Document copying films

Film of extremely fine grain and very good resolving power, but very steep gradation. Two types are available which differ in their colour sensitivity (orthochromatic – panchromatic). Often available in bulk quantities only; Agfa Agepe and Agepan Film and Eastman Kodak Microfile can be bought in 36-exposure daylight cassettes. No speeds are given for these films. As a yardstick for your exposure meter setting use 4-16 ASA. The higher speed is obtained with contrasty development, when the exposure latitude will be very narrow. Development is always individual and should be adjusted to suit requirements.

Spill on the steep slope. – If you turn the picture round you might get the impression of an up-and-coming ballet dancer on skis.
20mm Telyt.

Photograph by Stefan Kruckenhauser

This calls for a certain amount of experience. Readily adjustable developers such as Rodinal 1:50 5–7min produce very good results. Developing times and further details are given on page 213.

Uses: Line originals – faded documents – halftone originals – landscapes with little contrast – subjects in fog – commercial photography – photomicrography.

6. Positive Films

The true purpose of these films is copying and slide-making; but they can also be used in the camera. They are unsensitized, i.e. colour-blind, without anti-halation backing, and slow (about $1^1/_2$ ASA in artificial light). They are nevertheless eminently suitable for copying black-and-white originals. There is little exposure latitude, and the exposure time depends on the type of development. Before the first film is exposed a trial run of graduated exposures is necessary. Suitable developers: for half-tone copying Rodinal 1:50, approx. 7–10 min; for manuscript copying: any normal paper developer, about 3 min.

7. Infra-red films

Made in the Leica size by various manufacturers. As these films are also sensitive to normal light, this must be cut out by means of infra-red filters. Some brands are sensitive to rays of up to 850nm. High infra-red sensitivity reduces the keeping quality, and the film should be kept in a cool place. Further hints on exposure techniques see page 150.

Types of Leica film on the market

The perforated film of 35mm width used in the Leica is also the standard film used by the motion-picture industry. It is made in a great variety of types of the most diverse properties by almost all the film manufacturers throughout the world. The film consists of the base, formerly the highly inflammable nitro-cellulose, now almost invariably safety base such as acetyl cellulose or triacetate. Its thickness varies between 0.1 and 0.13mm. In contrast with roll and sheet films, which are coated on both sides – the photographic emulsion on the front, dyed gelatine on the back to equalize the stress – cine- and Leica films have no gelatine backing. The base itself is dyed grey-blue as a measure against antihala-tion. This greyness does not disappear in the processing baths, and slightly increases the exposure time in the positive process only. In order to improve the antihalation protection of 35mm film further, a layer of coloured varnish is coated on the back of the film base; it is dissolved by the developer.

Photographic emulsions do not keep indefinitely; their keeping quality depends on the properties of the material, and particularly on storage conditions, which should be cool and dry. Humidity is harmful, especially at high temperatures. Recurring changes in conditions, too, reduce the keeping quality. The manufacturers state the emulsion batch number and the expiry date on their film containers, and they will deal with complaints only if they are submitted within this date. The container should always be included if a film is returned to the makers.

In ideal storage conditions photographic material will keep much longer than indicated on the container, but it is advisable to ascertain the state of the film by means of trial exposures. Often the film has lost some of its speed, which can easily be allowed for during the exposure.

In the standard 35 mm cartridge the film is wound on a spool, emulsion side facing inwards. The outer shell is made of metal or plastic. The cartridge mouth is not absolutely lightproof so that cartridges should not be left lying unprotected for prolonged periods whether the film has been exposed or not. After the last exposure the film must be wound back into the cartridge so that it can be taken out of the camera in daylight.

For development the cartridge is opened in the darkroom, and the film torn off the spool. The cartridge, which is sold containing 20- and 36-exposure lengths of film, should be used only once.

Less common, but also to be used in daylight are the daylight refills. Here, too, the film is wound on a spool, but it is protected from the light only by a strip of paper; it can be inserted in the Leica cassette in daylight. The film lead is pulled out together with the paper lead. The instructions should be strictly followed, as at a certain position the Leica cassette must be closed. Darkroom refills with trimmed and numbered films are available for loading in Leica cassettes. They are usually packed singly in a lightproof wrapper and must be inserted in the Leica cassette in darkness. Leica cassettes are also loaded in complete darkness from bulk lengths (50 ft, 100 ft etc.) of film. Instructions for the use of the Leica cassette are given on page 310.

FILTERS, AND WHEN TO USE THEM

Filters are important aids to good photography. They enable us to alter the tone values of our picture. Since the properties of filters differ widely it is important to know their effect in order to use them correctly. The differences are demonstrated by means of many illustrations.

Originally the photographic emulsions were almost colour-blind as their sensitivity extended only from ultra-violet to blue. Even today such nonsensitized emulsions are still available for special purposes. They render blue almost white, and red appears black; this is just the opposite of our visual impression. These films require no filters, as they are used for the reproduction of black-and-white originals only.

An emulsion is made colour-sensitive by the addition of certain dyes during the manufacturing process. Films are called orthochromatic if they are sensitive to all colours except red. Panchromatic films are also sensitive to red. We speak of colour sensitivity even in black-and-white photography, although here only grey tones instead of the individual colours are produced. Such brilliant colour differences as between red and green or yellow and blue may in certain conditions result in almost identical grey tones. A better differentiation is achieved by the use of a suitable filter. In the past we often spoke of "faithful tone rendering". But any translation of colours into grey values is an abstraction, and you should not hesitate to choose strong filters in certain circumstances, provided they result in better tone rendering. In order to make a correct choice of filter, you must consider its effect, not on your eye, but on the film.

All colour filters have the property of primarily transmitting their own colour and, depending on their strength, of more or less reducing the light of the opposite colour.

For moving subjects the small exposure factor of the yellow filter is particularly convenient. Here, this filter has the ideal effect. The white gym-slip, the bronzed figure and the blue sky are well differentiated. A stronger orange filter would render the sky darker and the skin lighter; in this particular case the difference would in some respects be reduced.

Medau gymnastics, 50mm Elmar, yellow filter

U. V. filters (colourless)

This filter cuts off the invisible ultra-violet rays, which continue the limited visible range of the spectrum in the direction of short-wave radiation. All photographic emulsions are sensitive to this region; this has no practical significance in photography, for the following reason:

The camera lens transmits only a limited portion of the ultra-violet rays which, compared with the total light intensity, is negligible. Only at altitudes above 8,500 ft under a cloudless clear sky does the U. V. component reach proportions to be considered. But even at these altitudes you must make a distinction between subjects including much sky, and pictures of the horizon through long-focal-length lenses, where there is no danger of over-filtering. But in the first case a U. V. filter should be used in order to avoid an excessively dark sky.

The filter is colourless; it can be used also with colour film (see illustration p. 147 top). On the beach and during cruises it protects the camera lens against minute salt crystals.

Yellow filters

The yellow filter 0 is the weakest yellow filter. It does not appreciably extend exposure times and is therefore used where short exposures are essential. The yellow filter I has a slightly stronger effect; it is the universal filter for landscape photography where only the correct rendering of the blue sky is important. It produces more or less faithful tone values in the picture without excessive contrast in the sky. Snow scenes are rewarding generally only in sunlight. Here a yellow filter is indispensable because of the blueness of the shadows, unless, of course, you prefer a strong orange filter to emphasize contrast even more (filter factors see page 153).

Yellow-green filters

The effect of the yellow-green filter is very similar to that of the yellow filter 1. It is used in much the same way, but renders the green tones of a landscape a little brighter, which is often very welcome. The filter factor is approximately 3, i. e. a little longer than that of the yellow filter.

Hut in the snow. Top: panchromatic film without filter. Bottom: with yellow filter.

142

Orange filters

With an orange filter you can already exaggerate the effect of a summer sky with clouds. Blue and green tones are rendered darker. Since yellow and red rays penetrate haze more readily, long-distance subjects will be reproduced more clearly.

Red filters

This effect is even more pronounced with a red filter. Clouds are dramatized, green appears almost black, and atmospheric haze is penetrated even more effectively. The exposure factor differs widely according to the film, and varies between 5 and 100. It is therefore my urgent advice to determine the correct factor for a given film by a series of graduated trial exposures when a red filter is used for the first time. Here is an example of the exposure time read for a 40 ASA film, landscape, sunlight, slight haze; f/11, $^1/_{125}$ sec.

1. exposure without filter, f/11 $^1/_{125}$ sec
2. exposure with filter, f/8 $^1/_{125}$ sec   2×
3. exposure with filter, f/5.6 $^1/_{125}$ sec   4×
4. exposure with filter, f/5.6 $^1/_{60}$ sec   8×
5. exposure with filter, f/5.6 $^1/_{30}$ sec 16×
6. exposure with filter, f/4 $^1/_{30}$ sec 32×

If it is possible to work with a tripod it is simpler to adhere to f/11 and to choose the shutter speeds $^1/_{30}$, $^1/_{15}$, $^1/_8$, $^1/_4$ sec for exposures 3 to 6.
Infra-red filters are suitable for infra-red films only (see page 150).

Blue filters

Blue filters are used for artificial-light subjects in order to give them daylight character. Skin tones are reproduced darker and with more emphasis, blue eyes will appear very light. In daylight blue filters are used only if the red sensitivity of the film is to be reduced – e. g. for subjects in fog, or in order to preserve the misty character of an atmosphere.

View from Briançon (French Alps) towards the south. 90 mm Elmar.
Top: f/8, $^1/_{50}$ sec, without filter. Bottom: f/8, $^1/_2$ sec, with red filter.

Photograph by Bert Rupp

Polarizing filters

Reflections from glossy surfaces can in certain conditions be almost completely eliminated by the use of a polarizing filter. Reflected light is partly polarized by non-metallic surfaces. Its plane of vibration is directional. Some substances have the property of also polarizing the light they transmit in a certain plane of vibration (polarizing filters). If such a filter is rotated so that its direction of vibration is at right angles to the vibration direction of the reflected light the latter is extinguished by the filter, which does not affect normal, unpolarized light. In order to observe its effect the exposure subject is viewed through the filter while it is being rotated. When the most favourable position has been found, the number on top of the filter mount is read and the filter placed on the Leica lens with the number also on top. Polarizing filters with lens hood in the mount for E 39 and E 43 can be swivelled through 180° on the screw-on ring. Place the polarizing filter on the lens mount so that its fixing screw points to the camera baseplate. Now swivel the filter upwards through 180° up to the stop. When the subject is lined up, rotate the filter until the best effect is obtained. Now swivel the filter back in front of the lens for the exposure. The degree of polarization depends on the angle of the specular reflection; this also influences the degree of extinction.

A polarizing filter often has a favourable effect on the colour rendering of colour films. It is particularly useful for landscape pictures, because the light from the sky, too, is partially polarized; this enables the photographer to bring out clouds more effectively against the blue sky without falsifying the colours of other features in the picture. Polarizing filters absorb also ultra-violet, and to combine them with U. V. filters is pointless, as they already act as U. V. filters in their own right. On the other hand, they can be readily used with yellow, yellow-green, orange, or red filters in black-and-white photography. The filter factor of such combinations is obtained by multiplication of the two individual factors. The effect of a polarizing- and yellow filter combination particularly in landscape photography is striking. The filter factor of the polarizing filter alone is approximately 3.

Examples of the use of filters with colour film:

Top: View of the Matterhorn from Gornergrat. Left: without UV filter, right: with UV filter.

Bottom: View from the Nebelhorn. Left: without polarizing filter, right: with polarizing filter.

Photographs by Bert Rupp

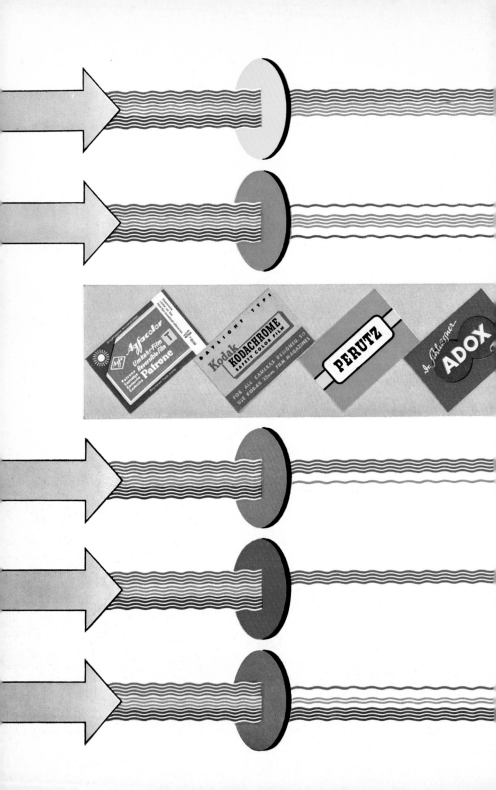

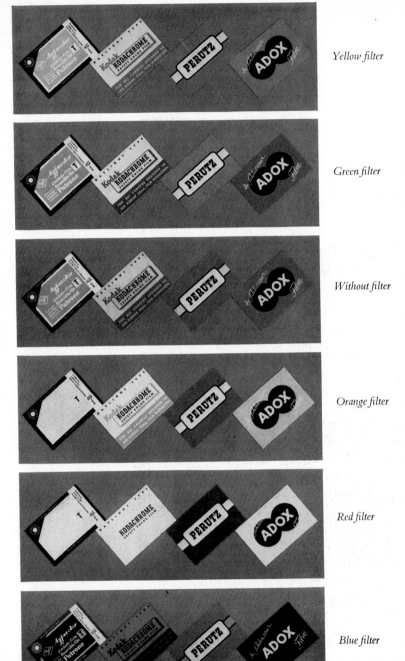

Yellow filter

Green filter

Without filter

Orange filter

Red filter

Blue filter

149

Infra-red photography

The region of the spectrum which lies beyond that of the red rays is called infra-red. Although the eye cannot see it, it can be used for photography with films which have been specially sensitized for it.

Infra-red rays penetrate atmospheric haze considerably better than normal light and therefore reveal distant objects more clearly. They thus make possible photographs of long-distance subjects which could never be obtained otherwise. Since, as we have said, our eye is insensitive to infra-red light, such pictures show unusual and surprising features. For instance, the blue of the sky and of a sheet of water appears black, the green of meadows and of the foliage of trees white as in a snowscape.

Special infra-red films are sensitive not only to infra-red, but also to visible light, which will mask the infra-red effect unless you prevent it from reaching your film by means of a dark red filter. Since this utilizes only part of the sensitivity of the film, you have to increase the exposure time considerably beyond that for a normal film. It is rather difficult to determine this in advance, particularly since the exposure latitude of good infra-red negatives is very narrow. This is due to the fact that the far distance generally lacks contrast in spite of its colour differentiation, and that the eye cannot judge the intensity of the infra-red rays. It is therefore always advisable to take several pictures at graduated exposure times. The exposure factors for infra-red films of different brands vary widely; it also depends on the angle of incidence of the light and on other lighting conditions. Here, too, it is recommended first to experiment with a single brand of film (the exposure factor for a dark red filter may vary from 4 to 30 for a 40 ASA film).

Negatives of long-distance shots should be developed for strong contrast – longer than normal, no compensating development. The film should be inserted into, and removed from, the camera in subdued daylight.

Lake Lugano from Carona.

Top: Kodak Infra-red film, without filter, f/8, $^1/_{250}$ sec.

Bottom: Kodak Infra-red film, Leitz IR filter, f/8, $^1/_{60}$ sec.

Note the differences in the surface of the lake, and the strong infra-red reflection of the green foliage.

50 mm Summicron.   *Photograph by Theo Kisselbach*

In some fields of scientific photography, such as medicine, forensic science, history of art etc., infra-red photography can reveal facts which would otherwise remain hidden to us.

Since the lenses have not been computed for the longer-wave infra-red rays, a small correction in the focusing must be applied. First the lens is focused as usual, but it must be turned a little further, until the second index line, marked R, takes the place of the normal index mark. The camera extension is thus slightly increased. This increase is not always the same, since infra-red films of various brands are differently sensitized. It is therefore recommended to stop down to f/11 or f/16.

If the lens has no R marking $1/300$ of the focal length should be taken as the mean increase in extension. Instead of on infinity, long-distance subjects through infra-red filters should be focused on

21 mm Super Angulon	4.5 m
28 mm Elmarit	4.5 m
35 mm Summicron	8 m
50 mm Summicron	11 m
90 mm Elmarit	18 m
90 mm Tele-Elmarit	25 m
135 mm Tele-Elmar	30 m
135 mm Tele-Elmarit	32 m
200 mm Telyt	46 m
280 mm Telyt	66 m
400 mm Telyt	130 m
560 mm Telyt	185 m

Kodak give a mean exposure time of f/11, $1/30$ sec for their IR film, sensitive from 700 to 850nm, in full sunlight; exposure time without filter f/11, $1/125$ sec (exposure factor 4). If you depend on higher speed, try Kodak IR HS; this is, however, available in bulk only.

Exposure factors of the Leitz filters

Filters absorb part of the light entering them; the exposure time must therefore be duly lengthened. The values given in the table are averages determined in diffuse daylight and Nitraphot-B (photoflood) light respectively. Changes may occur according to the colour sensitivity of the film and the lighting conditions.

With short exposure times the effect of a filter is usually enhanced: It is therefore advisable, when in doubt, to take an additional exposure at a shorter exposure time.

Filter	Daylight	Artificial light
Blue	1.5	2.5
U.V.	1.2	1.2
Yellow 0	1.5	1.2
Yellow 1	2	1.5
Green	3	2.5
Orange	3–4	2–3
Red	4–30	4–20
Infra-red for infra-red film	8–60	depending on film and illumination
Polarizing filter	2,5–4	depending on the setting

Spectral transmission τ of the Leica filters (approximate values)

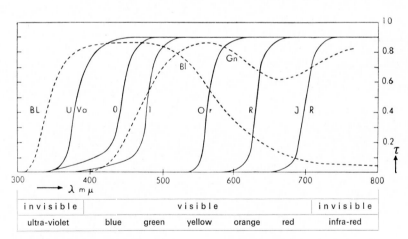

invisible	visible	invisible
ultra-violet	blue green yellow orange red	infra-red

Bl = blue filter
UVa = ultra-violet absorbing (colourless)
0,1 = yellow filters of increasing density
Or = orange filter

R, Rd = red filter
Gn = green filter (for panchromatic films)
IR = Infra-red filter

Does a filter affect picture sharpness?

Leitz filters are coloured discs manufactured with optical precision. A good filter hardly affects the performance of a camera lens*. With correct exposure the sharpness of a filtered picture is roughly the same as that of an unfiltered one. With gross overexposure, e.g. the yellow rays transmitted by a yellow filter penetrate more deeply into the photographic emulsion, and halation and reduced sharpness as a result of diffusion are more pronounced than with unfiltered negatives.

Filter diameters and filter mounts

The same filters fit a large number of different Leica lenses. The E 39 filter (screw-in filter, thread diameter 39mm) can be used on 10 Leica lenses. It is screwed into the mount so that the effect of the lens hood is not interfered with. The diameter of a filter must be large enough to avoid vignetting even at full lens aperture. Very fast lenses and lenses of very long focal lengths require larger-diameter filters (E 41, E 43, E 48, E 58, E 85). The screw-in mounts are designed to keep the filter glasses strainfree. The threaded ring is not tightened; it has a little play, and to prevent it from working loose it is secured with sealing lacquer.

Unengraved filter mounts, into which special filters can be inserted, are available for all standard diameters. They are suitable for simple glass filters only, and cannot be used for cemented or polarizing filters.

Series filters

Series filters are provided for some recent lenses; these filters have a smooth metal mount without thread, and are inserted in the two-part lens hoods or held by a special retaining ring. A few manufacturers of colour film offer whole series of very finely graded filters with which the colour rendering can be influenced.

---

* Exception: – Infra-red filter, see page 152.

EXPOSE CORRECTLY

Black-and-white films have considerable exposure latitude. It is therefore generally recommended to expose them generously. Although this will result in somewhat denser negatives, they can still be used; an underexposed negative is useless.

But this "generous" exposure also has its drawbacks. Many pictures become blurred through camera shake or subject movement because of needlessly long exposure. Considerable overexposure leads to increased halation and reduces sharpness. Even the grain becomes more obtrusive. The call therefore is for "correct exposure". *By correct we mean the shortest exposure time producing a perfect negative*. The exposure time depends on

● object brightness   ● film speed   ● method of development.

In order to obtain uniform results you must learn from experience. Needless changes in the types of film and development must be avoided, as this impairs your judgement of the varying brightness and of the all-important contrast range of the camera subjects.

The meaning of the terms under-, short, correct, generous, and overexposure is best learned by means of a little experiment. Expose an average subject (e.g. sunlight from the side, f/11, 40 ASA film) at the following shutter speeds: – $1/500$, $1/250$, $1/125$, $1/60$, $1/30$, $1/15$ sec. Careful scrutiny of the exposed strip gives a good idea of under-, normal and overexposure (here the correct negative will usually have had shutter speeds of $1/60$–$1/125$ sec).

If at first you find it difficult to judge your trial strip you will be well advised to consult an expert. When you estimate your exposure time bear in mind that bright subjects are usually photographically brighter than they appear to the eye, and dark subjects usually darker. The sensitivity of the eye adapts itself to the existing brightness. As a result, estimates are generally too short indoors and in artificial light. To obtain a yardstick and control of your own estimate, in the beginning rely on a simple exposure table or on the instructions of the film manufacturer.

The novices and the extra-careful make quite sure by making two or three exposures at appropriately graduated shutter speeds if they have any doubts at all. In very bright light (outdoors), an additional exposure, once more halving the exposure time, is recommended. In poor light and for dark subjects the second exposure should have double or four times the standard value. For document copying and colour films the steps should be smaller (e.g. open or close the diaphragm half a stop). The exposure data should be noted in order to check the results.

Photo-electric exposure meters are very valuable aids to good photography.

We distinguish between two types:

1. Exposure meters with a selenium cell. Here the incident light is converted into a weak electric current. The pointer of a micro-galvanometer indicates lens stop and shutter speed according to the intensity of the light. The film speed is set before the measurement is taken. The stronger the incident light the more current is generated. The size of the cell, too, has much to do with the intensity of the current.

2. Exposure meters with cadmium sulphide cells (CdS) are designed according to a different principle. Light incident on the cell changes the latter's resistance and thereby the current flux from a small mercuric oxide battery; the change is inversely proportional to the intensity of the light. With much light the current flow is strong, with little light weak. The outstanding advantage of this type of meter consists in the high limiting sensitivity of the CdS cells. It is moreover possible to reduce the measuring angle considerably. Dimensions and weight of the instrument are much smaller. It is essential to its correct functioning that the battery has its rated potential; this drops in cold weather; CdS hand-held exposure meters should therefore be carried close to the body during the winter. The operating instructions for the meter should be followed closely.

Photo-electric exposure meters permit the following types of measurement:

1. Normal direct reading. The instrument is pointed at the subject from the direction of the camera, measuring the total light coming from the subject. This results in the correct exposure time in 80% of all cases. Only if very bright or very dark portions are dominant within the field of the exposure meter will the reading be inaccurate; the view of a sun-bathed landscape through the clearing of a wood, for instance, will be overexposed, because the preponderant dark area of the wood upsets the balance of the reading. Conversely, in an interior view with windows, the light entering from outside influences the reading to such an extent that the interior in the shade will be underexposed. Similarly, in snow scenes the reading of the exposure meter is too high, with the result of underexposure, particularly with colour film.

Photograph by Bros. Ungermann

2. Close-up reading of the object. Errors can be eliminated in unbalanced lighting by means of a close-up reading. The measurement is carried out in exactly the same way as before, except that it is not taken from the camera viewpoint; the meter is moved so close to the object that light only from those parts which are of importance to the exposure is read, everything else being safely excluded. This method can be used only if it is possible to approach the object closely enough.

3. Reading with a sheet of white paper. This very accurate method has the advantage that the sensitivity of the exposure meter will be adequate even in very poor lighting conditions. Here, too, a close approach to the object is essential. A sheet of white paper is held directly in front of it, and the exposure meter moved up to it until only the white area is measured; but the meter must not cast a shadow on it. The exposure values thus found have to be multiplied by a factor which depends on the type of object in order to produce the correct exposure times. Stout white paper or, better still, white cardboard, size about 18×24 cm ($7 \times 10''$). Exposure meter at a distance of about 10×15 cm (4–$6''$). Make sure no shadows are cast.

> Bright objects $3\times$
> Normal objects $4\times$
> Dark objects $6\times$

I have been using this method for years with very good results. It was recommended originally for process work, because the extremely contrasty films used in this field demanded absolutely accurate exposure times. With colour films, where the exposure latitude does not normally exceed plus or minus $^1/_2$ stop, it has proved extremely reliable.

4. Incident-light reading. The majority of exposure meters can be used for this method with an opal disc or other diffusing medium covering their windows. Here, the meter is pointed towards the camera from the direction of the exposure subject. This method, too, is preferable to method 1 in contre-jour light and with snow subjects.

Top left: Normal direct measurement from the camera position. Sawing logs.
Photograph by Kisselbach

Top right: Close-up reading of the object. Close-up picture of foxglove in front of a bright sky. Universal focusing bellows, 135 mm Hektor. *Photograph by Bert Rupp*

Bottom left: Measurement with white paper (near the pews). Church at Otterndorf, Elbe. 35 mm Summaron. *Photograph by Walter Lüden*

Bottom right: Incident-light measurement. Ascent to the Krieger Horn near Lech, Austria.
Photograph by S. Hartig

Experience through practice

It is also essential for the correct use of an exposure meter to calibrate it with the film in the camera and with the developing method normally adopted for it. This may mean that you will have to set your film speed according to your experience with your exposure meter instead of the manufacturer's rating. This is particularly important with colour films.

Although it might appear a little exaggerated at this stage to devote so much care to the determination of the correct exposure time, it is certainly worth the trouble. With colour reversal film correct exposure is vital to acceptable results because of its narrow exposure latitude. In black-and-white photography, too, uniformly exposed negatives are better and quicker to enlarge.

High shutter speeds!

Provided the stop is chosen appropriately a correctly exposed negative can be obtained over a wide range of shutter speeds, although it is advisable to keep these as high as possible. A picture taken at $^1/_{125}$ sec is less subject to the hazard of camera shake than at $^1/_{30}$ sec.

Many an inexplicable unsharpness has been caused by slight camera shake. This danger becomes particularly critical with long-focal-length lenses.

LEARN FROM YOUR MISTAKES

Here is a true story with an element of humour, a minor "tragedy", and pointing a sound photographic moral. On a somewhat blustery summer's day, a photographer took a stroll along the Riviera, his Leica hanging from a neck-strap, at the ready. Suddenly he caught his breath: Surely this couple approaching round the bend in the road were the Duke and Duchess of Windsor! Knowing that the Duke was averse to being photographed by Tom, Dick and Harry the photographer took a position at the side of the road with some trepidation. Raising his Leica half to the shooting position as if to ask permission by implication, he was surprised and delighted that the Duke did not seem to mind and in fact actually nodded to the photographer, with a smile playing around the corners of his mouth as if to encourage him. At this very moment the shutter clicked. When the famous couple had passed out of sight, our Leicaman turned to his camera to check his snapshot setting for this unforgettable picture.

Suddenly, he almost fainted with dismay: the aperture was at f/8, the shutter at $^1/_{125}$sec, even the parallax setting of his universal viewfinder was at the correct 13ft setting, ready for just such an event. He had, however, forgotten one little thing: to protect his lens from dust on this windy day, he had put his lens cap on

Lens not pulled out. *Lens not locked.* *Not focused.*

a short while before this encounter. In the excitement of the moment he had forgotten to take it off... hence the Duke's friendly, quizzical smile.

The Leica photographer had enough sense of humour to stick a sheet of black bromide paper into his photo album, entitled "The Duke and the Duchess of Windsor". It was a "picture" which caused general interest, because each time he opened his album he related this little anecdote.

There is not one even among the old "Leica hands" who at one time or another has not had a similar experience. The layman surrounds the owner of a Leica with an aura of infallibility – "nothing can go wrong with his camera!" What he fails to realize is that it takes two to get the right results, and that the Leica can produce them only if and when it receives the correct orders from its master. It "obeys" you blindly, and it is up to you to avoid mistakes.

What are these mistakes? Let us make a list of the most frequent ones while we are on the subject. The illustrations shown here represent a kind of cross-section through the contents of a darkroom waste bin.

Failing to remove the lens cap has already been discussed. But you may also have forgotten to extend the lens in its collapsible mount, or to lock it securely. This,

| *Camera movement during exposure.* | *Excessively stopped down, excessively long exposure ($^1/_{15}$ sec)* | *Disturbing background, excessive stopping down* |

too, spoils the picture beyond hope; all it shows is a blurred something. It is important to pull out and lock the lens automatically as soon as you open the ever-ready case. Not only carrying out the various operations, but also their correct sequence must become second nature to you. If you are not careful when you insert the film it may happen that the teeth of the transport sprockets do not engage the film perforation holes; the film will not be wound on. You will notice this when the rewind knob does not turn during your attempt to transport the film. If the worst comes to the worst, your film counter will tell you that you have made 36 exposures; in reality the film is still unexposed in the cassette. You may possibly discover this during rewinding. You will have the consolation, though, that you have saved yourself the trouble of developing and enlarging it. Some enthusiasts continue to wind the film on (forcing the issue), although they have reached its end. This tears the film from the cassette spool; it is wound open onto the take-up spool and can be removed from the Leica only in a darkroom. Remedy: watch your film counter – and zero it when you insert a new film!

Flap of the ever-ready case in front of the lens.

Pre-exposure through the velvet mouth of the film cassette. Never leave cartridges or cassettes lying around unprotected.

Keep the camera level – watch the horizon!

Front and rear lens surfaces must be spotlessly clean. Dust and finger marks, for instance, turn the best anastigmat into a soft-focus lens. Scratches in appreciable numbers, too, adversely affect the performance. Dust on the lens is best avoided by the use of a lens cap. But if cleaning has become necessary it should be done very gently with a piece of soft, clean lint. On the beach and at sea lenses are exposed to the danger of drifting sand and particles of salt. A filter here fulfils the additional purpose of protecting the lens, it can be cleaned more easily than the convex, recessed front lens. Never on any account dismantle the lens for cleaning!

The ever-ready case, too, may play tricks. You are puzzled by a peculiar round shape on your negative, not related to anything you saw during the exposure. A ghost to be exorcized? No need to be frightened. The explanation is simple; the flap of the ever-ready case partly obscured the camera lens, because you failed to hold it back with your left hand during an upright exposure. The inherent speed of the Leica often helps you to obtain a picture even in most surprising situations. This speed is the unfailing measure of the skill with which you handle your camera and of your ability to rely on your own "automatic movements". The most common shortcoming of pictures taken in a hurry is

Pre-exposure through changing lenses in direct sunlight.

Vignetting through wrong lens hood.

Wrong shutter speed with fla

camera shake. If you pull your camera up quickly and prematurely push the release button, you can produce camera shake even at $^1/_{1000}$ sec. Concentrate on what you are doing when the decisive moment arrives.

Wrong focusing, too, is due to lack of concentration in a photographic emergency. At worst it renders the picture useless; the value of the picture is reduced if you forget to set the stop or shutter speed correctly, causing over- or underexposure. The sequence: focusing – stop – shutter must become a matter of routine through frequent practice.

Another mistake is failure to set the shutter on $^1/_{50}$ sec or longer for electronic flash pictures. Higher shutter speeds, such as $^1/_{125}$ sec, prevent the exposure of the entire frame because of the restricted slit-width of the focal-plane shutter. No exposure at all will take place if the wrong, i.e. the expendable-flash contact is used for electronic flash. Fortunately, such mistakes, caused by lack of experience, i.e. a merely technical factor, usually happen only once. Once bitten twice shy, and you will take good care to prevent a repetition. On the other hand, the illustrations on pp. 162–165 show pictures with faults which have nothing to do with the handling of the Leica. These pictures are all both sharp and correctly exposed. But your eye has let you down. It is not trained

Taken from too steep an angle.	*Sun from behind, unfavourable use of the format.*	*Persons too small, unfavourable distance.*

165

well enough to see a subject in its pictorial setting. Thus, in the picture on the right on page 162 the author failed to appreciate that the background, too, forms an important part of the whole motif, and should have been chosen with greater care. In the picture on the left on page 165 the photographer should have taken the trouble to squat on his haunches, and in the following examples he should either have approached the scenes more closely or have asked his subjects to come closer to him.

Fast-moving subjects

When extremely fast action (motor racing) has to be photographed it has been found useful to expose at $^1/_{500}$ instead of $^1/_{1000}$ sec and to follow the subject with the camera through the viewfinder. This requires a certain amount of practice. The background may become blurred, enhancing the pictorial appeal. The Leica should be held in the normal exposure position; to hold it upside down is no advantage; it merely interferes with smooth handling. In other kinds of pictures of moving subjects the highest possible shutter speeds are often necessary in order to avoid "subject movement". The capture of the most favourable moment calls for a sure judgement of the progress of the movement and quick and reliable operation of the camera. If you want to gain experience in this type of photography, start with taking pictures of a person walking, and try to catch the movement when he sets his foot down. A good tip: Count one-two in the rhythm of his gait, and press the button in this rhythm.

FLASH PHOTOGRAPHY

Fast Leica lenses and ultra-fast films produce good pictures even in poor light. But if it is too dark, or if the existing lighting conditions are not suitable for your photographic intentions, an additional artificial light source becomes necessary. Today the use of flash offers you many new possibilities compared with the often tedious and inconvenient setting up of electric lamps. Flash will be the only way out if fast-moving objects have to be taken at the highest shutter speeds in poor light, if not in complete darkness. In addition, we now have handy flash units which are easy to operate. Through the synchro-device in the Leica the flash is automatically fired by the shutter (tables for all models in the Appendix).

1. Expendable flash

These units work with flash lamps. Filled with oxygen, the bulbs contain metal wire or foil which is ignited like a flash of lighting by an electrically triggered primer capsule. Such a flashbulb, which is completely burned out after firing, can of course be used only once. Depending on the size and make of the bulb, a certain lapse of time occurs between the firing of the bulb and the maximum brightness (peak) of the flash discharge (average about $^1/_{60}$ sec). In the Leica-M models the expendable-flash contact has been permanently set for certain types of lamp; their firing delay is allowed for. In a flash cube, four bulbs are housed, taking up very little space.

2. Electronic flash

In these flash units the flash is produced by an intensely bright electric discharge in a tube filled with an inert gas. Such a tube can be used again and again since the gas is not burned up, but merely caused to emit light by the electric discharge. A special advantage of these units is their very short flash duration ($^1/_{1000}$–$^1/_{2000}$ sec), during which practically the entire quantity of light is discharged. This makes it possible to obtain sharp pictures even of fast-moving objects. But this also implies that with such flash units the shutter speed must not exceed certain values. At high speeds, the shutter exposes the film through a slit of varying width moving across its breadth, so that during the short flash only part of the film area is exposed. At $^1/_{50}$ sec the entire frame is exposed simultaneously; this, then, is the highest shutter speed we can use with electronic flash on the Leica.

167

A simple test for correct function is carried out as follows: (Leica without film) connect electronic flash unit according to instructions and set shutter. Remove base plate, and introduce a piece of bromide paper into the film channel (this can be done in subdued light). Unscrew the lens, hold flash in front of the aperture. – Release shutter – the effect of the flash will be visible on the photographic paper directly, even without development.

A special type of electronic flash unit operates with automatic flash adjustment. If you use flash from a short distance, the flash power is automatically reduced; the distance at which this happens depends on the type of unit. This is how it functions: A built-in light sensor in the unit measures the reflection of the flash while it is being fired; if it is too powerful, any unwanted light is "siphoned off" by a special second tube, without lighting effect, built into the flash unit. The automatic mechanism can be disengaged, when brightness calculation must be based on the guide number also with these units.

Guide Number

The guide number, also called flash factor, is of great importance in flash exposure technique. It is given by the manufacturers as a measure of the power of the flash. Its use is based on the simple formula:

Guide number divided by flash distance = lens stop
Guide number divided by lens stop = flash distance

This makes it very convenient to calculate the stop for the correct exposure at a given flash distance, or vice versa.

The guide number represents an average value only, and is valid for subjects in normal rooms and at medium distances. It also depends on the speed of the film and the developing method used. If you use a film of four times the normal speed, for instance 160 ASA instead of 40 ASA, it is a safe rule to double your guide number. As with other artificial-light sources, the photographic effect of the flash and the resulting exposure (or stop) depends on the type of the reflector used, and to a very large extent on the brightness of the surroundings reflecting the light. Thus, light reflected by bright walls may mean an additional lightening of the subject. Conversely, this reflection is entirely absent in complete darkness, such as outdoors at night or in a very large room. It is therefore

Photograph by Siegfried Hartig

recommended to open up to a maximum of two stops where there are no bright reflecting features; in small, very light interiors, you may stop down 1 stop.

The built-in reflector bundles the light. This has the effect of insufficiently illuminating pictures with extreme wide-angle lenses (28 mm, 21 mm). When these lenses are used the flash should be bounced from the ceiling (at half the guide number at most).

With close-up shots below 2 m (6 ft 8 in) the stated guide number is too high if there is no reflection. In order to obtain satisfactory results, make sure that the shadows are effectively softened; you can determine the true guide number with a series of trial exposures. Details will be found in the following chapter on close-ups, p. 180.

The performance of electronic flash units suffers if they are not used for prolonged periods. To restore the capacitor to its full power, release a few flashes at intervals of a minute each.

Also remember that an electronic flash can work at full power only if you give it sufficient time for its capacitor to be recharged, and with battery-operated units if the battery still supplies sufficient power.

Flash technique

Flash is extremely versatile, offering many photographic possibilities.

Although mounting the flash gun directly on the camera is very convenient indeed, the results are rarely satisfactory. Flash, too, conforms to the rule that frontal lighting produces flat illumination. It is better to hold your flash in your free left hand and to use an extension cable. You will thus gain a certain amount of freedom of movement in your lighting arrangements.

The "flash character" of a picture can also be softened if the flash is set up behind the camera (extension cable). Or the flash can be directed at a white sheet or cardboard, and only the soft, reflected light be used for the picture. With close-up portraits the effect of the flash should be subdued (with a piece of tissue paper placed over the reflector).

The simultaneous use of several flash lamps allows you to set up more complicated types of lighting, for instance placing one lamp as main light from the front, and a second lamp as effect- or back-light on one side of or behind the subject. It is possible to couple several flash lamps only when the units have facilities for parallel connection.

Many electronic flash units provide for the connection of a second flash lamp. Here each tube receives only half the original power, and the lens should be opened by one stop if the second lamp is used as a side- or back-light. It is generally accepted that one light should be dominant, hence the distances between each lamp and the subject should always be different.

Smoky rooms

In smoke-filled rooms flash pictures become very flat, particularly when they are taken from some distance, since the smoke diffuses, and diffusely reflects, the light. The only way out is to air the room first.

Flash and daylight combined

It is often advisable to combine flashlight and daylight, when the flash has the task of lightening dark shadows, or of making up for the absence of sunlight. Since with electronic flash units the minimum exposure time is fixed, the correct exposure must be obtained by adjustment of the lens stop.

Most pictures will be correctly exposed if after calculating the guide number you determine the lens stop disregarding the daylight, and close it by one step for the exposure.

Colour photography with flash★

For colour photographs on daylight film the light of the electronic flash can be directly combined with daylight as it has almost the same spectral composition. Blue-tinted flashbulbs, too, can be used without difficulty. The earlier, clear flashbulbs, however, have a colour temperature of 3800°K, which places them between photoflood and daylight.

Which flash unit?

Whether to use electronic flash or expendable flashbulbs is first and foremost a question of money. If you use flash rarely or occasionally only, you will choose flashbulbs. These units can be used at any time without preparation, are easy to carry about, and need hardly any maintenance. The flash gun is also cheaper than an electronic unit. If you use flash frequently, the larger but non-recurring outlay for an electronic flash unit is worth while.

★ Further details in the chapter "Colour photography" on pp. 267.

Top: With the flashholder attached to the camera the lighting is flat, shadows cast on the wall are disturbing.

Centre: With the flashholder held higher the lighting becomes more plastic. Disturbing background shadows disappear.

Bottom: In modern flats with low ceilings, the flash can be pointed at the ceiling and a very soft, indirect light produced. But the lens must be opened up 2–3 lens stops.

Photographs by
Th. Kisselbach
with Braun Hobby

CLOSE-UPS

Where does the close-up range start?

The 50 mm lens of the Leica can now be focused down to a distance of 0.7 m (28"), when it covers a field area of about 28×42 cm (11×16"). The photography of smaller subjects so that they fill the frame is called close-up photography. Since various focal lengths cover the same object field from different camera distances, it is the reproduction scale, not the distance which is the deciding factor.

The close-up range from 1:1 (reproduction at natural size) up to 50× magnification comes under the heading of macrophotography. With still higher magnifications we enter the field of photomicrography.

What is the meaning of reproduction scale?

The reproduction scale indicates the ratio at which the original is reproduced on the film. An example:

The Leica format measures 24×36 mm ($1×1^1/_2"$), the object to be photographed 120×180 mm ($5×7^1/_2"$); it is reproduced at a ratio of 1:5 or, in other words, reduced to $^1/_5 = 0.2$ (decimal) its true size. All three terms are used in practice; lately the decimal version has come into favour because it simplifies the calculation of the extension factor for exposure.

How do we obtain sharpness in the close-up range?

Distances of less than ∞ are set by rotation of the focusing mount of the lens. To obtain sharp focus at the correct distance we use either the coupled rangefinder, or the groundglass screen. In both cases sharp focus is produced by an increase in the distance between lens and film plane. – By how much is the extension increased? This increase corresponds to the reproduction scale; here, too, the decimal expression is the simplest. Let us return to our example: – In order to obtain critical sharpness at a reproduction of 0.2× natural size you need to increase your camera extension by 0.2× the focal length of the lens used. One focal length corresponds to the value 1. With, for instance, a 200 mm lens in the camera, the extension must be increased by 40 mm and with a 50 mm lens by 10 mm.

The increase in extension, as we have said, always corresponds to the reproduction scale. If you reduce 1:10, the additional extension is 0.1× the focal length,

173

at 1:2 it is $0.5\times$, and at 1:1 a whole focal length. But if you want to magnify your subject on the film to, say 3:1, you will have to increase your existing extension by three focal lengths.

Whether a close-up subject can be focused sharply at a certain reproduction scale therefore depends on the possibility of obtaining the required extension by means of extension tubes, focusing bellows, or other accessories.

How much increase in exposure?

The exposure time must be increased if the additional extension reaches a certain value because the aperture ratio (ratio of lens diameter to focal length) is no longer valid. You must now be guided by the ratio of lens diameter to camera extension. The increase in extension is added to the focal length of the lens. In our example: $1+0.2 = 1.2$; this value is squared, since the aperture represents an area. $1.2^2 = 1.44$, approx. 1.4.

Strictly speaking, this calculation of the increase in exposure applies to symmetrical systems only; the Elmar-type lens, however, does not yet show any appreciable deviation. But the shortened construction of the telephoto lenses and the different position of the diaphragm in them have such a pronounced effect as to call for a further increase in the exposure.

The actual practice is not quite as complicated as this, because you can make use of tables of extension factors (p. 316). On the universal focusing bellows I and II, the values can even be read off directly for some lenses; all you have to do is to determine the scale at which you want to take your picture.

How much depth of field?

The table just mentioned also contains details of the depth-of-field zones for various lens stops.

The depth of field does not depend on the focal length of the camera lens, but on the reproduction scale. The larger this scale, the narrower the depth of field. Since the values in this table are based on a $1/_{30}$ mm circle of confusion, which does not always meet practical demands, a brief test is urgently recommended. A photograph is taken of an isosceles, rectangular triangle as shown on the facing page, so that the area photographed is inclined to the film plane at an angle of $45°$. The middle zone in sharp focus is marked. You will see clearly how the depth of field changes as the lens is progressively stopped down. Conditions are a little more favourable in practice than we would expect from a depth-of-field table.

174

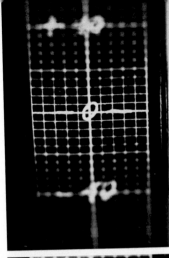

*Changing
depth of field
with different
lens stops.*

f/4

f/16

f/32

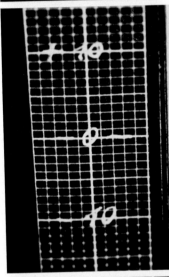

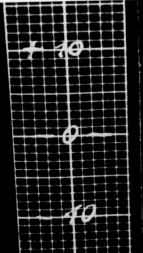

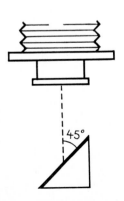

The lens should not be stopped down more than the depth of field requirements indicate, since its resolving power will be reduced by diffraction effects. Some practical values: – down to a diaphragm diameter of 4mm (= f/11 in a 50mm lens) no noticeable reduction. At apertures smaller than 4mm progressive decrease in point sharpness, but increased depth of field. The lens should be stopped down below 2mm (about f/22 in a 50mm lens) only if depth of field is more important than resolving power.

What focal length for close-up pictures?

Since depth of field depends on the reproduction scale and not on the focal length, you are faced with the question when to use short or long focal lengths. The advantage of short focal lengths is the reduced increase in extension they require. With a 35mm lens a $2\times$ magnification is obtained with only a 70mm increase in extension. With a 135mm lens a 270mm extension is necessary for the same magnification. In practice it is almost invariably more important to leave enough distance between exposure subject and camera lens to be able to arrange one's lighting properly. In order to understand this relationship clearly it is necessary to visualize the set-up (subject – camera lens – film plane) illustrated by the diagram below. The distance between the two principal planes of the camera lens has been ignored as it is negligible, and we focus on the groundglass screen.

In the diagram, 1f in front of the lens (towards the object G) and 1f behind the lens (towards the image B) is always the same. The distance (extension) between lens and image and that between lens and object varies according

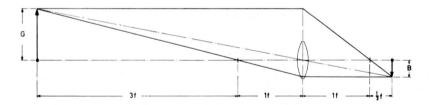

to the reproduction scale. For a reduction of 1:3 we require an additional 3f for the object distance, and 1/3f for the image distance. The values 1/3 and 3 correspond to the reproduction scale and its reciprocal value. Hence, the distance between object and film plane will be the same at 1:3 and 3:1. Only the

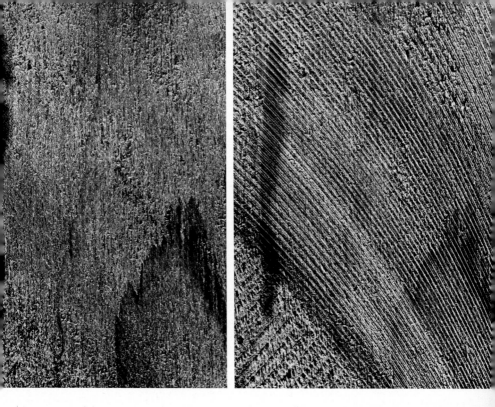

Two pictures of the same piece of wood at natural size. The difference in the rendering is entirely due to a change in the lighting. On the left incident light, on the right glancing side light in order to bring out the texture of the saw cut clearly.

lens position is changed, since in the first case the extension is increased only by 1/3f, and in the second case by 3f (see diagram). The extension factor is accordingly about 1.8 in the first case, and 16 in the second.

Almost all camera lenses are computed for objects at infinity. Their performance in the close-up range depends on their individual type. Since, however, they are always stopped down considerably in order to gain depth of field they are generally more efficient than we have a right to expect. The defects in image formation from which some lenses suffer in the close-up range as a result of their correction for infinity are quite useful in actual practice, because the depth of field is increased when a small proportion of the image-forming rays converge in front of or behind the focal plane. A few trial exposures will reveal more than a long-winded explanation.

How to light your subject

Full sunlight is often excessively contrasty, producing an unfavourable relationship between highlights and shadows. For some subjects the answer may be to subdue the sun with a diffusion screen, for others to soften the shadows by reflecting light from a sheet of white cardboard. Metal foil or mirrors, incidentally, are more efficient reflectors than white cardboard. For backlit subjects, the lens may be pushed through a hole in a sheet of light paper. This produces appreciable softening of the shadows. A sheet of cardboard can serve as a quiet background if the subject lends itself to such treatment.

A combination of electronic flash and daylight is very favourable under an overcast sky. The flash readily produces the effect of the absent sun, and also minimizes the dangers of subject movement and camera shake. Outdoors the wind presents a twofold danger with the long exposures called for in the macro range: it may cause slight movement of the tripod, or move the subject itself.

Artificial light

Ordinary household lamps and photofloods are bright enough for large objects. For small items, light directed from a projector or a small spotlight is preferable. Here, too, the harshness of the light must be softened by means of reflectors or diffusing screens.

We distinguish between the following types of illumination: – Incident light, side lighting, and transmitted light. Several types of lighting can, of course, be combined. But always follow the rule of making full use of a light source by means of reflecting surfaces before you set up a second source. One source should dominate the picture; any second and/or third source should be used for shadow-softening and the placing of highlights. In addition a dominant light makes it easier for the viewer to get his bearings in space. As the falling-off of light plays an important part in artificial lighting, the background must often be lit separately. Since we always photograph with only one lens (i.e not stereoscopically) judging the lighting with only one eye is more reliable. This merely by the way.

Close-ups of stamps are always interesting. This stamp – Saxony 3 New Groschen – was issued in 1858. Black print on yellow paper. Agfa Agepe FF film, f/11, 4 sec.

Flash

Flash is recommended only after the lighting effect has been previewed with daylight or artificial-light sources, because the lighting effects of flash are difficult to assess in advance. Experience is essential here; it can be gained only with daylight and artificial light. At the short distances at which they are used in close-up work, the intensity of electronic flash and flashbulbs considerably exceeds that of the sun. It is therefore often possible to stop down to f/11 or f/16 in spite of increased extension. But the guide numbers are smaller in the close-up range than those given by the flash manufacturers. It is, however, easy to determine them by experimenting with various f/stops. An average object distance of 50 cm (20") is recommended. In the close-up range the general law which states that light intensity decreases as the square of the distance increases is influenced within certain limits by the effect of the reflector. But good results are obtained if the experimentally determined guide numbers for the 50 cm (20") object distance are varied according to the following table:

Distance:	1 m (40")	70 cm (28")	50 cm (20")	35 cm (14")	25 cm (10")
Intensity:	$^1/_4$	$^1/_2$	1	2	4

(Values determined for Braun Hobby Automatic [EF3]).

Experience has shown that the vast majority of subjects can be lit effectively at these reflector distances. Here, too, results are improved if the shadows are softened with light-coloured cardboard sheets. Normally, the light path via the reflector should be $1^1/_2$ to 2 times as long as the direct distance between flash and the object (flash distance).

Shiny objects create the danger of reflections whose extent depends on the size and distance of the light source. Such reflections can often be made less disturbing if the flash is diffused by the removal of the standard reflector, and a sheet of silver foil wrapped round half the flash tube to prevent light from escaping to the rear. But this also reduces the guide number. In addition to the subject lighting, the background illumination plays an important role. The brightness of the background and a very bright surrounding area can strongly affect the brilliance of the picture.

Remedies: Mask the surrounding background area, and use a very long lens hood, preferably of the bellows type, on your lens.

The different lighting techniques used for the illustrations are fully described in the captions.

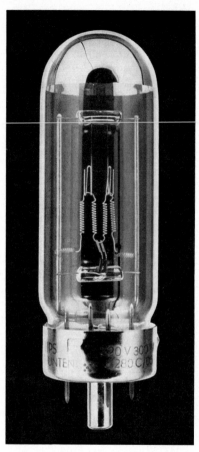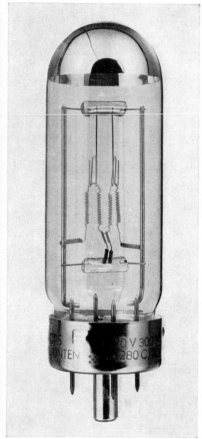

Projector lamps. Leica M2 with Reprovit II and 50mm Focotar f/4.5; f/11, 2 sec. Reproduction scale on the negative 0.3. Normal four-lamp illumination, made more diffuse by means of a translucent paper tent. Projector lamp on a glass plate separated from background to obtain shadowless reproduction. Agfa Isopan FF, Rodinal 1:50, 20° C (68° F), 7 min.

Changed rendering by a change of background, illumination unchanged. On the left: dark background with bright surroundings. Without the bright surrounding field strong differentiation from the dark background was unobtainable. Right: bright background with dark surroundings. Reflections from this dark surrounding field give a dark outline to the glass bulb.

How to determine the correct exposure time

Normal measurement with the exposure meter is difficult within the close-up range. Nor can the eye judge the situation with sufficient accuracy. If possible, the reading should be taken off a piece of white cardboard held closely in front of the object. The value found is first multiplied by 4, and then by the factor for the camera extension. The white cardboard reflects far more strongly than the object. It also prevents the background from influencing the measurement. But with higher magnifications this method is no longer possible. Only a graduated exposure series will help you gain experience here.

The following steps are recommended:

1. for normal black-and-white film in unknown conditions 1:4:16:64;
2. in vaguely known conditions 1:2:4:8;
3. for exposures on document copying and colour film 1:1.4:2:2.8:4 (interval factor $\sqrt{2} = 1.4$).

Obviously the series given here are relative and must be referred to a basic reading found with the meter.

In electronic flash, a change in the distance of the flash lamps frequently disturbs the setup. Here the exposure values should therefore be varied by means of opening and closing the lens stop, at half steps for document-copying and colour film, and at whole steps for black-and-white film.

Reciprocity Law Failure

When long camera extensions and the use of very small lens apertures lead to exposure times of 10 seconds or more, Reciprocity Law Failure, also known as the Schwarzschild Effect, causes an additional problem. At low lighting intensity it requires more exposure than the "normal" exposure calculation would indicate. If a light intensity of "20" calls e.g. for a 10-second exposure, the exposure required for a light intensity of "1" will not be 200 seconds, but actually more than 400 seconds, because the lower intensity has in practice a considerably weaker effect on the photographic emulsion.

With colour film, this Reciprocity Law Failure causes yet another difficulty: because the three layers of the colour film will be differently affected, there will be a colour shift as well. The colour shift greatly differs with the various brands of colour film. In the Agfacolor reversal film CT18 it moves in the direction of yellow-green with long exposures; the taking filters necessary to correct this fault are blue-purple.

182

Tetradrachm from Athens (5th Century B.C.). Original size approx. 25 mm (1") diameter. Diffuse side lighting with shadow softening.

This is another reason for the popularity of electronic flash in colour photography because it produces no disturbing effects (exception: earlier flash units of flash durations of $^1/_{1000}$ sec and shorter. Here again the Schwarzschild Effect – as ultra-short-time effect now – produces a colour shift, here in the opposite direction of the spectrum).

Picture brilliance

Illumination must be set up so that light from disturbing light sources is prevented from entering the camera lens. A lens hood or a bellows lens hood should be used; disturbing background elements can be masked by means of black cardboard. But disturbing reflections can also occur inside the camera, caused, for instance, by the walls of extension tubes or of other extension devices. If you make your own extension tubes, e.g. to tide you over an emergency, it is absolutely essential to line them with black velvet to eliminate reflections. A pattern is cut from a paper strip, the black velvet glued on to it and both together glued into the tube. You can test for reflections by looking through the lens at full aperture held, together with the extension device, against a bright light source.

What film for macrophotography?

Close-up exposure technique calls for some experience. A certain amount of practice is therefore necessary. A few exposure series will give you a very good idea of the potentialities and limitations in this field. Start with a black-and-white film, preferably of medium speed and of known properties. If sufficient illumination or a flash unit is available, a slow film (e.g. Agfa-Isopan FF) can also be used.

Document-copying films have roughly the same resolving power as slow thin-emulsion films, but their brilliance is superior and their grain finer. As a guide for the exposure measurement rate e.g. Agfa Agepe film 10–20 ASA, with the slower speed corresponding to the shorter developing time. Develop document copying film yourself, since only with expert development (Rodinal 1:50, 5–7 minutes) and soft lighting will you obtain the best possible results.

Colour photographs of course have an attraction all their own. Again and again you will be surprised at the abundance of colour to be found in small objects, and how much of it you fail to see when you look at them in normal conditions. Here, too, a balanced, fairly soft illumination will produce the best results. The narrow exposure latitude of colour film demands very exact work, and detailed notes of the exposure data if you want to learn from your experience. If you are a stickler for faithful colour rendering, you must not allow colour reflections from surrounding areas to affect the subject. Conversely, you can use such reflections to good advantage for creative purposes. To judge them correctly in advance calls for a trained eye.

Four times the same stamp – colour yellow, postmark black, surface embossed by the printing method. Effect on the reproduction by lighting technique and filters. Agfa Agepan film. On the left without filter, on the right with red filter. Two top pictures: diffuse illumination; two bottom pictures: parallel light in order to emphasize the surface texture.

184

NEAR-FOCUSING DEVICES

Universal focusing bellows II for the Visoflex II and III

The focusing bellows II is the most universal of all the near-focusing outfits. With the appropriate focal lengths it covers the entire range from infinity to 1:1. Within limited focusing ranges shorter focal lengths can also be used and the versatile field of close-up- and macrophotography explored with them. Both this breadth of application and its simple and reliable operation are greatly appreciated by scientific and technical photographers.

The focusing bellows II is an accessory for the Visoflex II and III. A variation of the extension through 95 mm can be obtained with it by means of a rack-and-pinion movement. This extends the focusing range of the 90 mm Elmar and Elmarit lens heads from ∞ to 1:1. With the 65 mm Elmar the reproduction scale ranges from ∞ to 1.4:1. Considerable magnifications are possible with Leica lenses of shorter focal lengths. With the longer focal lengths of 125, 135 and 200 mm the focusing range extends from ∞ to 1:2 and 1:1,5 respectively. After mounting the Leica on the Visoflex attachment, fix the two together on the focusing bellows, which has a little catch on the left; when this is pressed the Leica and Visoflex attachment can easily be rotated from the horizontal to the vertical position.

The ring 16558 on the front of the focusing bellows belongs to the basic outfit. Its thread takes the lens heads of the 135 mm Tele-Elmar f/4, 90 mm Elmar f/4, 90 mm Elmarit f/2.8, and the 65 mm Elmar f/3.5 lens. An additional adapter ring 16472 is required for the 135 mm Elmar and Hektor lens heads. In order to be able to use other lens heads on the universal focusing bellows, unscrew the ring 16558 and replace it by the appropriate other ring. The ring 16590 accepts all Leica lenses with screw thread. The ring 16596 has the standard Leica-M bayonet and can be coupled with all bayonet lenses.

The ring 16598 accepts the following lens heads: 90 mm Summicron f/2, 135 mm Elmarit f/2.8, 200 mm Telyt f/4, and 280 mm Telyt f/4.8. But the two last-named lenses can also be screwed into the ring 16590 together with their mounts.

A scale giving the reproduction scales and the extension factors for the 90 mm lenses is engraved on the left of the monobar. On the right the bellows extension can be read off in mm. If you want to repeat pictures at a given reproduction scale you merely have to read the value of this mm scale, and set it again when required.

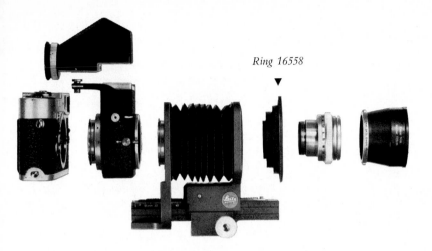

Ring 16558

To make focusing on an object possible in the near-focusing range without a change of the reproduction scale, a further rack-and-pinion movement has been added on the underside of the tripod slide of the universal focusing bellows to permit fine focusing after the total distance has been roughly determined. The lower drive knob can be arrested with the wing nut. A push-on bellows lens hood provides effective protection against stray light with contre jour exposures.

This bellows lens hood, however, is suitable only for lenses of 42 mm diameter. With other lenses, the ordinary lens hood must be considerably extended if the lighting conditions demand it. Because within the near-focusing range the camera extension appreciably narrows the angle of field from that applicable to the infinity value this extension of the lens hood creates no difficulties.

For the exposure a sturdy tripod with a rigid ball-and-socket head is required. With a very low camera viewpoint operation will be much more convenient if the straight 5× magnifier is used on the Visoflex III in place of the right-angle 4× magnifier. Although the image will be side-reversed, this will not be found disturbing with tripod work.

187

Insects – flashed by the water's edge

Let Walter Wissenbach, the wellknown animal photographer take the word: "Science knows of about 700,000 different kinds of insect, a number representing four-fifths of all the types of animal inhabiting our planet.

The unlimited variety of forms offers the nature photographer innumerable possibilities for creative picture-making. Along the water's edge, among the reeds and glades, particularly attractive subjects such as dragonflies and daddy-longlegs are often found darting from blade to blade.

These often tiny subjects are tricky to take. Much experience, patience, and yet more patience are necessary before you are rewarded with a good picture. My favourite equipment in this field is the Leica with the 135 mm Hektor, Visoflex, and the focusing bellows which allows rapid, mobile close-up focusing. With electronic flash, which I use to supplement daylight, I can work with 40 ASA films at apertures of f/16 and f/22, depending upon the size of the subject, with flash distances from 1 m to 1.5 m (3$^1/_2$ to 5 ft)."

Bright expanses, sky and water, can be included in the picture to good effect. This usually avoids the black background obtained with small stops and flashlight.

Damselfly	*f/16*	*top left*
Crane flies	*f/22*	*top right*
Dragonfly	*f/16*	*bottom left*
Skin of a larva	*f/16*	*bottom right*

All pictures: Leica, 135 mm Hektor, Visoflex, universal focusing bellows, daylight and flash.

188

Copying gauge	quarto	210×305 mm	$(8^1/_4 \times 12'')$
	octavo	152×210 mm	$(6 \times 8^1/_4'')$
	postcard-size	105×152 mm	$(4^1/_8 \times 6'')$

The equipment consists of 3 extension collars and four extensible metal legs. Each of the 3 extension collars is designed for a certain marked format. It is chosen accordingly, the four legs screwed in and extended as far as the notches appropriate to the object field. The notches are engraved with the numbers 4, 5 and 6. After the legs have clicked into position, slightly tighten the knurled captive nuts. The tips of the legs now indicate the 4 corners of the object field as well as the exact object distance. This close-up device is suitable for the 50 mm Leica lenses in bayonet mount (except Summarit, Summilux and Noctilux). When the extension collar is attached its red dot must face the red dot on the bayonet mount of the Leica body; it is then turned to the right to be locked in position.

The Leica lenses are inserted in the inner bayonet of the collar. The collapsible bayonet-mounted lenses are not extended, and locked with the inner bayonet of the collar. The lens head of the 50 mm Summicron f/2 can be unscrewed from the non–collapsible version of this lens, and is screwed into the bayonet mount (16 508) and locked in the collar. Slightly press against the mount during insertion and lock the lens head by a turn to the right. In the end position the lens is secured in the mount. It can be unlocked only by slightly depressing it and turning it to the left.

This copying gauge is very useful whenever the object field can be determined with the extensible legs with sufficient accuracy, e.g. flowers and plants out-

190

doors, perhaps small animals, and inanimate objects of all kinds. For copying, the 4 legs can even be used as a camera support, but care must be taken (preferably by using a lamp from each side) to prevent the legs from casting shadows on to the subject.

A way out with exposures in sunlight is to unscrew the leg which casts the disturbing shadow; the outline of the field can be kept quite adequately with only 3 legs. Bear in mind that you must change the setting of the legs each time you alter the reproduction scale.

If no special lighting for uniform illumination is available, e.g. in a library, the copying gauge can be used very effectively in ordinary daylight, near a window. Again, shadows cast by the legs should be avoided. They disappear if pieces of light cardboard are propped against the legs on three sides, or the leg nearest the rewind knob is unscrewed. To prevent the assembly from toppling over, a ball-and-socket head is screwed into the baseplate. The depth-of-field scale for this accessory will be found in the appendix. It is advisable to stop down to f/11. A cable release should always be used.

Left: The copying gauge with fully extended legs for reproducing originals of 210×297mm (8.4×11.9"). Do not place the lamps too close and too steeply to avoid reflections from the shiny letters. Right: Reflections may occur in the reproduction of dark, glossy originals. It is therefore advisable to use dark sheets of cardboard as screens on either side inside the legs. A lens hood is indispensable.

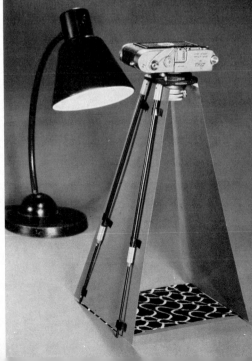

Copying gauge for the reproduction scales 1:3, 1:2, 1:1.5, 1:1

This device can be used with either bayonet-mount or screw-thread Leica cameras. It consists of a base with an adjustable column, four extension tubes for the various reproduction scales, three drop-in masks and a bayonet adapter. All 50mm lenses can be used. The appropriate focusing distances are engraved on the back of the column. The object fields accommodated are covered by the following extension tube:

Picture area	Reproduction scale	Extension tube	Exposure factor
72×108 mm (3×4³/₈″)	1:3	A	1.8×
48×72 mm (2×3″)	1:2	A+B	2.3×
36×54mm (1¹/₂×2¹/₈″)	1:1.5	A+C	2.8×
24×36 mm (1×1¹/₂″)	1:1	A+D	4×

The base of the column limits the picture area to 72×108mm (approx. 3×4³/₈″). For the other reproduction scales the field is reduced by means of the drop-in masks. The image is focused with the detachable groundglass magnifier. This must first be adjusted to the user's eyesight; slowly lower it from its most extended position until the black ring on the groundglass screen is clearly visible. This setting can be arrested by a strip of Scotch tape if you are the only user of the equipment.

This sharpness in the centre of the groundglass screen is checked with the magnifier, which does not outline the picture area as this is done by the drop-in masks. The lens should be stopped down to f/11, even for flat subjects.

The device can be used also for the copying of glass-mounted or unmounted colour- and black-and-white transparencies. Since these have to be transilluminated the device must be mounted on a light box. Disturbing side light should be masked; light from above, too, reduces the contrast. A recess in the underside of the base can be used as a guide for the optical copying of filmstrips or negatives.

The copying gauge can be dismantled for transport; the column is unscrewed from the base of the stand, when everything will take up the smallest possible space.

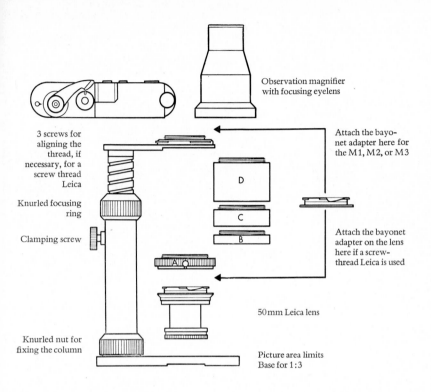

Observation magnifier
with focusing eyelens

3 screws for
aligning the
thread, if
necessary, for a
screw thread
Leica

Attach the bayo-
net adapter here for
the M1, M2, or M3

Knurled focusing
ring

Clamping screw

Attach the bayonet
adapter on the lens
here if a screw-
thread Leica is used

50 mm Leica lens

Knurled nut for
fixing the column

Picture area limits
Base for 1:3

Interchangeable 1:2, 1:1.5 and 1:1 masks

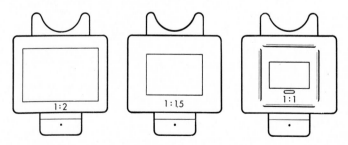

Optical near-focusing device for the Leica M2, M3 and M4

All 50mm lenses with bayonet for the M Leicas (except Summarit, Summilux and Noctilux) can be used. The lens head is unscrewed from the rigid version of the 50mm Summicron and attached by means of the small bayonet adapter (16508). The optical near-focusing device is inserted in the Leica body like a Leica lens. In order to lock the lenses in the near-focusing device, exert slight pressure and turn them to the right; to remove them, again depress them slightly, and turn them to the left.

The coupled rangefinder and automatic parallax compensation are effective from 88–48cm (35–19''). This corresponds to a range of reproduction scales from 1:15 to 1:7.5. The relevant object sizes as well as the corresponding depth-of-field zones are given in the table for close-up subjects on page 317. If you want to take photographs at a given scale, set it on the index, and make the two rangefinder images coincide by moving the camera backward and forward. Distances are always measured from the film plane (camera back).

There is little depth of field in the close-up range. The lens should be stopped down to at least f/5.6; further stopping down is recommended when exposure conditions permit it. Table page 317.

194

Reprovit IIa

The new Reprovit IIa has replaced the earlier Reprovit II. It is a versatile piece of equipment for the close-up and copying work so frequently required in scientific departments, industrial laboratories and in the photographic business. All components have been matched to ensure a considerable saving of time.

A 67×68 cm ($27 \times 27''$ approx.) baseboard supports a robust column of 1.4 m (56") height. The counter-balanced carrying arm can be moved effortlessly. The Leica is attached to a changing slide, which has a groundglass screen at the level of the film plate. Depending on the camera distance, originals from 45×68 cm ($18 \times 27''$) (1:19) down to 24×36 mm ($1 \times 1^1/_2''$) (1:1) can be covered. A built-in projection device indicates the object field, and a projected test mark permits fast, accurate focusing.

To enable you to determine the reproduction scale conveniently, 1" and 10 mm index lines are engraved on the groundglass screen and projected on the original. The reproduction scale will be 1:9, if the distance between the 10 mm lines is 90 mm on the original. If a magnifier instead of the projection lamp is used for focusing in the close-up range, a rule can be placed on the original and its reproduction compared with the 1" or 10 mm lines on the groundglass screen.

The special 50 mm Focotar f/4.5 lens is used for photography. Its focusing range can be extended from 1:1 to 3:1 by means of 4 extension rings (16615). The 24 mm Repro-Summar is available as an additional lens, permitting close-ups up to a scale of 7:1 ($7 \times$ magnification on the film). The changing slide can be removed from the carrying arm and attached to any ordinary tripod.

The object is illuminated by a set of 4 lamps, which produce the uniform lighting so useful for general copying purposes. Special black screening cloths prevent the light from reaching the camera assembly. The distance of the lamps is fixed, so that the exposure times change only with the reproduction scale; the extension factors can be read directly off a scale. When the changing slide is moved the projection focusing light is automatically turned off and the four-lamp subject illumination switched on.

Opening and closing the lens stop is coupled with the movement of the changing slide by means of a drive. With the groundglass screen in position above the lens, the stop is open; when the slide is moved to the exposure position the lens is automatically stopped down to f/11.

Long exposures are accurately controlled by means of the electric exposure timer and a built-in magnetic shutter release. The Leica shutter is set at B. An

exposure lock prevents release of the shutter unless the changing slide is in the exposure position.

The Reprovit IIa can be extended according to requirements by such accessories as the framing box, light box, and object stage. The framing box, with object field of 30×42cm (12×17″) is most useful for copying from journals and books up to 12cm (5″) thickness. It works on the principle of sliding wedges on which the object stage can be raised and lowered. The original is pressed against a plane-parallel glass sheet from below, which keeps the object in focus even at varying thicknesses. The framing box is also suitable for the shadowless photography of small objects if the wedge is lowered or removed altogether. The object stage is recommended for the photography of very small objects, such as postage stamps.

Rapid focusing is made very much easier by means of a knurled fine-adjustment screw. Transparencies can be made from black-and-white negatives, and black-and-white negatives from colour transparencies at natural size (1:1); for this, however, a light box is required.

A 40×42cm (16×17″) light box with fluorescent tubes is used for the copying of X-ray-films, negatives, or transparencies. The originals are placed on the uniformly transilluminated sheet of opal glass, and kept flat by means of a sheet of clear glass. Bright surrounding areas should always be masked. For this purpose the new version of the light box includes black masking cloths.

The light box can also be used for the shadowless photography of three-dimensional objects. In order to avoid disturbing glare, the incident illumination must be adjusted so that its intensity is balanced correctly with that of the light box.

The light box is extremely useful for the visual recording of slide lectures. Four rows of six or six rows of eight 5×5 cm $(2\times2'')$ slides each are placed on it and photographed. To make the titles legible, the four-lamp illumination from above is also switched on.

Exposure tips for copying

We distinguish between two basic forms of copying:

1. Halftone copying (pictures, drawings) – faithful reproduction of the original. Fine-grain films up to 50 ASA are recommended.
2. Line copying (manuscripts, woodcuts, etc.) – contrasty reproduction: Document-copying films are especially suitable.

Subjects including both type and pictures are best copied like halftone subjects, but the film should be developed to a slightly higher contrast.

Uniform illumination is essential to good reproduction. In daylight, near a window, a piece of white cardboard will be very satisfactory for this purpose. For artificial light an equal number of identical lamps are used from opposite sides. The uniformity of the lamp distances is judged from an appreciable distance or tested with a pencil stood on the original below the camera lens; the two shadows cast by the pencil must be equally dark. The angle of lighting should be about 45° (steeper = reflections). The distance between the lamps and the centre of the original must be at least the same as the length of the original. Cover with a dark mask whatever does not form part of your subject (surrounding field). Always use a lens hood.

For the copying of dark, glossy originals the camera assembly should be kept in the dark to prevent disturbing reflections. This effect is avoided by means screening the apparatus against the light.

If possible use f/11!

Accurate exposure is important. Do not overexpose. Use an exposure meter. Always take your reading from a sheet of white paper, not from the original you wish to copy. Calibrate your exposure meter for your film and your developing method. In unknown conditions find the correct exposure by a graduated exposure series based on an exposure factor of 1.4 – i.e. double every second exposure time (e.g. 0.7 – 1 – 1.4 – 2 – 2.8 sec). With very small objects an additional extension factor owing to the long camera extension must be introduced.

Top: *Examples of halftone reproductions. Left: Title page of a book of photographic anecdotes published in London 1855 (Stenger Collection).*
         Right: Close-up of a run in a stocking. Total magnification 15×.

Bottom: *Examples of line reproductions. Left: Reduced title page of an 18th Century book on optics. Right: 15× magnification of a blockmaker's screen (from the instructions for the Leica M3).*

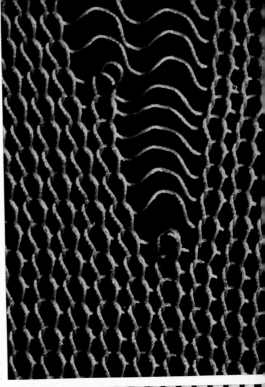

OCULUS
ARTIFICIALIS
TELEDIOPTRICUS
SIVE
ELESCOPIUM,
EX

litis rerum Naturalium & Artificialium
principiis protractum novà methodo, eâque solidâ explicatum
ac comprimis è triplici

FUNDAMENTO
FSICO feu NATURALI, MATHEMATICO DIOPTRICO
Et
MECHANICO, feu PRACTICO
ſtabilitum.

s curioſum Theorico - Practicum magna rerum varietate
atum, omnibus Artium novarum ſtudioſis perquàm utile: Quo Philo-
e atque Matheſi præſertim mixtæ, nec non univerſo penè hominum ſtatui
fimis adjumentis conſulitur; nova plurima abſtruſa curioſa Technaſmata reclu-
untur, ipſáque Ars Teleſcopiaria facillimè addiſcenda, ac ſumptibus non adeò
magnis in praxin adducenda proponitur,
adeoque

TELESCOPIUM
ex tenebris in lucem aſſeritur.
AUTHORE
JOANNE ZAHN
FRANCO-CAROLOPOLITANO
ri & Candidi Ordinis Præmonſtratenſis Canonico Regulari
nec non Parthenonis Cellæ inferioris ejuſdem Ordinis propè
Herbipolim
PRÆPOSITO.
Editio Secunda Auctior.
Cum Facultate Superiorum.

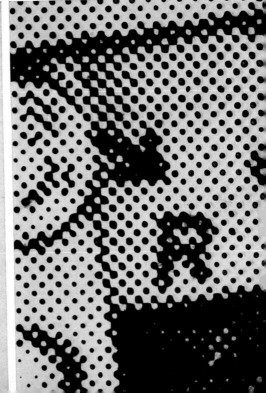

Photomicrography with the Leica

All the wonders of the microcosm opened up by the microscope can be recorded on film with the Leica. Photomicrography is an indispensable handmaiden of scientific research. It provides valuable visual aid for schools, universities, and scientific institutions.

The micro-attachments for the Leica extend the versatile technical possibilities of the Leica system to photomicrography. Two of its main advantages are the saving of material through the use of the 35 mm format, without which serial photographs of microscopic events, to mention only one example, would have to be ruled out on grounds of economy, and a shortening of exposure times so welcome particularly in colour photography.

The MIKAS micro-attachment is suitable for black-and-white and colour films and can be used with all Leica cameras on all microscopes with normal tubes. It consists of a conical adapter with an intermediate optical system, a focusing telescope, a central shutter for time- and instantaneous exposures, an eyepiece clamping ring with a clamping screw for the microscope tube, and two cable releases. A PERIPLAN 10× eyepiece also forms part of the outfit, although for macro- and low-power work up to 200× a 10× Huygenian eyepiece is preferable.

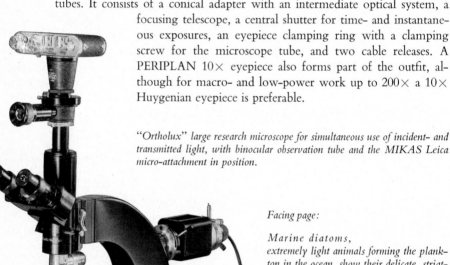

"Ortholux" large research microscope for simultaneous use of incident- and transmitted light, with binocular observation tube and the MIKAS Leica micro-attachment in position.

Facing page:

Marine diatoms,
extremely light animals forming the plankton in the ocean, show their delicate, striated needle-like microstructure, ingeniously designed to keep the animal suspended. – Plankton means "drifting, suspended". From the very beautiful picture volume "Wunder der Mikrowelt" (Wonders of the Microcosm) by Dr. Horst Reumuth, Director of the Fraunhofer Institute for Applied Microscopy, Karlsruhe. Published by Konradin Verlag Rob. Kohlhammer.

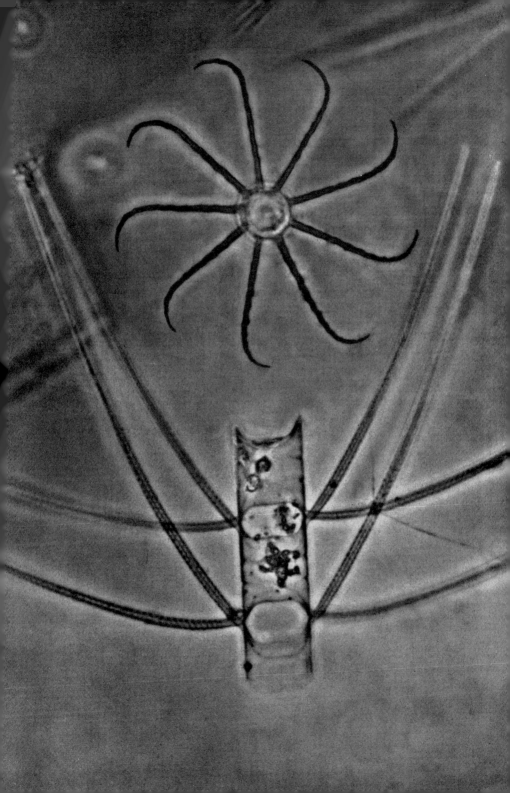

The micro-attachment is designed for a reproduction scale of $^1/_3$ of the final microscope magnification. A $3\times$ enlargement of a 35mm negative will therefore produce a photomicrograph at a reproduction scale corresponding to that of the microscope.

The MIKAS attachment is fixed to the Leica body, and the combination inserted with the eyepiece in the tube of the microscope, where it is clamped in position with the small clamping screw. The graticule in the focusing telescope is focused sharply for the eyesight of the observer by rotation of the eyelens of the telescope; only now should the subject be focused with the fine adjustment of the microscope, so that graticule and object both appear sharp at the same time. The lines of the largest rectangle of the graticule indicate the object field when the $^1/_3$ adapter is used.

Sharpness and field of the microscopic image are checked in the focusing telescope, into which a swing-out prism, actuated by a cable release, deflects about 25% of the image-forming rays. If the prism is left in the optical path during the exposure, the object can be observed even while it is being exposed. But for weakly-lit subjects or if the shortest possible exposure times requiring the full amount of light are necessary the prism is swung out immediately before the exposure; here the subject can be observed right up to the moment of exposure and again immediately afterwards. The self-winding time- and instantaneous shutter has speeds from 1 to $^1/_{125}$sec and Time, and is synchronized for electronic flash. With a twincable release, which is useful for instantaneous shutter speeds, the observation prism is swung out automatically when the shutter is released.

The MONLA microscope lamp is a particularly efficient light source for photomicrography. It has a 6v 5amp. low-voltage filament lamp, connected to the mains through a regulating transformer (a.c.) or a fixed resistance (d.c.). The lamp can be clamped on its stand in any position. Its high intensity allows very short exposure times.

In order to increase contrast with black-and-white pictures generally a yellow-green filter is inserted in the optical path of the microscope, with a consequent increase in exposure time. The economical Leica format allows you to take two or three exposures of every subject at different shutter speeds, so that particularly beginners can quickly familiarize themselves with the procedure. Whenever long exposures are permissible ultra-finegrain film should be used in black-and-white photography. Only in very difficult cases (e.g. fluorescence microscopy) of low lighting intensity will you have to fall back on ultra-fast film, sometimes in order to make an exposure possible at all. The fact that because of the $^1/_3$ adapter the exposure time for the Leica is very much shorter than for the 9×12 cm format is of great significance.

Especially in colour photomicrography the determination of the correct exposure time calls for much experience. A further micro-attachment for the Leica has therefore been designed, to which the MICROSIX-L exposure meter can be attached. A vibration damper is built into the top of the micro-attachment, which prevents the unavoidable shutter bounce during the action of the focal-plane shutter from being transmitted to the microscope. Here, too, the image is observed and focused through the focusing telescope of the micro-attachment. Only a few manipulations are required for exposure measurements. Turning a lever on the micro-attachment directs the full light flux towards the measuring eye of the MICROSIX-L. The user reads the measurement off the scale of the exposure meter, determining the correct exposure time according to the film speed within seconds.

The limiting sensitivity of the MICROSIX-L is so high that even the long exposure times of weakly fluorescing objects can be measured with it.

Furthermore, a special version of the Visoflex III is available for photomicrography. A changing device makes it possible to use a groundglass screen at low and a clear glass plate at high magnifications for observation and focusing. This device is used on the Aristophot in conjunction with a special support and an extensible bellows. The magnification range can be varied with it considerably more than with any other device.

In addition to the Leica attachments mentioned here a large number of outfits exists for the most varied purposes of photomicrography. Leitz have been building microscopes from their foundation in 1849, ranging from the simple classroom microscope to the most sophisticated large research stand.

The endo-photographic attachment

Endoscopes are instruments for the observation of body cavities, such as the human bladder (cystoscope), the stomach (gastroscope) the bronchi (bronchoscope) etc. The wish to record the visual impressions photographically is practically as old as endoscopy itself. Many difficulties had to be overcome before this aim was reached. Special photo-endoscopes with larger transmission pupils, very fast colour films, and a special lighting technique – partly with electronic flash units developed for the very purpose – in connection with a special version of the Visoflex III have created the conditions essential to the practice of endo-photography on a broad basis.

The special feature of this modified Visoflex III is a changing guide permitting the introduction of a clear glass plate in place of the groundglass screen. The photo-endoscopes of the following manufacturers can be used with it:

Richard Wolf, G.m.b.H., Endoskopbau, 7134 Knittlingen/Wuertt., Postfach 18, Karl Storz, Endoskope, 72 Tuttlingen, Hermannstrasse 14, Deutsche Endoskopbau-Gesellschaft Sass, Wolf & Co. m.b.H., 1 Berlin 61, Ritterstraße 12.

A special junction piece each is required for connecting the attachment to an endoscope; it is available from the manufacturer of the endosope used. A mirror-reflex-device serves for observation and focusing. A right-way-round image is seen through the right-angle 4× prism magnifier. A groundglass screen of fine texture is used for adjustment and sharpness control. For observation it is replaced by a clear glass plate, which reveals all details with great clarity.

Other uses of the Endo-Visoflex housing

The use of the endo-photo-attachment is not restricted to medical subjects, but can be extended to other tasks in scientific and technical photography. A few examples are pictures of the inside of steel bottles, steam cylinders, bores, tubes, and other cavities. Here, the reproduction is larger and may sometimes even fill the Leica frame, since with the stationary, although less powerful, instruments exposure times are not limited.

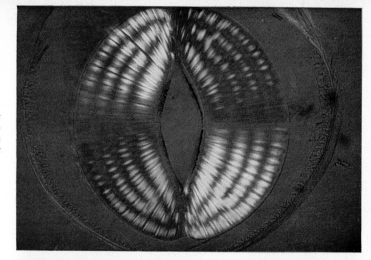

...llis blomstrandi
...elid worm).

...-section through the pharynx:
..., transversely striated muscle
..., sectors alternately in addition
...on (blue), and subtraction position
...w). Pol+, gypsum plate, 1st
...red. 160×.

...da granosa
...-shelled turtle).

...n through the deep layer of the
...ry skin. Undulating collagen
... zones alternating in addition
...on (blue) and subtraction position
...w), separated by extinguishing
... zones, Pol+, gypsum plate, 1st
...red. 160×.

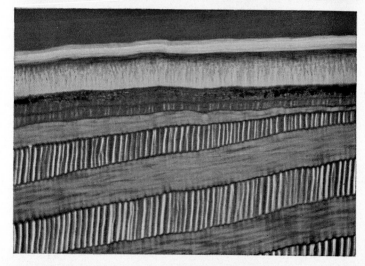

...da granosa
...-shelled turtle).

...-section through the skin. On top
...mis with horny layer and the
...y germ layer; below, the leathery
... whose layers rise towards the
...mis, tapering; the collagen fibres
...ghbouring layers are cut alter-
... lengthwise and across; in the
... layers the vertical fibres of the
...ry skin are visible (yellow).
...y gypsum plate, 1st order red.

FILM DEVELOPMENT

The exposure of the film does not by itself produce a visible picture; this must first be developed. Film development can be strongly influenced by its duration and by the type and the temperature of the developer. In the interest of reliability the results should be as uniform as possible; you can achieve this only if you adhere to a well-tried developer formula, and keep all conditions as constant as possible by using a watch or darkroom timer to control the duration and a thermometer to determine the temperature. Never rely on intuition.

Many efficient photo-dealers with excellent processing facilities will gladly take all these worries off your shoulders. This way out is recommended if your photographic activities are intermittent, or if you are unable to develop your own films owing to lack of time or a suitable darkroom. But in all other cases, especially if you enjoy the technical aspects of photography, you cannot do better than carry out your own processing. Only then will you get to know your negatives really well.

The Leica film has up to 36 frames which are all developed together. The risk of damaging the tiny negatives would be far too great were they to be cut for individual development. Developing tanks are therefore used for the processing of Leica films; a darkroom is no longer necessary. All processes are carefully timed, and carried out in ordinary light except loading the film into the tank. With the Agfa-Rondinax tank the film can also be inserted in daylight.

Developing at home is simple

You need:

1. a developing tank

2. a darkroom thermometer (the region around 20° C [68° F] should be clearly readable)

3. developer (the ready-packed, commercial variety is usually preferable)

4. Acid fixing bath: water   1000 cc
                        sodium thiosulphate (hypo) cryst.   250 g
                        potassium metabisulphite cryst.   25 g

Hydroquinone crystals (developer substance).
Photomicrograph 60×, in polarized light, gypsum plate I.

In the absence of a darkroom a temporarily darkened room will be sufficient for the development of Leica films. But since complete darkness is essential, you have to wait for about 6–8 minutes before you are able to see and stop any chinks in the blackout. To avoid stains the developing tanks etc. are placed on a nonsensitive surface. The procedure is as follows: –

1. Fill the tank with a sufficient volume of developer.

2. Measure the temperature accurately.

3. Place a vessel next to the tank for the intermediate rinse.

4. Have a second tank (or a container of similar size) ready at a distance for fixing.
   Place the vessels so that you cannot confuse them in the dark.

5. Wind the film on to the spiral in darkness. Even if you use the dark green safelight necessary for lighting the darkroom, insert the film far away from the safelight (if you are inexperienced, practise the procedure a few times with an old film in daylight).

6. Immerse the spiral with the film in the developing tank with a slight twisting movement and lightly tap the bottom several times to dislodge any air bubbles.

7. Immediately upon immersion start timing the development. A stopwatch or a clock with audible warning is best for this purpose. Close the lid.

8. Slowly rotate the spool insert with the rotating knob several times once every 30 seconds. This can be done in daylight. (The developer is, however, mixed more effectively if the spool is lifted once every 30 seconds and rotated as it is being re-immersed; this must of course be done in darkness).

9. At the end of the prescribed developing time remove the film from the tank in total darkness, rinse for a few seconds, and fix it. Here, too, repeated agitation is necessary.
   Normal film fixing baths require 10 minutes when fresh. The light must not be turned on at first. The fixing bath can be used repeatedly.

10. Final wash. – This should be 20 minutes in running water. Direct a jet of water into the centre of the spiral; this at the same time cleans the tank.

Flow sheet of the developing process from "Dunkelkammer-Handbuch". Follow the black arrow. The timer is graduated in 30 minutes.

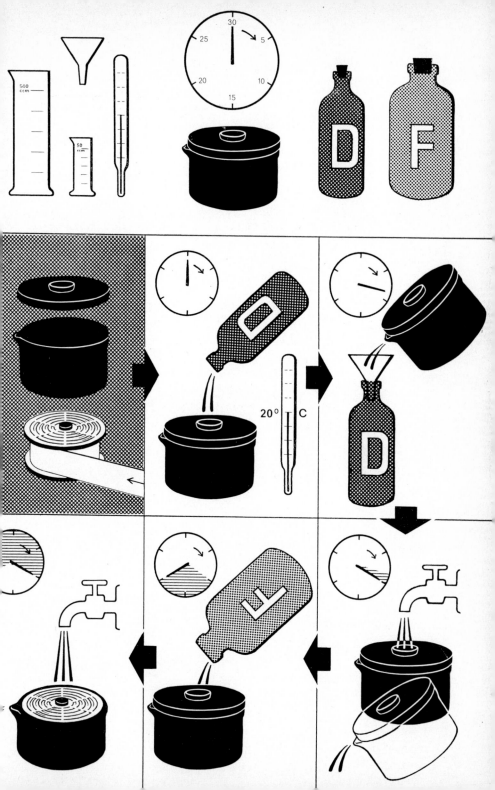

11. Drying. – Carefully remove the film from the spiral. Hang it up in a dust-free area, with a second weighted film-clip at the bottom to inhibit curling. Remove excess water–damp surgical cottonwool is best (immerse a strip of cottonwool in water, squeeze it out and fold it so that both sides of the film can be wiped down with moderate pressure).

12. Storage. – When the film is dry cut it into strips of 6 and keep it in trans-lucent negative envelopes. If after drying the film curls lengthwise, gently roll it emulsion side outwards (diameter of the roll 3–4cm), and leave it in this state for 5–6 hours before cutting it. To store the films permanently rolled up is not recommended, since they become scratched as they are repeatedly unrolled and rolled again.

The rate and effect of development differs for the various types of film and developer. To give yourself a chance to learn from experience it is highly advisable to stick to one film and one developer suitable for Leica films at first. You will find the use of ready-packed finegrain developers simplest and most reliable, because this is a convenient method of obtaining great uniformity of development.

For those who insist on mixing their own, here are two excellent formulas offering full speed utilization and pleasing printing contrast. Quantities are given in the metric system which is far easier to use than ounces and grains.

Agfa 14	Metol	4.5 g
	Sod. sulphite anh.	85 g
	Sod. carbonate anh.	1 g
	Pot. bromide	0.5 g
	Water to 1000 cc	

Kodak D 76	Metol	2 g
	Sod. sulphite anh.	100 g
	Hydroquinone	5 g
	Kodalk or Borax	2 g
	Water to 1000 cc	

To ensure consistantly uniform results, the following points are important:

a) *Making up the developer.* – Unless it is to be used immediately, store in brown 500cc or pint bottles. If filled right up to a tight-fitting stopper the unused solution will last for as long as 6 months.

Spiral developing tanks are now preferred as their grooves are more widely spaced and the developer is mixed more thoroughly during the inversion of the tank. Two types of tank are available which differ in their method of film loading.

1) With this Jobo Neofin Tank the film is pushed into the spiral from outside. The lead of the film is cut off and the corners rounded to make loading easier. The spiral must be completely dry.

2) Should the film become jammed during loading, it can be eased and worked loose through the lateral cutouts.

3) Spiral of the Jobo Tank 160D. The film is fastened to, and loaded from, the centre by means of a winder.

4) This Kindermann spiral, like the tank into which it is inserted, is made of stainless steel and therefore indestructible. The film is loaded from the centre; here, too, a winder is available. To avoid mishaps, loading should first be practised repeatedly in daylight with a length of waste film.

b) *Yield.* – Never use the developer to exhaustion. The safest method is to develop no more than two rolls of film (either together or in quick succession), and discard it, as used developer is unpredictable in its action. The uniform results obtained fully justify the slight added costs of this method.

c) *Developing time.* – Consult the developer manufacturer's instructions carefully, since different films require different developing times. The use of fresh developer eliminates variation in speed utilization and negative contrast.

Advanced workers slightly modify their developing times when lighting and/or subject contrast was abnormal. With low contrast (fog, bad weather, distant views, etc.) it is advisable to extend, with high–contrast negatives (back–lighting, architectural subjects in strong sunlight, etc.) to curtail the rated development time.

If you intend to adjust development to accommodate abnormal conditions, you should endeavour to collect subjects of a similar contrast range on the film, and remember to mark the film container accordingly.

Development Tips

● To maintain correct and constant processing temperature, place the tank and any other containers in a shallow bowl filled with water at the same temperature as that of the developer. The temperature of such a large-volume water jacket hardly changes during development.

● Before the film is threaded into the spool sharply fold the end of the film torn off the cassette or cartridge spool to prevent the jagged edge from damaging the sensitive wet emulsion.

● Using a rapid hardening-fixing bath protects the emulsion from abrasion throughout the life of the negative. Such solutions are essential for high-temperature processing in tropical countries.

● After washing, a short immersion in a 1:200 wetting agent solution prevents the formation of drying marks.

● The occurence of drying marks caused by hard water supply will not be prevented by a wetting agent. The remedy is immersion for 2–3 minutes in a 1% acetic acid solution.

Not all films are strong enough to withstand rapid drying by immersion in alcohol after washing. If you plan to use this technique, first test by immersing a piece of the same film in alcohol for about 30 seconds. Films treated in this way usually dry within 2–3 minutes.

Developers of special properties

Ultra-finegrain developer

It is best to keep the grain of ultra-fast and medium-speed films as small as possible by means of ultra-finegrain developer. High film speed utilization of the
developer is also important so that the advantage of the higher film speed is not
lost. With medium-speed films, ultra-finegrain developers are of special
importance when the brightness contrast of the scenes is low (snow, distant
views, beach), since here the grain will be particularly obnoxious.

Detailed instructions for their use will be enclosed with the developers of
various makes.

Developers effectively influencing gradation

With inherently constrasty slow films (up to about 50 ASA) a modification of
the developer to produce normal or soft gradation is specially important. One
type of developer has been found particularly reliable for this purpose. By
changing its dilution between 1:20 and 1:50 you can adapt it to a wide range of
conditions. Depending on the developing time the negatives obtained will be
soft to normal. But its most important property is that as a pure surface developer it "squeezes" the maximum sharpness out of the negatives. The adjacency
effect enhances the impression of sharpness still further; this is a phenomenon
in which the boundary lines between strong brightness differences appear traced
lighter or darker.

This is the versatile Agfa Rodinal, or similar paramido-phenolbased formulae.
Its use at a dilution of 1:50 at a temperature of 20° C, developing time 5–10 minutes depending on the exposure material and the desired contrast, is well tried.
The developer is diluted immediately before use, and discarded after a single
film. Rodinal is not a finegrain developer, and its good qualities must therefore
be reserved for slow films of inherently fine grain. Some workers recommend
dilution down to 1:100, but I find that results are more even at 1:50, and less
influenced by the hardness or softness of the tap water.

Excellent results are obtained by the processing of the very finegrain document-
copying films, which are now also available as panchromatic films, in such soft-
working developers. Development has to be kept short (5–7 min), since the
gradation of these films is inherently very steep. For outdoor subjects sunlight
should be absent or at least very subdued, and with artificial light the lighting

Turning of square blocks in a steel works. The most minute details in the highlights of the steel blocks appear even on this reproduction. – The Eberhard Effect typical of Rodinal development is, however, more prominent on the original photograph.
50 mm Elmar, f/8.   *Photograph by Liesel Springmann*

should be a little softer than usual. Because the exposure latitude is very limited, a trial run with graduated exposures is recommended in order to determine the effective speed of the emulsion.

Another way to high film speed utilization is to use "Emofin", the new two-bath developer by Tetenal. Here the developing process has two stages. In the first bath the emulsion layer takes up the developer substance, in the second bath, which contains the alkali, development continues only as long as there is any developer substance left. This method thus utilizes the film speed very efficiently without producing excessive contrast in the negatives.

Extended development

Extended development, sometimes increased temperatures, although leading to high film speed utilization and consequently permitting very high shutter speeds should be strictly limited to press and sports photography in very poor light and to similar tasks.

Deliberately the exposure is therefore cut down considerably from what the exposure meter indicates. With normal development underexposed negatives are produced. But such pictures can very often be saved by an extension of the developing time or an increase in the developer temperature. Whether you will be able to manage with half, a quarter, or even an eighth of the measured exposure value depends on many factors. Start with a certain combination and make an exposure series of graduated shutter speeds, beginning with the measured speed, e.g. $1/30$ sec, following with $1/60$, $1/125$, $1/250$ sec. Not all films react favourably to this unusual method. Mostly ultra-fast films will be used in poor lighting conditions, but medium-speed and slow films, too, can be forced by extended development. Often the results are even more striking; the exposure latitude, however, always becomes very narrow, so that the most precise treatment is essential.

The following points must be observed:

1. All exposures must be appropriately short. Normally exposed films will become very dense and are difficult to enlarge.

2. The lighting contrast of the subject must not be too strong, as long or warm development produces considerably more contrasty negatives.

3. If possible, a normal- to soft-working developer should be used. Suitable formulae are Atomal, Promicrol, and Ultrafin, and Agfa 14 and Kodak D 76 for preparation by the user. The developer should be fresh, i.e. unused.

4. At normal temperature (20° C) development can be extended by a factor of 4. A higher developer temperature saves time. Although some emulsions will stand temperatures of up to 35° C without special hardening and are fully developed after 3 minutes, this must not be risked without preliminary tests with the same emulsion. In practice it is better not to raise the temperature above 26–28° C, when the developing time will be roughly the same as that for the normal temperature. But the various emulsions react so differently that preliminary trials are essential. Note that the temperature of the stop- and the fixing baths should be only slightly lower than that of the developer.

Tropical developer (for insufficiently hardened emulsions)

Some manufacturers sell special preparations for tropical development. If these are not available or you want to make up your own formulae, most commercial finegrain developers can usefully be modified for work at 26–30° C (75–86° F) by the addition of about 45g anhydrous sodium sulphite per 1 l working solution. Developing time should be shortened, according to the temperature. A reduction of about 3 minutes is normal at 30° C, 86° F, but it is best to make a test. Remember that the rinse and fixing solutions must be at the same temperature as the developer, and add some hardener to the fixer. Note that once modified by the addition of sodium sulphite, all developers will operate more slowly at normal temperatures.

Stop bath

When the film leaves the developer and is briefly rinsed in water, development does not stop. Developer remaining in the emulsion will continue to act, and all the rinsing does is slow this action down. With short developing times, this "after development" must not be ignored.

An acid stop bath breaks off development at once by chemical action. For printing paper a 2% acetic acid bath is normal; for films a 4% solution of potassium metabisulphite should be used. The immersion time is 20–30 seconds, and the bath is active only as long as it is acid.

With running water, the usual intermediate rinse ($^1/_2$ to 1 minute) between development and fixation is completely adequate. But if time or water is in short supply, a stop bath is recommended.

Fixing bath

During the developing process about a quarter of the silver bromide in the film is reduced. The remainder is dissolved in the fixing bath. It is not a simple dissolution, but a complex chemical process. There must be a surplus of the sodium thiosulphate necessary for fixing, so that water-soluble salts can be formed. The keeping qualities of the fixing bath will be improved by acidulation with potassium metabisulphite. The fixing bath is so cheap that it should not be unduly exhausted. It should have the same temperature as the developer. At low temperatures it acts slowly and sluggishly. Temperatures above 30° C (86° F) are not recommended.

Sun Temple at Konarak, India. Photograph by Ella Meillard.

Thin-film and fine-grain emulsions are fixed more quickly than thick and coarse-grained ones. Rapid fixing baths cut down the normal fixing time by about half. Recently, ammonium thiosulphate has been introduced as a fixing agent. These new rapid fixing baths have the additional advantage of halving the subsequent washing time.

Washing

During washing the silver salts formed during fixing diffuse out of the emulsion into the water. The following points should be noted:

1. Fixing salts are heavier than water and sink to the bottom.
2. The water should be drained from the lowest part of the tank or vessel, so that the chemically-enriched water is replaced by fresh water.
3. The time of washing can be cut down by a bath in 3% sodium sulphite anh. solution.
4. A complete removal of the thiosulphate salts is not possible, but their concentration can be weakened enough to eliminate all adverse effects.

   Washing, therefore, depends mainly on a sufficient change of water, and not simply on time.

After-treatments *(Reduction, redevelopment)*

A chemical change in the contrast of Leica negatives should be restricted to those cases which produce no satisfactory results on bromide papers in the grades from ultra-hard to ultra-soft. Single negatives are very sensitive, and extreme care is required during all after-treatment. The worst danger is damage and scratches in the baths. Small cork pegs are therefore clamped on the perforated edge of the pieces of film during washing to prevent them from sliding on top of each other.

All after-treatment is carried out in daylight.

Reducer: Farmer's reducer

Solution A.   *100 cc water*
                         10 g pot. ferricyanide
Solution B.   *1000 cc water*
                         50 g sod. thiosulphate (hypo) (neutral).

Add 5–10 cc of solution A to 100 cc of solution B.
Always mix immediately before use. Farmer's Reducer clears the negative and increases contrast.

The well-known Farmer's Reducer is suitable in only a few cases. The permanganate reducer given below is preferable, since it reduces the negative without increasing its contrast. It is essential that the film has been thoroughly washed; in case of doubt wash again.

If possible, make up the solution some hours before use, so that no undissolved crystals will be deposited on the film.

Permanganate reducer: 1000 cc water
1 g pot. permanganate

Determine the duration of the bath by experiment, rinse, immerse in strongly acid fixing bath; only then will the degree of reduction become apparent. Reduction can be continued, but the film should again be washed first. The progress of the reduction is not directly visible. In order to be able to stop the process at the right moment, a trial should be carried out with a piece of waste film of the same emulsion.

Redevelopment

Very contrasty negatives can also be softened by redevelopment. The negatives should be washed well.

Bleaching bath: 250 cc water
25 g copper sulphate
20 g sod. chloride
5 cc sulphuric acid conc.
(to be added to the solution, stir continuously)

The negatives remain in the bleach bath until they are completely white even when looked at from the back. After 15 minutes' wash they are brought into a soft-working developer such as Atomal or Rodinal 1:50, developed for 3 minutes with continuous agitation, rinsed, and fixed in the usual fixing bath for 10 minutes. The effect can be judged only after fixing. Wash as usual, finally immerse in a little distilled water with wetting agent; dry. If a negative is extremely contrasty, it can be enlarged after bleaching and drying even without redevelopment. The contrast will be reduced by up to two grades; in addition, there will be no risk.

The duplicate negative

Since all forms of after-treatment involve a certain amount of risk, an intermediate positive should first be made of any important negative on suitable material, and a duplicate negative obtained.

219

Normal or contrasty negatives are printed on soft film. Generous exposure and soft development produce positives with detail both in the highlights and the shadows. It is quite acceptable if they look a little grey. The duplicate negative is obtained by contact-printing, and is also processed in a softworking developer.

In order to avoid a coarsening of the grain it is advisable to produce the first intermediate positive, too, by enlargement instead of contact-printing. For same size duplicate negatives the reversal process for 16mm reversal films is suitable. Optical 1:1 printing on Agfa-Dia-Direct-Film.

Scratched negatives (see also p.226 below)

If the emulsion side only is scratched, soaking the negative in water, or, for cleaning and loosening the emulsion, in a 1% sodium carbonate solution will often be sufficient. This is followed by 5 minutes' wash. Before the film is hung up to dry, it should be bathed in a wetting agent solution.

Scratches on the back, i.e. on the emulsion base, are not removed by this method. Here, commercially available scratch-removers are recommended. Instructions should be strictly followed. Great care should be taken that the negatives are absolutely dry, clean, and free from dust before they are sprayed with the solution. It is advisable first to find out with a piece of waste film of the same type how the scratch-remover solution affects the emulsion.

50mm Summicron, f/8, 1/125 sec. Photograph by E. Herb

ENLARGING TECHNIQUE

Larger pictures – greater impact

Leica negatives must be enlarged. The tiny contact prints may be excellent for filing purposes, but the pictures will be of little value unless they are enlarged. This need for enlarging is an advantage of the Leica method.

Have you ever compared the average small album-size picture with its $10 \times 8''$ enlargement? The difference is astonishing. Good photographs must be reasonably large. Many subjects, of course, are taken only as "reminders"; for them, wallet-sized prints are completely adequate. But where the pictorial content counts, the impact will be increased by enlargement.

Enlarging – simple and instructive

"One ought to be able to do one's own enlaging" is an often-expressed wish. If you have never done it before, you may, more likely than not, think it difficult. I would say without hesitation that it is much easier than you think. A blank sheet of bromide paper is exposed. Seemingly nothing happens. The first trace of a picture appears only after 20–30 seconds in the developer, and, gradually, the positive is built up to its full contrast.

The modern yellow-green darkroom printing safelight is so bright that every stage in the build-up of the picture can be seen and controlled. No matter how often you watch this process it will never lose its fascination. If you do your own enlarging you will look at your negatives with completely different eyes. You will check at once: – Will this negative enlarge well? Is it sharp? Was the exposure correct? What about the picture area? I can safely say that I have learned most of my photographic techniques during enlarging. As your experience grows, so does your skill. You will realize that enlarging is not a matter of pure routine, but – once you have mastered the finer aspects of the technique – also a creative activity.

On the coast of Calabria. Photograph by W. Benser on Agfacolor.

The principle of enlarging

The light-proof lamp housing of the enlarger contains an opal lamp which passes light through the negative via a condenser lens. This type of illumination is very bright, produces balanced enlargements, suppresses the effect of the grain in the film, and largely mitigates the results of minor damage to the film.

The enlarger can be vertically adjusted in order to alter the enlarging scale. The longer the distance between enlarging lens and baseboard the larger the picture. The lens must always be focused on the enlarging distance.

The light-sensitive paper is exposed in a masking frame, developed, and fixed. The result is an enlarged, positive paper print.

The negative, in most cases a strip of film, is inserted, emulsion-side down in a holder that should be easily accessible for this purpose. Both sides should be perfectly clean and free from dust.

Practical design and precision finish are essential in an enlarger in order to preserve the full sharpness and all the detail of a 35 mm negative in the enlargement. The optical axis must be truly vertical to the film plane and the baseboard, the performance of the enlarging lens must be equal to the special demands it is expected to meet, and the lens must move very accurately in its focusing mount.

Focomat Ic

The Leitz Focomat Ic provides automatic focusing throughout an enlarging range of 2–10× linear. The enlarger head can be vertically adjusted on a parallelogram guide, while the lens is automatically focused by means of a cam.

This focusing adjustment is generally much more accurate than visual focusing. It has the additional advantage of saving considerable time, since the laborious visual focusing procedure is eliminated and the enlarging scale can be adapted to the needs of format and picture area in the simplest possible manner.

The function of the automatic focusing mechanism is very exact but it must be adjusted for the precise focal length of the enlarging lens. Readjustment is necessary if a lens of different focal length is used (the true focal length of the lens may be slightly different from the value engraved on its mount). To compensate these differences the cam can be adjusted within a range of 49–52.5 mm

Olive grove near Tremosine, Lake Garda. 50 mm Elmar, f/5.6, $^1/_{60}$ sec.

Photograph by W. Schacht

focal length. The procedure is described in detail in the operating instructions for the Focomat I c.

The correct vertical setting on the column is also essential to the perfect functioning of the focusing mechanism; here the height of the masking frame must be allowed for. The column has two holes, either of which takes a locating pin. If no masking frame is used, the pin is inserted in the lower, and, with the standard Leitz masking frame on the baseboard, in the upper hole. An extra-large Leitz masking frame (30×40 cm [$12 \times 16''$]) is slightly higher than the standard version, so that an adapter ring must be placed on the locating pin on the column to maintain the correct distance for the automatic focusing mechanism.

Normally the Focomat I c is supplied with the factory-adjusted 50 mm Focotar f/4.5 (17581) enlarging lens. Its speed is slightly less than that of the 50 mm Elmar (which, with clickstops, was also available as an enlarging lens under the codewords VAROB and DOOIT); this can, however, be ignored, since the most usual stop for enlarging is f/8.

Dust particles on the negative or on the condenser lens may be troublesome. They appear on the enlargements as white spots, whose "spotting out" is time-consuming and tedious. It is therefore important to keep the enlarger free from dust, which on the condenser lens is discovered immediately on the baseboard when the focused enlarger is switched on without a negative. For cleaning, the lamp housing is tilted backwards. The negatives, too, must be free from dust. This can be ensured by various means e.g. by blowing with a rubber ball, brushing with a sable brush, wiping with a soft rag etc. The film should never be strongly rubbed as this may produce an electrostatic charge which attracts and retains even more strongly dust particles floating in the atmosphere. The use of anti-static cloth for cleaning the film is not recommended.

Tips for enlarging

Scratches on the back of the film are not reproduced by the enlarger if they are treated with a small amount of vaseline and the negative guide of the device for correcting converging verticals (17645) is used. This consists of a 35 mm wide glass plate and a metal plate of the same width with a window in the Leica format. The film is placed on the glass, emulsion side down; when the device is shut the treated back of the film is protected by the window in the metal plate. After enlarging the back of the film is cleaned with a piece of cotton wool moistened with a little carbon tetrachloride. Danger – noxious fumes!

For extremely big enlargements the outfits can be supplied with a longer column. You can, however, obtain the same effect by setting up the enlarger with the column at the edge of the table, turning the enlarger head to the back, and enlarging past the edge of the table on to the floor or on to a low stool; the baseboard must be weighted to prevent the enlarger from tipping over.

For checking the correct position of the paper immediately before exposure an orange filter is used; this is turned into the light path below the enlarging lens.

With big enlargements or when slow chlorobromide paper is used exposure times may become very long, when it is advisable to replace the 75 W lamp with a 150 W or with the very powerful 250 W Aktina lamp. The latter is overrun to obtain its high intensity. A dimmer switch prolongs its life considerably.

An exposure timer is a great help particularly in printing a large number of enlargements. It should be fitted with a continuous-light switch for focusing. Even when the exposure time is carefully maintained, puzzling exposure errors may be caused by fluctuations in the mains voltage. Voltage-stabilizers are therefore popular with professional photographers and photofinishers.

If the film does not make even contact with the condenser, Newton's rings may occur which will be a disturbing feature on the enlargement. A remedy is the disc 17652. It is slipped onto the condense, keeping the film perfectly plane by means of a specially treated surface.

The enlarging of single negatives is made easier by the use of the double glass plate (17545) or the double plate (17645). The latter covers only one side of the film; it has been designed for the device for correcting converging verticals, but can also be used independently.

The paper must be carefully protected from stray light, particularly when exposure times are prolonged. Bright surfaces near the masking frame may affect the picture through reflected light; too bright or unsuitable darkroom safelights may have the same effect. That undeveloped paper should not be left lying about openly need, I hope, not be stressed.

Diffuse flashing with stray light outside the enlarger below the developable threshold value will cut down the contrast.

228

The way to good enlargements

A permanent darkroom of your own with tiled walls, white sink and running water, dustfree floor etc. would be ideal; this does not mean excellent results cannot be obtained in a makeshift darkroom. It is advisable, though, to protect sensitive fittings from developer or hypo stains by means of formica sheets etc. At night blacking out presents no difficulties, since the room need not be lightproof to the same extent as for the development of negatives. Besides the necessary equipment and baths, suitable darkroom lighting is an essential requirement. Safelights should be arranged to provide good light for development, but leave the enlarger in the dark, otherwise the judgement of the projected negative will be difficult. Absolute cleanliness is the first demand; its observance prevents many failures. The enlarger and the place where the paper and the films are kept must be safely protected from splashes and other contact with liquids. The dishes should be placed so that "flooding" is avoided during development. Washing facilities and a towel for cleaning and drying the hands is necessary to guard against stains on paper and films. The use of printing tongs avoids the need for immersing your hands alternately in developer and fixing bath. A separate pair of tongs should be used for each bath.

Left: The disc 17652 prevents the formation of Newton's rings. An adapter, thickness 3 mm, shortens the distance of the condenser "N". Older models require a condenser in a short mount. – Right: The standard 50 mm Elmar in bayonet mount for the Leica M3 can be screwed into the normal helical mount of the enlargers by means of the adapter 17671. The adapter ring 17672 accepts the lens head of the 50 mm Summicron f/2.

Like the film, the bromide paper has a light-sensitive emulsion, but its speed is much slower to permit convenient processing in the darkroom. Since negative gradation varies greatly, enlarging paper is also available in several grades (degrees of hardness). If the negative is very contrasty this is compensated by the use of paper of soft gradation. Conversely, a very soft negative will have to be enlarged on hard or even ultra-hard paper.

The correct exposure time, on which the perfect quality of a picture depends, is not easy to assess in the beginning. The choice of the correct paper grade also presents difficulties. The systematic method of obtaining trial prints from a normal negative on the various grades of paper and with progressively increasing exposure times is therefore urgently recommended. Such comparison series make the judgement of future deviations easier. The centre sections of such a series in the gradations soft, normal and hard are shown on the facing page.

The trial exposures are developed in paper developer for exactly the same time ($1^1/_2$ to 2 minutes depending on the brand) throughout. After a brief rinse in the stop bath they are transferred to the fixing bath – where the print tone changes slightly, so that the beginner is advised to defer judging his print until after fixing. In a correctly exposed picture the brightest portions should still have a little detail, without the darkest portions becoming lost in a uniform black. Normal fixing time 5–10 minutes.

Photographic papers are available not only in different grades, but also with different surfaces. Those who want to learn enlarging are, however, urgently recommended to stick to "white-glossy" in the beginning, as this reveals all mistakes with merciless candour. Later on other surfaces may be chosen; all matt finishes should appear a little lighter when wet, as they become slightly darker on drying. The distance and the colour of the darkroom safelight greatly affect judgement during development, so that uniform conditions should be ensured.

The properties of the paper developers, too, vary; some are normal, some hard, some soft working. By the use of two different developers intermediate gradations can be easily obtained. This is a more reliable method than compensation by varying the developing time.

Note: Maintain a temperature of 18–20° C (65–68° F) and the sequence: – Developer – stop bath – fixing bath. Never dip the fixing-bath tongs into the developer or vice versa. In the fixing bath, too, the prints should be agitated repeatedly. Washing after fixing vitally affects the keeping qualities of the prints. Excessive time in the fixing bath also prolongs their washing time. A 1% sodium

Negative contrast

The contrast of your negatives may vary widely. Several causes are responsible for this:

1. Subjects differ considerably in their brightness values and lighting. There are many intermediate stages between a subject in fog, and a view from a dark interior to a sunlit landscape. We have chosen only four examples here; there is the added difficulty that the long brightness range of a very contrasty negative will not be adequately reproduced in print.

2. The gradation of the film used affects the result. Differences present in the subject can thus be increased or decreased.

3. You can also influence the negative contrast by the type of developer and the duration of development. Thus, a very weak negative is produced of a delicately graded subject by too short development. Conversely, very long development gives a very harsh negative of a subject rich in contrast.

Since paper is available in various grades, a further opportunity is provided to compensate for excessively contrasty or flat negatives by the use of an opposite paper grade. We must not, however, forget the "mood" of the picture. It would be wrong, for instance, to attempt to accommodate the entire tonal scale from white to black in the foggy scene above. Here, delicate shades of grey represent reality.

carbonate bath after fixing reduces the washing time by about 50%. Unless prints are washed in running water, they should be turned over frequently, and the water changed 6 times, once every three minutes. In running water single-weight prints are washed for 12–15 minutes, double-weight ones for 20 minutes.

The special treatment of individual picture portions (holding back, printing up) makes it possible to improve the picture quality. The shapes of the dodges for holding back, and of the holes in the dark cardboard for printing up vary according to the purpose. They must always be moved slightly during exposure, otherwise the dodge will show up.

Increasing exposure times on various paper grades.

The figures below the pictures represent the exposure times in seconds, which are increased by the same factor within a paper grade. For ultra-hard paper the exposure differences would have to be still smaller.

Top row: Soft (exposure factor 1.4).
Middle row: Normal (exposure factor 1.4).
Bottom row: Vigorous (exposure factor 1.25).

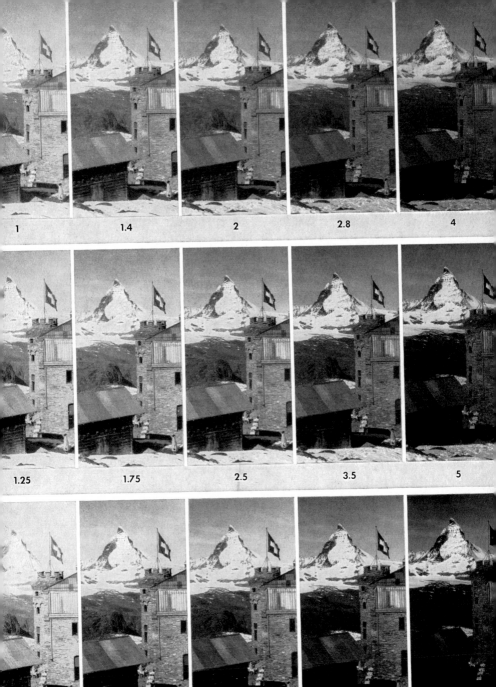

1   1.4   2   2.8   4

1.25   1.75   2.5   3.5   5

1.9   2.4   3   3.75   4.7

Copying with the enlarger

An enlarger can also be used for occasional copying. The original takes the place of the enlarging paper, and the negative material is inserted in the film guide.

A small, handy copying darkslide (17670) is available for the VALOY and the FOCOMAT enlargers. Both 5×5cm (2×2") lantern plates* and lengths of film can be used. The little mirror glass plate included is used for measuring the length of the film and also as a holder for the focusing negative with which the enlarging ratio is set according to the size of the original to be copied. It will now be simple to focus and to set the picture area accurately. The exposure material is inserted in the darkslide after the lens is stopped down to f/8 or f/11. The subject is illuminated from both sides for identical periods at an angle of about 45° with the lamp in the detached lamp housing as shown in the illustration. Do not use a steeper angle of illumination because of the danger of reflection with glossy subjects.

Halftone prints are developed in 1:50 Rodinal for about 6–7 minutes, letterpress reproductions for 7–8 minutes. Pieces of document copying film or 5×5cm lantern plates to be projected as negatives must be developed for 3 minutes in the paper developer. In urgent cases they can be hardened in formalin after fixation and enlarged while still wet.

* A piece of dark cloth is wrapped round the film stage when 5×5cm plates are used to prevent the emergence of stray light.

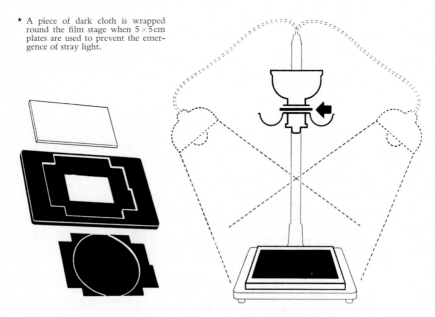

Correcting converging verticals

When you point your Leica obliquely upwards when photographing a tall building, the verticals in the picture cease to be parallel, and will converge towards the top. This is a natural effect of the laws of perspective, but it may adversely affect the pictorial impression, particularly in architectural photography. By means of a trick it is possible to cancel this disturbing effect at the enlarging stage. This is called, a little clumsily perhaps, "correcting converging verticals". The side of the negative with the more distant parts of the object has to be enlarged more strongly. Within narrow limits this can be done without any modifications to the equipment simply by raising one end of the masking frame, focusing on the centre of the frame and sufficient stopping down of the enlarging lens. But if the tilt of the camera was considerable, the masking frame will also have to be strongly tilted, and satisfactory sharpness over the whole negative area can be obtained only if the negative is also tilted to the optical axis. The laws of image formation in this case demand a tilt which is opposite to that of the masking frame. The Leitz perspective correcting device for the VALOY and the Focomat Ic consists of a negative holder with a universal tilting movement and a baseplate with a tilting joint to which the masking frame is attached.

With the negative holder horizontal, and after the required enlarging scale is set, the converging verticals are made parallel by means of tilting the masking frame. Uniform sharpness on the entire picture field is now obtained if the negative holder is tilted in the opposite direction. As a rule, the tilt of the masking frame and the focusing will have to be readjusted. The lens should be stopped down to f/8 to f/11 for the exposure. The differential enlarging scale on the tilted printing frame is compensated for by means of printing up. With this procedure the picture format will not remain rectangular, and certain marginal portions will therefore have to be sacrificed (see illustration). Certain marginal parts will be lost during the correction of converging verticals (see illustration). If the distance between the Focotar and the negative plane is too long, the intermediate ring behind the lens must be unscrewed.

In order to obtain sufficient space for the tilting negative holder, the position of the condenser lens must be raised. In the VALOY II it should be removed from the bayonet and placed in the bottom of the lamp housing. – In the Focomat Ic, the pressure spring in the lamp housing is removed, and the condenser placed on the guide ring by raising and slightly rotating it.

For very strong corrections it is advisable to replace the normal 50mm lens in the enlarger with a wide-angle lens, such as the 35mm Summicron.

235

The following points should be observed in this case:

a. Screw the lens in, turn the focusing mount in as far as possible, raise the Focomat enlarger head fully, and leave it in this position;

b. adjust the format by raising or lowering the lamp house with the locking piece on the column;

c. tilt the negative in the holder so that its distance from the rear component of the lens remains as short as possible;

d. focus with the enlarger focusing mount.

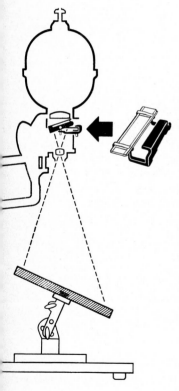

Birnau monastery, Lake Constance; 28mm Summaron, f/8, $^{1}/_{60}$ sec. The camera distance could not be further increased because the ground dropped steeply away towards the lake. In such cases, the camera should be tilted as little as possible, and the empty foreground trimmed off during enlarging. The dotted lines on the left show the picture area utilized after correction of the converging verticals.

Photograph by Kisselbach

Leica transparencies

Transparencies are required if pictures are to be shown with the projector. The advantage of the projected image over the paper print lies in its greater brightness range. In a paper print viewed by reflected light, this range is limited to about 1:30. In transmitted light images will reach 1:300, or more, depending mainly on the power of the projector. Light and shade, and all the more delicate intermediate values, can be fully revealed only through projection. Leica slides are projected in their original 24×36 mm format, mounted in cardboard or plastic frames, or between $2 \times 2''$ glass plates. Enlarged transparencies are used for exhibitions and for advertising purposes. They are produced in much the same way as paper enlargements, except that the paper is replaced by a piece of positive film of suitable format.

There are several methods of producing 24×36 mm Leica slides: 1) by contact printing, for example, with the slide copier 35; 2) by optical printing at same-size scale (1:1) with the Reprovit IIa, or an enlarger; 3) by means of a black-and-white reversal film which, like colour reversal film, provides a positive for projection directly after processing.

Contact printing

Contact printing has the advantage of consistent sharpness and of requiring only the simpler copier, although it is more difficult to recognize and to remove dust beforehand. Spotting of the final slide is ruled out because of its small size. The utmost cleanliness of work place, equipment and the films to be copied is therefore vital. Any friction with glass or film produces an electric charge, which acts on dust like a magnet. Friction should therefore be avoided and a sable brush used for dusting. Obstinate particles of dirt can be rubbed off with a piece of rag soaked in spirit.

Optical printing

With a suitable device for optical printing not only same-size reproductions, but also slight reductions and enlargements are possible. But critical focusing is not easy. It has therefore been found useful to lay down the commonest distances of reproduction and to use these settings whenever required without alteration. The process of optical printing will thus become as rapid as contact printing; at the same time, it offers the advantage of more effective dust control.

Here is my procedure for critical focusing with a Leitz Focomat or -Valoy: – A line negative of excellent sharpness is placed in the film guide. A piece of

238

white paper is pasted on a 5×5cm (2×2") coverglass and the 24×36mm format outlined on it. A black transparency mask can also be pasted on it for this purpose but its window is only 23×35mm in size. For same-size reproduction the distance between film plane and emulsion side of the lantern plate must be 4× the focal length of the enlarging lens.

The average focal length of the 50mm Leica lenses is 52mm. The total distance will therefore have to be about 208mm. Sharpness can be judged only with a magnifier, for which the head of a 90mm lens unscrewed from its mount is suitable. Without an extension ring ("Repro" ring, depth 26mm, 16615) the helical focusing mount will not be sufficient. The image is focused with the focusing mount (maximum extension 2f) as well as by the vertical adjustment of the enlarger head until the necessary total distance (4f) has been established.

Since this procedure is a little tedious for the beginner the distances should be marked once the correct values have been set. Two pieces of wood or strips of stout cardboard are cut; the length of the first strip represents the correct distance between the enlarger head and the film plane; the second, shorter strip indicates the exact distance between the lens and the film plane.

Slide copier 35 of Messrs. Kindermann, Ochsenfurt, West Germany for the making of 35mm contact prints on positive film or perforated 35mm paper strips. Exposure in the light cone of the enlarger is convenient provided the same lamp distance is always maintained.

Materials for transparencies

Positive film or 5×5 cm (2×2") lantern plates are used. For high-quality work plates with antihalation backing are superior. They are available in normal, soft and hard grades.

Positive 35 mm film is available perforated and in bulk. If the individual transparencies are eventually to be mounted in 5×5 cm (2×2") cardboard frames it is simpler to make a series of graduated exposures and to select the best transparency for mounting, as positive film is very cheap. But if you want to make a filmstrip, the procedure is a little more difficult. In order to make intermediate trial exposures the positive film in the slide copier is masked with a piece of black paper of suitable size. A trial frame of the same positive film is placed on the black paper below the negative to be printed, and exposed. Development should be identical with that of the final film strip.

Positive film in the 35 mm format has a slightly softer gradation, but considerably more speed than the normal lantern plate. It should therefore be processed under a bright-red darkroom safelight. In this light 35 mm document-copying film (ordinary or orthochromatic) can be used as printing material for soft 35 mm negatives. Such films are also available with panchromatic emulsions, but these are not recommended for printing purposes, as they must be developed in almost total darkness. The projection of diagrams, text or drawings is more effective if they are colour-washed with albumen dyes. Here negatives are more suitable than positives.

In the interest of legibility the size of the writing and the boldness of the strokes should have a certain relationship, which can be judged already on the original. If it can be read in comfort at a distance 5× its long dimension, the slide, too, will be satisfactory.

Whereas photographic papers are easy to judge during development, with transparencies this is not possible with any certainty until after fixing. Viewed against a white background, the highlights should have satisfactory detail, but should not be grey; the shadows in spite of their blackness should also show good detail. Transparencies have a "drying factor", which makes them appear a little darker after drying than in the wet state.

If exposure has been slightly generous, development should not be altered. Positives which are a little too dense can be lightened by means of Farmer's Reducer. This is accompanied by an increase in contrast. Underexposure and underdevelopment should be avoided.

A good printing tone is obtained only by adequate development. Since it is often necessary to adapt the gradation of the positive to the character of the negative it is advisable to use two developers of different properties. Normal paper developer produces a brilliant gradation after 3 minutes' developing time. Another suitable developer is Rodinal 1:30, at 3 minutes' developing time. A few more tips for processing 5×5 cm ($2 \times 2''$) lantern plates: If a great number of tranparencies has to be made of negatives varying in character it is recommended to determine the speed relationship to a bromide paper by means of a trial. For "normal" lantern slides, for instance, the trial is made on normal or No. 2 paper. This is by far the quickest and cheapest method. If the relationship is, e.g. 1:3, the exposure for the lantern plates must always be three times that of the trial on paper. All exposed plates are eventually developed together for the prescribed time. The paper trials, too, must therefore all be developed for the same time, which, however, need not be the same as that for the plates (e.g. paper 2 minutes, plates 3 minutes).

If several lantern plates are kept simultaneously in any of the baths or in the rinse, they are always in danger of sliding on top of each other and of becoming scratched. This is avoided if the plastic storage boxes for 5×5 cm ($2 \times 2''$) lantern plates are used also for processing. If the bottom is solid, a few holes must be drilled to prevent floating. The new Pradovit slide magazines are also suitable; plastic troughs to fit, for developer and fixing baths, permit the processing of 25 or 30 lantern plates at a time. Two or three cork pegs can be attached to individual plates for washing; these are kept floating in the water, emulsion side down.

The reversal process yields excellent results when reproductions from books, journals or other originals have to be made into slides.

Suitable black-and-white reversal films are available from most film manufacturers.

BASIC COMMENTS ON SUBJECT CHOICE

"What am I to photograph?"

All technical operations from inserting the film to drying it after processing can be taught and learned. The ability to read, and even to play, music does not make a musician. Neither can you call yourself a photographer because you believe the complete mastery of the technical aspects to be the be-all and end-all of photography.

This is only the beginning!

Take a young photo-fan who one fine Sunday morning answers a phone call by a neighbour who has a splendid show of flowers in his garden: "Could you nip over for a moment with your Leica; there's a lovely picture for you – flowers wherever you look!" Our friend takes a picture of the whole garden, a real panoramic view in order not to miss any of its splendour. When they look at the final picture both the proud owner of the garden and the photographer are equally disappointed. The many thousands of blossoms have shrunk into insignificant dots of varying brightness, trees and shrubs represent a featureless grey mass. For it is one thing to "scan" a flowering garden with the eye, when you can look at all the different details as long as you like, and quite another to have the whole mass concentrated in a photograph.

Almost all beginners are at first misled by the colours. But even the most gorgeous sea of flowers will be represented only as grey tones in a black-and-white photograph. What is more, beginners often do their best to cram as much as possible into each picture. But in the vast majority of cases they should do the exact opposite. More often than not, the less your photograph contains, the better the picture.

Language is a good teacher in this respect. When we speak of a "redhead", a "blonde" or a "paleface" we always describe the whole person by graphically emphasizing a single strong feature. Latin scholars call this "pars pro toto" which means "take a part to describe the whole". This is precisely what you should do when you take photographs. Ignore the total view of the garden, close in on individual features. This allows you to take pictures in the garden the whole Sunday long (weather permitting), discovering ever new and more beautiful subjects as you go along. And the proud owner of the garden will be delighted with a close-up of his favourite flower, filling the whole picture format.

The principle of "closing in on the subject" cannot be over-emphasized. All you have to do is look at the photo albums of most common-or-garden

Visoflex, 135 mm Hektor, f/16. Photograph by W. Wissenbach

button-pushers. They take children surrounded by a welter of irrelevant detail, and between all the superfluous sky and meadows, their subjects become so small that it is difficult to recognize them. Concentrate on essentials, forget what is mere bywork.

The rule of making your subject fill the frame is no less important. Particularly the Leica man betrays a lack of discipline if he uses the excuse that he can choose the right picture area in the darkroom during enlarging. Of course he can. But does anyone buy five yards of material for a suit for which he needs only three? You should be just as economical with your film material by choosing the correct picture area right in the viewfinder. In reality, of course, every picture you take is only a part of what you see. But this is what you have to ask yourself: – does it bring out the essential feature of what I want to show, and does my composition present this essential feature so that it produces a real *picture*? To be able to judge this at a glance and with confidence you must train your

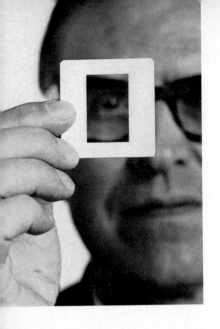

eye, you must compel it to see "like a camera". There is an extremely simple means to do this, literally always at hand. You can form a kind of rectangular "viewfinder" window with both hands. Or you can cut such a rectangular window out of a postcard or hold an empty transparency frame in front of your eye. Since its window corresponds to the Leica format all you have to do is hold the frame in front of your eye at the distance of the focal length. For the 50mm standard focal length 50mm distance = the length of a matchstick. Even if you have left your Leica at home, it is an instructive and amusing exercise to investigate all sorts of subjects in this way for their pictorial potentialities.

Choice of the correct viewpoint is just as important to composing a picture. Since the Leica is a very versatile camera, the versatility of the photographer, too, is unrestricted. He can lie flat on the ground to shoot from the worm's eye view, or climb towers to look for his subjects from a bird's perspective. The pictorial effect is always decisive. Children, for instance, should be photographed from a squatting position instead of standing, at eye level. If you want to take a subject – say, a glamour girl on a beach – framed by the sky with dramatic clouds – you will have to lie down, and prop yourself up on your elbows. You should carefully watch the changes in perspective which are caused (especially in the near foreground) by the most minute lateral and vertical movements of the camera. A few inches to the right or left may already be decisive for an effective pictorial composition. But the judgement of the light must come before all other considerations. A photograph is, after all, unthink-

The four pictures clearly show the influence of the illumination and the camera position: on the right worm's eye and bird's eye view, on the left normal view. The illumination ranges from the diffuse fog atmosphere to harsh contre jour light.

Top   left: Lorry in the fog. Photograph by Kisselbach.
*   right: View of a hemlock plant from the edge of a field. Photograph by Kisselbach.*

Bottom left: Street in Tetuan. Photograph by Siegfried Hartig.
*   right: Rooftops. Photograph by Toni Schneiders.*

244

able without light. And there can be no good pictorial lighting without shadows. Both are basic requirements not only for the mere production, but also for the composition of a picture. The expert, too, watches the interplay of light and shadow every day in order to find the best pictorial effect.

A village pump, photographed in the morning in frontal sunlight, may provide a humdrum photograph; late afternoon shadows may make it a subject for a master. Shadows may spoil a picture, or make a picture out of a bare snapshot. Here, too, practice and experience are important, because the human eye registers brightness differences as great as 1:1000, but photographic paper reproduces a ratio of only 1:30.

If you consider that, e. g. on a summer's day in the South, the shadows cast by a row of houses appear almost as black as night, whereas they can become delicate and transparent under the famous soft sky of Paris, you will begin to appreciate the length of the photographically effective scale of the shadows. You will learn that you cannot find and master the variety of light- and shadow effects with the camera by following a formula, but only through personal, constant, and keen study.

It is often thought that conditions are similar for visual observation and photography. This is by no means so. Normally, our vision is really sharp only within a narrow angle of view, and our eye scans the various objects one after the other. But our memory registers only those we consider worth noticing, so that even of a restless total view, often only a few important restful features remain to capture our attention. In photography the process is completely different. With a single exposure we record all details within a given angle of field simultaneously, without any emphasis or discrimination. This compels us first to choose the picture area and lighting suitable for the characteristic representation of the object.

Line and form

The judgement of a picture is affected not only by its content, but also by its form. You can, of course, change the side ratio of the picture to adapt it to the subject

The means of composition at our disposal are the contrasts between light and dark, fore- and background, ascending and descending lines. We can compose a picture on an area or in space. The rules of composition are numerous, but it would go far beyond the framework of this book to deal with them, because most opinions have their proponents as well as their opponents. Hence we shall give only two examples of the principal differences: we can choose a picture area so that only the line, the ornament as it were, is decisive for the composition as in the "Tree in Early Spring", or we can work with the effects of perspective and of light and shade, as in the opposite example of "Logs in the Lock".

Top: *135mm Hektor.*
        Photograph by J. Behnke.

Bottom: *35mm Summaron.*
        Photograph by A. Tritschler.

247

Pictorial content

The only rule we can establish about the content – also called the "message" – of a picture is that it is indispensable if a photograph is to be a true picture. Now the Leica is an extremely "eloquent" camera with which you can photograph almost anything your eye can see. The pictures will be correspondingly varied and different in kind. A photograph can, for instance, recount a little incident briefly and concisely (snapshot), it can report an event (press or pictorial journalism), record an object purely as an object (technical or commercial photograph), or it can appeal to our emotions ("atmosphere"). These are only some of the most important categories, which naturally are not sharply separated, but in practice often overlap. According to the inclination and the talent of the man behind the camera, his pictures will gravitate towards this or that type of pictorial content. The more marked, however, his personality, the more marked will be the personal imprint he leaves on his photographs.

The amateur's path leads from the album photograph, whose value as a personal document nobody doubts, to what is called a "creative picture". It is a path leading to simplicity. When you look at good examples of photography or the creative arts you will realize that the approach to perfection is the closer, the more sparing the artist has been with his means of expression. The more you advance in your photographic work, the more you will search out simple compositions, because it is their very simplicity which has coined the phrase that "they convey more than a thousand words".

A picture which shows the essential, leaves out the superfluous, represents an idea, becomes a symbol. Obviously, not every one of your photographs can be a creative masterpiece. But there is a reliable yardstick with which to measure the force of expression, or its absence, in your pictures. Enlarge a selection of photographs you yourself regard as good to at least $10 \times 8''$ and submit it to a photographic club for judgement; they will be only too pleased to discuss them with you.

On the Nuerburg Ring. 560mm Telyt f/5.6, f/8, $^1/_{500}$ sec. Photograph by Guenter Osterloh. The lucky snapshot below is the work of Gisela Büse at Marseille. In spite of the peaceful atmosphere it was essential to grasp the situation instantly. If you are keen on this kind of picture, always carry your Leica with you ready for action. There are many opportunities simply waiting to be taken.

248

Persons outdoors

Influence of lighting and background (pictures on the left).

Top left: Back-lit picture, with light reflected by a tin-foil reflector. Similar effects are produced by an open newspaper. Without shadow-softening the face would be too dark. The background appears a little too disturbing.

Bottom left: In this picture, too, the shadows were softened, although the back-lighting was less contrasty than before. The background has become more restful owing to the longer distance.

Top right: Typical snapshot with the sun on one side. The background hardly stands out against the hair. But the expression on the face is so lively that such minor shortcomings are overlooked.

Bottom right: Sunlight also from one side. The blue sky provides an even background sufficiently held back by a yellow filter for the face to stand out clearly.

Wetzlar from the Kalsmunt tower

Photographs from the same viewpoint, with changing light:

1. *on a dull day*
2. *frontal illumination*
3. *sun on one side, with blue sky*
4. *sun also on one side but shadows softened by reflected light from clouds.*

   The strong influence of different lighting can be seen clearly. The pictures were taken over a number of years, and reveal changes owing to widespread building activity.

All photographs by Liesel Springmann.

251

How does the eye see, how the camera?

1. The eye sees colours when colours are present. Any abstraction into grey tones as on the black-and-white film is impossible.

2. The eye has only limited resolving power, so that details can be discerned up to a certain distance only. Telephoto lenses overcome distances. Infra-red films penetrate haze.

3. The eye has only a narrow angle of view within which it sees really sharp. It adds and registers impressions in the brain. According to the lens in use the camera sees everything sharp at once between 4° and 92°.

4. In the eye the image persists only a short while, disappearing after $^1/_{50}$ sec. The photographic picture can be fixed.

5. The eye has its minimum distance of vision in the close-up range at 25 cm (10″) (distinct vision). Close-up and macrophotographs are possible at considerably shorter distances, making magnifications possible.

6. The eye sees very rapid movements very imperfectly. The electronic flash permits exposures of $^1/_{1000}$ sec and less, recording movements which could never be perceived by the eye.

7. The eye requires a certain light intensity before it is able to see anything. The camera can record pictures with less light, provided the exposure is long enough.

A black-and-white picture cannot directly reproduce colour, space and movement. The effect of grey tones, contrast, perspective, unharpness is only indirect. The eye perceives, the camera records. Eye and brain form an integrated unit. Memory and emotion have an important influence. We do not always see things as they are, but as we want to see them. The eye sees selectively, we see what we are interested in, overlooking everything else. The camera lens emphasizes important and unimportant features alike.

The eye does not see objects at various distances at sizes corresponding to their true distance, but is influenced by our ability to remember. Since our pair of eyes gives us stereoscopic three-dimensional vision, and since they always use the same lenses, our orientation in space differs from photographic representation. Camera perspective changes with the focal length and subject distance.

The eye adapts itself to lighting contrast, it changes its power of differentiation automatically, e.g. when we look from a room into a sunlit landscape. The bridging of large brightness differences creates difficulties in photography.

The influence of the illumination

The "illuminator" for outdoor photography is the sun. It moves in its course across the sky without considering the photographer's wishes, hides behind clouds, or beams from a clear sky. In the course of the day and the change of the seasons it makes the same features look a thousand times different. We have become so accustomed to the appearance of these features surrounding us that most of us have long ceased to notice the delicate differences in their illumination.

If you practice photography seriously and want to go beyond the production of mere souvenir snapshots you must develop a kind of "lighting sense". By close observation, but also through your own pictures which failed because of unfavourable lighting, you will soon learn that things look different at noon from how they look in the morning, different under a glowing summer sun from how they appear in the mellow light of winter, or on a dull rainy day.

The even illumination of a sunny day, too, changes according to your viewpoint. Viewpoint and illumination have a very close relationship. If the sun is behind you it illuminates your subject frontally. This is called incident light. This kind of lighting, which in the early days of photography represented the basic method, is today considered unfavourable for most subjects. It produces "flat" pictures, which look boring because they include no enlivening shadows, have no roundness and no depth.

A simple experiment clearly shows the effect of different lighting on a subject. Have a look, for instance, at a section of a cobbled street, with the sun at your back. Now walk slowly round the cobbles in a half circle, so that you have the sun at one side, and finally directly in front of you. You will note that the side light, and even more the back light, brings life to the dead stones. If you use a viewfinder for this experiment, the effect will appear even more dramatic.

What applies to cobble stones applies equally to all sunlit subjects. Side and back lighting are almost invariably preferable to frontal illumination. But since, unlike the cobble stones, the majority of subjects cannot be approached from all directions, your only remedy is to wait until the sun does you the favour of lighting your scene at exactly the right angle.

Quite often you may not photograph a certain subject you have seen at 10 a.m. until 4 p.m. because looking at it you realize that this will be the time for the most favourable lighting. But if you cannot wait, perhaps because you are unable to stay very long in the locality, you need not miss the picture if it is important enough to you. It will always be adequate for a souvenir shot. But you must admit, with frank self-criticism, that it could have been better.

Correct lighting is of particular importance in architectural photography. Experts in this field speak of the "critical half-hour", by which they mean the short time during which the sun sends glancing light along the main façade of a building, exactly from the side. Even a simple rough-cast wall will then come to life, broken up by the most delicate shadows.

Sunlight from a clear-blue sky does not create ideal photographic conditions. What the photographer would order for his outdoor subjects, if only he could, are large cumulus clouds. These act as huge reflectors, whose broad beams of light soften the shadows and perfuse everything with a delicate illumination. "Hazy" sun similarly produces a pleasant light for foreground subjects.

Because the sun is hidden behind clouds is no reason to leave the Leica at home. Thousands of close-up subjects will reward your efforts also in dull weather. Rainy days, of course, have an attraction all their own, and offer you subjects galore. You can photograph umbrella-carrying passers-by mirrored in the gleaming asphalt road, or the ripples caused by falling raindrops in a puddle. However, a foggy day can be one of the photographer's most rewarding experiences. Fog simplifies, reduces everything to essentials. Contrasts are almost extinguished, details disappear, and what remain are ghostlike shapes in the background, merging into a grey emptiness. Exposures in fog should be on the short side.

Here, the steep gradation and fine grain of slow films are favourable. The slowness can be compensated by larger stops. It is sufficient to focus on the pictorially important features in the foreground, since owing to diffusion by the fog the background is more subdued.

Artificial light

Whereas in daylight the lighting can hardly ever be changed, and your task consists of using the available illumination to the best advantage, of choosing your subjects accordingly, artificial light affords the possibility of arranging the lighting to suit your own requirements.

Normally you will start with a main light and try to illuminate your subject so that its characteristic features are well brought out. Your second task will consist in balancing the light of the first lamp so that the shadows in the final picture will have the correct gradation. The light of the lamp will therefore have to be reflected by suitable means. Small reflector screens should be used for this purpose if the walls are not sufficient. This reflection of the light from the first lamp has the advantage over the use of a second lamp in that it can be balanced far more delicately. Only when all the possibilities of the main light are exhausted should you begin to think of a second lamp. A fill-in light is used to reduce or eliminate disturbing shadows caused by other lights, and must always be weaker (or more distant) than the main light. An effect light can be stronger than the main light, but must be confined to a smaller area. A slide projector can serve admirably as an efficient spotlight for intensely illuminating limited areas from long distances. It can, for example, be used to emphasize subject contours without unduly interfering with the general illumination.

Depending on the shape and colour of your subject the background illumination, too, plays an important part. The second light is often used to illuminate the background so that the subject stands out in clear relief. Because work with artificial light requires a certain amount of practical experience, it is advisable

Examples of the effect of lighting in portraiture. Photographs by Wilh.Reng.

| *Excessive front light* | *Excessive side light* | *Balanced lighting* |

to start by experiments with inanimate objects which will permit you to take your time in adjusting the lighting. In the example below, the tomatoes and a basket have been photographed with front-, side-, and back lighting. Notice how each form of lighting produces its own distinct spatial effect.

In photographing people by artificial light you will want to emphasize or bring out their characteristic features by the way in which you arrange your lamps. A main light placed high above the sitter results in a comparatively narrow outline of the face. The nose shadow in the final picture will usually show exactly how this light was placed. Here again, it is wise to choose a patient subject for your first experiments to enable you to practise all the delicate differences in lighting.

A tip for those who want to make artificial-light pictures in the home with a minimum amount of fuss: Replace the normal overhead lighting with one 500 watt lamp, or two 250 watt lamps, and walk around the room with your model. You will almost always find a spot in which lighting conditions are favourable for a successful picture without any other lighting equipment.

Lighting studies in artificial light. Photographs by Liesel Springmann.

| *Front lighting* | *Side lighting* | *Back lighting (shadows softened)* |

256

COLOUR PHOTOGRAPHY

The Leica is an ideal colour camera

Colour photography is gaining more and more followers. As a dynamic and at the same time universal camera, the Leica is always at the centre of events, enabling you to record life in colour. Together with the accessories of the Leica system it is eminently suitable for all the essential conditions of colour photography. Lenses of excellent correction, rapid and accurate focusing, precise viewfinder and groundglass screen facilities, and the possibility of utilizing the full frame are indispensable to first-class achievements in this field. Another considerable advantage of the Leica is its economical format. Even the cost of colour film is so low that your enthusiasm need not be damped by financial considerations.

You can take colour photographs with any Leica. The colour in your picture depends on the properties of the exposure material, not on special devices in the camera. It can almost be said that colour photographs are simpler to take than black-and-white ones, since the colours are not converted into grey tones but are rendered as colour differences.

Colour reversal film and the negative/positive process

The normal modern colour film is coated with three superimposed emulsion layers, of which the top layer is sensitive to blue, the middle layer to green and the bottom layer to red. The colours are produced in the three layers by a single exposure, i.e. the colours are recorded in each emulsion according to their content of blue, green, and red. Each of the three superimposed layers is considerably thinner than a normal photographic film. They can therefore accommodate brightness differences only within a limited range, and as a result the exposure latitude is narrower than with normal (negative) films. The structure of a colour film is described on page 265.

1. *The colour reversal film.* Here the original picture is directly converted into a colour transparency in a multi-stage operation. It is unique, and can be conveniently shown in any projector. The accuracy of colour- and tone rendering is unsurpassed. In the course of the years the resolving power of the less sensitive colour films has been increased to a degree where it leaves no more to be desired. The cost of the individual picture is low. Excellent colour paper prints can be obtained from suitable colour transparencies.

2. *The colour negative film.* In this version a complementary-coloured negative is first developed. It yields both colour paper prints and colour transparencies. Resolving power is inferior to that of colour reversal film. It is possible to influence the colours in the positive process; this advantage demands, however, much extra effort if individual wishes are to be satisfied. With the introduction of large processing machines the printing process has now become largely automatic, so that it has been possible to lower the cost of normal colour enlargements in the standard formats considerably.

Whereas only a single type of colour negative film is available, and colour adjustment for day- and artificial light is carried out during the printing stage, colour reversal film makes a distinction necessary between daylight (colour temperature 5600°K) and artificial light (colour temperature 3200°K or 3400°K) emulsions.

Colour temperature

The term "colour temperature" occurs frequently in colour photography and is the measure of the spectral composition of the light. It is subject to considerable fluctuations in artificial light as well as in daylight, greatly affecting the colour rendering of the emulsion. The unit of measurement is the °Kelvin (starting from Absolute Zero, −273°C). The higher the blue content of the light, the higher its colour temperature.

Mean daylight and normal sunlight have a colour temperature of about 5600°K. Daylight is not always constant, and the colour temperature varies appreciably, more than our eyes normally notice. Without doubt we are aware that the light of the sun shortly after sunrise and before sunset is very red. We are less conscious of the blue accent on the shadow illumination with normal sunlight from a cloudless, blue sky. Here the colour temperature ranges between 10000°K and 20000°K. It is not surprising that our colour film duly registers this difference. In the presence of clouds the colour temperature in the shade is appreciably lower, considerably improving your photographic chances.

Lighting contrast

In addition to colour temperature, lighting contrast plays an important part in colour photography. Every photographic object shows, besides differences in colour, differences in brightness, influenced by the method of lighting. This light-and-shadow effect, so very important in black-and-white photography, should not

258

exceed a certain limit in colour photography. The colour rendering is changed when the lighting contrast between the brightest and the darkest portion of the subject is more than 1:4. This can be determined by taking an exposure meter reading of white paper first in the brightest and then in the darkest portion of the subject. The difference between the pointer deflections is a yardstick for the contrast.

The lighting contrast has nothing to do with the general brightness of the subject. A brightly-lit snowscape may have little lighting contrast. On the other hand, the difference between a photograph taken in frontal light (sun behind the camera), side light, and back light is considerable. Especially in the last case the contrast increases, and may easily exceed what the colour film will accommodate. This will, however, not occur if the shadows in back lighting are effectively softened as, for instance, in snow- and beach subjects.

These, then, are the points of importance for good colour rendering:

1. Colour temperature,
2. lighting contrast,
3. exposure time.

Correct exposure

Colour reversal film has an exposure latitude of only $\pm$ $^1/_2$ stop. The determination of the correct exposure is therefore particularly important. You will recall the hints about the use of exposure meters in the chapter "Expose Correctly" on p. 155. You will find the third method especially efficient provided you can approach your object closely enough. Here, a reading is taken of a piece of white cardboard, and the value found multiplied by a factor which depends on the colour of the object. It is always useful to calibrate your exposure meter carefully for the brand of film in your camera by means of a trial series. If your exposure meter indicates, say, f/8, $^1/_{60}$ sec, take the following exposure series, always at $^1/_{60}$ sec: – f/5.6, halfways between f/5.6 and f/8, f/8, between f/8 and f/11, f/11. When the five pictures come back from the processing station, you can see immediately which setting has produced the best result, and compensate your readings accordingly.

The manufacturers include instruction leaflets with their films, with details of the speed of the material, and hints for the determination of the correct exposure time. It is absolutely essential in the beginning to compare the results

259

of your exposure meter with the data in the leaflet and, if the differences are appreciable, to decide which data promise to be more successful. If possible, make two exposures, note the data, and compare the results.

Tips for colour photography in daylight

● Sunlight with clouds in the sky is ideal.

● Watch the lighting contrast, and soften any heavy shadows.

● In hazy sunlight prefer nearby subjects.

● Close-up subjects should be observed with only one eye, because any disturbing influence in the background will be immediately noticed.

● Distant views are rewarding only in very clear weather.

● Distant views with foreground details have better depth.

● Fog and rain offer interesting motifs, particularly in large cities. – But fast lenses are essential here.

● Fully utilize your frame. Close in on your subject or use longer-focal-length lenses.

● Portraits are most successful in very soft light; harsh and glaring light causes squinting.

● Be sparing with colours, avoid a hotchpotch.

● Subjects almost devoid of colour often yield very attractive colour photographs.

● Insert and remove your film in the shade.

● Immediately pack and send exposed colour films to be processed as soon as possible, especially in a hot climate.

Breakers. f/8, $^1/_{50}$ sec, Kodachrome.   *Photograph by Dr. Fritz Graeber*

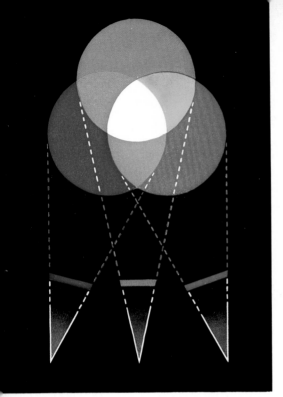

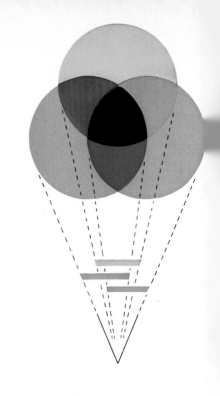

ADDITIVE COLOUR MIXTURE   SUBTRACTIVE COLOUR MIXTU

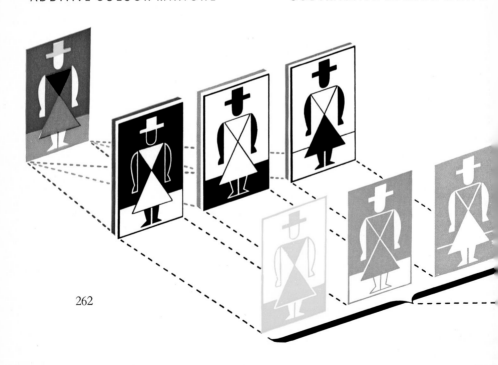

262

COLOUR NEGATIVE/POSITIVE PROCESS

Structure of colour reversal film
(subtractive colour reproduction)
Top layer blue sensitive — eventually yellow.
Yellow filter layer — is decolorized.
Middle layer green sensitive — eventually magenta.
Bottom layer red sensitive — eventually cyan.
Antihalation layer — is bleached out.
The hatched field is the emulsion base.

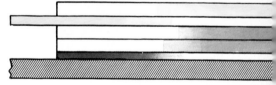

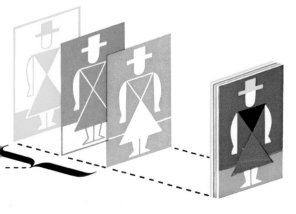

The part-images are produced by the three blue-green-red sensitive layers. Only the second development is carried out in the colour-forming developer. The silver image is bleached out later, and the colour image remains.

How the colour picture is produced

Explanation of the colour illustrations on pp. 262/263.

Modern colour films are almost without exception based on the subtractive principle. They are coated with three emulsion layers on top of each other. In the top, blue-sensitive layer dyes eventually form a yellow image. The middle layer is sensitive to green, the dye image becoming magenta, and in the bottom, red-sensitive layer it will be cyan. A yellow filter layer between the top and middle emulsions prevents any action of the blue rays on the second and third layers.

In a colour reversal film, e.g. Agfacolor Reversal Film, incorporating colour components in the three layers, a black-and-white silver image is first developed. After a thorough rinse the film is re-exposed to strong light.

The three different dyes are formed simultaneously in the three emulsion layers during the colour development following this exposure. The silver image formed during the first and second developments is bleached out; the film is fixed, and washed. A pure dye image is all that remains. As a projected transparency it exhibits extraordinary luminosity.

The subtractive method was first used for colour reproduction on paper, but it is now generally accepted also in projection, since it yields considerably brighter screen images than the additive process. In this latter method, white is produced by the superimposition of light in the basic colours red, green, and blue. Red and green light rays appear yellow when added. Red and blue add up to magenta, green and blue to cyan.

In the subtractive method, white is the starting colour. By means of the colours in the transparency (pigment colours) light is subtracted, so that a mixture of the basic colours of this process – yellow, magenta, cyan – produces black in the area of maximum density. It is, however, essential also with the subtractive method to obtain colour separations in the primaries blue, green, and red. They are formed in the three appropriately sensitized emulsion layers.

Facing page: Chameleon. Leica M3, 135mm Tele-Elmar f/4, f/16, $^1/_{50}$ sec, Braun Hobby with second flashlamp at 50 cm (20 in) distance, Kodachrome.   *Photograph by Klaus Paysan*

The use of filters

In colour photography the use of filters is confined to a few isolated cases. Filters suitable for black-and-white film cannot be used for colour film (except UV filters and polarizing filters).

The *colourless Leitz UVa filter* cuts out the invisible ultra-violet portion of the light which on colour film would reveal itself as additional blue.

Since coating with an Absorban film has reduced the ultra-violet transmission of the modern Leica lenses to a negligible value, it is normally possible to work without U.V. filters. On the other hand, these filters afford most effective protection of the delicate front surfaces of the camera lenses against salt crystals on the beach or on sea voyages. The use of U.V. filters is urgently recommended with the earlier Summaron and Elmar lenses at noon.

Various makers supply additional filters for colour photography, tinted a very delicate blue, yellow, or pink for avoiding colour shifts even in unfavourable lighting conditions. Their use must be based on a thorough knowledge of the characteristics of the film in the camera, and on information about the composition of the light; this is provided by colour temperature meters indicating the deviations. The filters also affect the exposure times according to their densities. Their exposure factors are supplied by the manufacturers.

Conversion filters

Some film manufacturers offer special filters which make the use of artificial-light film in daylight possible. Kodak market, e.g., the orange-tinted filter No. 85B, which reduces the film speed by 2DIN (0.66 × the rated ASA value of the film). The results are strikingly good; the opposite correction, however, for the use of daylight film with artificial light, is less recommended.

Polarizing filters

The fact that sky light is polarized is very important in colour photography. Polarizing filters make it possible to render the sky considerably darker without influencing the other colours. The strength of the effect depends on the angle of incidence of the light. You can very easily determine this by looking through the polarizing filter in the exposure direction, rotating it slowly. In the most favourable position the top figure on the filter mount is read and the filter placed on the lens in this position. The mean filter factor is about 3× (Fig. p. 147).

Pictures in artificial light

Colour film for artificial light is adjusted so that it produces a correct colour balance with photoflood lamps of a colour temperature of 3200°K (or 3400°K for Type A films) without filter. Allowing for the different properties of artificial light, the topmost blue sensitive layer of artificial-light film is considerably faster. The colour temperature of normal incandescent lamps is only about 2800°K, i.e. they are slightly deficient in blue. Photoflood lamps of comparatively short life are considerably overrun and have a colour temperature of about 3400°K. Fluorescent tubes are unsuitable for artificial-light colour film since their spectrum is not continuous. They can be used together with photoflood lamps if the latter are 3–4 times brighter.

In artificial light the admissible subject lighting contrast should never be exceeded. Here it can also be most easily controlled. Intense lighting produces more luminous colours than weak light. Artificial-light film is very sensitive to residual daylight, so that in dull daylight shadows can be softened with halfwatt light only if the intensity of the latter is 4–5 times higher than that of the daylight.

The colour temperature of electronic flash is about 6000°K, it is therefore suitable for daylight colour film, and can also be combined with daylight. The flashbulbs on the market today are almost all blue-tinted, which makes them also suitable for daylight colour film, and as a fill-in light or even main light combined with daylight.

Processing colour reversal films

Processing exposed reversal film requires scrupulous care. When buying colour reversal film note whether reversal processing is included in the purchasing price. There are differences, too, in how the final transparencies are returned to you. Sometimes they are cut in strips, sometimes they arrive in the form of cardboard-mounted slides.

Since these are projected by artificial light, they should be examined for any shortcomings in the light of a very bright incandescent lamp. A sheet of white paper should be lit with a screened lamp and the transparency viewed in transmitted light. Always pick up the transparency by the edges!

267

The negative-positive colour process

The negative-positive process is more suitable for colour prints on paper. It is also based on the subtractive principle, and employs three emulsion layers. But a dye image in complementary colours is produced during the first development. A feature which is red in the original thus becomes blue-green in the negative, blue becomes yellow in the negative etc. Illustration top left and right, p. 263. The dyes in the colour films do not have the ideal absorption curves necessary for accurate colour rendering. In order to correct these minor deviations, some films have "masks" between the colour layers. Such films appear almost entirely orange-red.

The colour negative is printed or enlarged on colour paper based on the same principle, and the original colours are reproduced. During the enlarging stage the colour rendering can be modified by means of delicately graduated filters, so that any colour cast can be eliminated.

A special version of the Focomat Ic Color enlarger has been designed for the production of such colour enlargements. Its lamp housing incorporates a slide into which printing filters are inserted. An illuminated scale on the baseboard indicates the enlarging scale.

To obtain good colour effects on a paper print, you must arrange your lighting with great care, for the brightness range of a reflected-light picture on paper is smaller than in a transparency. Neither flat nor very harsh lighting is recommended. But the brilliant light with effective shadow softening found under a bright sun with clouds is very favourable indeed.

Although the exposure latitude of colour negative film is greater than that of colour reversal film, correct exposure is a great advantage in processing, as it makes the filtering for printing considerably easier.

Colour transparencies, too, can be made from colour negative film, even in large numbers if required. Resolving power, however, is a trifle lower than in the colour reversal film.

Black-and-white enlargements, too, can be produced in large numbers. Here, too, negatives which had too short an exposure for colour enlargement will often yield still satisfactory results.

135 mm Hektor with Visoflex I, f/5.6, $^1/_{15}$ sec, Braun Hobby (2 m, 6 ft 8 in) and 500 W photoflood (0.75 m, 2 ft 6 in), mixed light 5600/3200° K. Photograph by Hermann Eisenbeiss

268

With colour reversal film, faults can have the following causes:

Picture generally too light, colours very pale: overexposure.

Picture too dark: underexposure. Slight underexposure can be compensated by increased brightness of the projector. In poor lighting conditions and for dark subjects the exposure time must be somewhat increased (see instructions by the film manufacturers). If the whole film is too dark, a loss of speed due to ageing of the emulsion may be responsible. Note the film expiry date. Satisfactory colour duplicates and black-and-white negatives can often be obtained from slightly underexposed colour transparencies.

Bright bands across some pictures at the beginning of the film: Fogging. Never insert the film in direct sunlight. Do not leave films, exposed or unexposed, lying about openly even indoors; always keep them in their tins.

Slight blue cast, especially in the shadows. Unsuitable lighting.

Strong blue cast: – Artificial-light film used in daylight.

Yellow cast: – Morning or late afternoon light.

Yellow-brown cast: – Daylight film was used for artificial light.

Strong yellow cast: Exposure through a yellow filter (colour camera was confused with a black-and-white camera). When two Leicas are used side by side, the colour camera should be marked by means of a coloured adhesive strip on the top.

The whole film is dark and shows no trace of an image. The film was not exposed.

Disturbing coloured reflections are caused by large coloured areas close to the subject, but outside the picture area. Bright, neutral colours such as white and light grey are particularly sensitive to these reflections. An outdoor portrait, for instance, under a coloured parasol can show this disturbing effect if the parasol does not form part of the picture. Reflections of objects inside the picture area do not usually appear disturbing.

The nature reserve at Mettnau, Lake Constance. The subject was photographed from the same viewpoint, but in completely different lighting conditions, in the morning and in the late afternoon. The effect of the atmosphere, too, is noticeable, because a 135 mm lens was used here. Agfacolor film. Photograph by Kisselbach

Vignetting: With wide-angle lenses at full aperture the light tends to fall off a little towards the margins of the picture. In colour reversal film this is shown by a darkening of the corners of the picture. This effect will disappear if a smaller aperture is used (with a longer exposure time). A lens hood of excessive depth can also cause vignetting.

Originally perfect transparencies may fade in the course of time. Their keeping qualities depend very much on the conditions of storage. Continuous exposure to light, heat, chemical fumes, and the prolonged effect of a dank atmosphere are particularly damaging.

Schwarzschild Effect (Reciprocity Law Failure): The rated speed of colour films applies only when the light is of sufficient intensity. For daylight colour film shutter speeds of $1/_{60}$ or $1/_{125}$ sec, depending on the film speed, are the accepted mean values. If the exposure time increases up to 1 sec or longer, for instance inside a church, the Schwarzschild Effect will make itself felt in that low light intensities produce a weaker photographic image. Here it will be necessary to expose for about 2 instead of 1 sec. Moreover, minor colour shift will occur, which also depends on the type of film. It is therefore impossible here to offer detailed information.

Naturally, minute variations are bound to occur in the manufacture of such a highly intricate material as colour film; these make themselves known as slight differences in colour rendering. They are disturbing only when excessive. The basic density of a colour reversal film in the unexposed perforation area is a good yardstick for the general colour reproduction.

How to store colour films

The long way from the manufacture of a colour film to its reversal processing harbours many possibilities of changes in the colour balance. Storage at too high a temperature is particularly harmful – this starts already at 20°C. Today the general advice is therefore to store films that are not to be used immediately in as cool a place as possible. The domestic refrigerator is ideal; although deep freeze to −15 or −20°C does no harm, you have to wait longer than 24 hours before you can use the film. Storage in a plastic bag in the vegetable drawer at temperatures from 8 to 10°C is most convenient, because the films can be inserted in the camera immediately.

PROJECTION

When I showed my children Leica transparencies for the first time, and they saw themselves on the screen, playing during our holidays, my small daughter spontaneously ran towards the screen to fetch her doll, the projected image appeared so lifelike and real!

Projection is the most impressive method for reproducing the photographic image. All the delicate tonal gradations in the transparency can be reproduced without loss. Because they are transilluminated, colour slides accommodate a very much greater brightness range than paper prints.

The three-dimensional effect largely depends upon the size of the projected image, and pictures appear more natural to our eyes when they are larger. There is a definite relationship between the effective image size and the viewing distance. But since we can not normally afford the cost of such large pictures, the only way out is to make Leica slides and to project them, a method which has the added advantages of being simpler than the making of big enlargements and of superior quality.

Small album-size prints can be examined by only two or three persons at a time. A slide show, on the other hand, is a shared experience for a large circle of viewers.

What you show and how you show it makes or mars the enjoyment of your audience. Success or failure is measured not by the quantity of slides you project, but by their selection, arrangement, and matching. Everything should be carefully prepared, particularly for a show before a large audience.

Your slide presentation should be as carefully organized as a well-told story. It is, of course, much easier to lecture with slides, because picture follows picture, and you take your verbal cues from the screen. One hour's duration is normal, but an hour-and-a-half may be permitted for special subjects. Anything longer than this will tire your audience. The more slides you include in a lecture, the less time you will have to explain each picture. There is, however, no need to speak continuously, and some subjects require silence for best effect. Eighty to a hundred slides are quite sufficient for one showing. Whether you work with a manual or an automatic projector, slide magazines have the advantage that, once inserted in the correct order, the slides are always immediately ready for projection in the right sequence. Magazines also keep your slides free from finger marks because they need never be handled during projection. The plastic unit containers supplied for Leitz slide magazines protect their contents against dust and provide a means of organizing your slide archive in the easiest manner possible.

How does a projector work?

In a projector, the light from a special lamp is collected by means of a condenser system, and an image of the transparency in front of the condenser formed on the projection screen. The lamp and the lenses must be well cooled. This is achieved by designing the lamp housing like a chimney. A heat filter inserted in the beam path protects the transparency from damage by excessive heat. A motor blower is used where the lamps are more powerful than usual.

The optical design of the condenser is very important to the brightness and uniform lighting of the image on the screen. Losses of light are minimized because the lenses have special anti-reflection coating. A concave mirror behind the projector lamp utilizes the light radiated by the lamp to the back for projection.

A projector can give its best performance only with projector lenses of large aperture. Various focal lengths permit quite a free choice of the distance between projector and screen at given image sizes.

The power of a projector is chosen according to the requirements of size and brightness of the screen image. The relationship between screen brightness and image size must not be neglected. But a decrease in the quantity of light will really be felt only when the brightness sinks below a certain threshold value. This can be easily checked with slightly underexposed and therefore denser colour transparencies.

Light power is not the only distinctive feature of a projector; we can choose between non-automatic projectors, in which the slides are inserted by hand, and semi-automatic and fully automatic ones. These use magazines accepting 30, 36, or 50 slides.

The third classification is based on the voltage of the projector lamp. Some projectors take mains-operated lamps, e.g. for 240v, others 12v/100W or 24v/150 or 250 W low-voltage lamps; the latter have built-in transformers through which these lamps are connected to the mains. The low-voltage lamps have some advantages of light output, low picture gate temperature, and increased depth of field. Responsible for this is the small size of the filament which makes a better bundling of the light in the beam path possible.

Pradix

The *Pradix 150* is a particularly small and handy unit, which can be comfortably carried in a briefcase. It has a 150W projector lamp which together

274

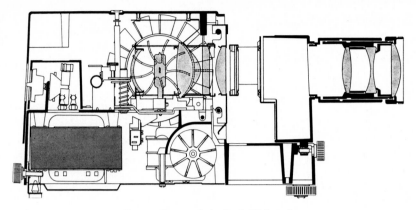

Cross section trough the Prado Universal

with the reflector and the aspherical condenser lens is fully adequate for screen images of 7 feet maximum width. The projector lens is a 100 mm Elmaron f/2.8. Cross section through the Prado Universal.

Prado Universal

The Prado Universal is a further development of the Prado 250/500 known for two decades. It has been designed for optimum performance and has the wide range of adaptability necessary for teaching and use in the lecture theatre. It is simple to operate. The unit component system enables it to be adapted for any purpose in the shortest possible time.

There is a choice of projector lenses of focal lengths ranging from 35 to 300 mm, so that projection distance and image size can be adjusted to requirements. (Table see Appendix.)

The slide changers, for formats from 18×24 mm to 6×6 cm, are interchangeable. A semi-automatic magazine changer is provided specially for 5×5 cm slides.

The light output of the new 24 v/250 W halogen lamp is superior to that of the 110 v/500 W projector lamp. Its brightness remains unchanged, as the envelope of the halogen lamp does not become blackened, even after prolonged use. The life of this lamp is rated at 50 hours, and increases to 100 hours if the lamp economy switch built into the Prado Universal is used. A four-step switch controls the following functions:

1. Off – 2. Blower running – 3. Lamp on economy power – 4. Lamp on full power.

Lamp and motor have separate fuses. The lamp can be centred horizontally as well as vertically. The halogen lamp is easily accessible and interchangeable, because the condenser system can be readily taken out.

A two-path blower extracts the hot air, and a further blower cools the slide and the transformer. A thermal cutout automatically switches the Prado Universal off during overheating, e.g. if the fan belt breaks (replacement belt in the lid of the projector housing). The cutout switch may also be actuated by shocks during transport. It is situated in the upper part near the heat filter. To switch it on, pull out the mains plug and push a screwdriver into the slot of the bimetallic trip.

The accessories are particularly useful in natural-science teaching. A vertical attachment makes low-power projection of liquid or melting objects possible. A large micro-attachment and a polarizing attachment permit the most varied demonstrations and experiments.

The halogen lamp is the latest development of the low-voltage lamp. The tungsten wire filament is sealed into a small quartz glass envelope filled with a halogen gas (iodine-bromine) mixture. Whereas in ordinary tungsten lamps the tungsten particles detached during incandescence become a black deposit on the glass wall, the halogen mixture in the halogen lamps causes them to return to the filament.

The advantages of the new lamp are its higher light output, longer life at undiminished brightness, low picture gate temperature and improved efficiency owing to the smallness of the filament, which ensures better bundling of the light in the beam path.

Halogen lamps are sensitive to finger perspiration and should therefore not be directly touched by hand during insertion.

Pradovit-Color

In an automatic 35mm projector slide change – forward and backward – is actuated via a remote-control cable. Since manual focusing of the projector lens whenever slides in different glass mounts or unglazed slides are to be shown consecutively is very tedious, this operation, too, has been included in the remote-control facilities.

Left: The Prado–Universal with 150 mm Elmaron f/2.8 as classroom and miniature projector.
Right: Semi-automatic slide changer with magazine holder. 90 mm Colorplan f/2.5 projector lens.

Left: Prado–Universal as micro-projector. The microscopic image can be projected at three different magnifications through a simple turn of the revolving objective nosepiece.
Right: The Prado–Universal as projector for demonstrations and experiments with birefringence and polarization phenomena.

In connection with a tape recorder the automatic slide change can be controlled so that it is synchronized with the lecture. A special switch relay is required, which transmits the control impulses from the second track of the magnetic tape to the projector.

All these technical facilities and many more are found in the Pradovit-Color. Here, too, we distinguish between a high-voltage version for mains-operated lamps and low-voltage versions with built-in transformers for halogen lamps:

1. Pradovit-Color with 24v/150W halogen lamp.

2. Pradovit-Color Autofocus with the same lamp but with built-in automatic mechanism for focusing the lens for differently mounted slides.

3. Pradovit-Color 250 with 24v/250W halogen lamp. The light output of this projector is 70% higher than that of the standard 24v/150W version. With thermal cutout see p. 276.

4. Pradovit-Color F for mains-operated lamps of up to 500W.

Depending on the necessary projection distance and the desired screen image size lenses of focal lengths between 50 and 250mm can be chosen. For normal conditions the 90mm Colorplan f/2.5 is the favourite.

The standard remote-control cable supplied with the projector is 3m (10ft) long; extension lengths of 5m (17ft) and 15m (50ft) are also available. Such extensions are convenient if the lecturer wishes to stand close to the projector.

Colour photograph by Walter Wissenbach, universal focusing bellows I, 135mm Hektor, f/16, daylight and electronic flash.

The focusing mechanism of the Pradovit-Color actuates the slide stage instead of the projector lens. This offers a number of advantages, for instance with the heavy long-focal-length lenses. But above all it provides a useful basis for the "Autofocus" version. Two photo-resistors act like a balance, moving the slides automatically into the optical plane of sharpness. Any divergence towards the + or − range changes the light flux; an amplifier-controlled motor carries out the necessary correction within fractions of a second.

Pradolux 24

This semi-automatic projector also uses a 24v/150W halogen lamp. The slides are inserted in magazines as in the Pradovit, but transported manually. In the projection position the transport knob is used also for focusing. If the lamp economy switch is used the life of the lamp will be doubled. There is little reduction in brightness.

Wide-angle projection

The extent of our stereoscopic vision depends largely on the size of the image and on the distance from which we look at it. We obtain a more threedimensional pictorial effect if we view a projected image of 3.5m (11′6″) width and 2.3m (7′6″) height from a distance of, say, about 4m (13ft 4″). If the image resolution is high and the emphasis on the foreground and the spacing in depth good, we will have the illusion of standing in the middle of the picture.

For this a large projection screen is essential (not below 2×3m [6′8″×10′]). In the home this size can be used only with projector lenses of short focal length (35mm or 50mm). The Prado-Universal and the Pradovit-Color can be fitted with such short-focal-length lenses.

Tips for perfect projection

The projection screen greatly influences projection quality. A bed sheet with ironing creases is a very makeshift substitute; stout drawing paper off the roll is much better. Projection screens have a high reflecting power because of their special treatment and their pure white colour. Washable plastic screens of excellent properties have recently appeared on the market. In view of the high light output of the Leitz projectors, metal-coated screens are not necessary.

Golden Gate Bridge, U.S.A., 35mm Summaron, f/8, $^1/_{60}$ sec.

Photograph by Emil Schulthess

Theirs is the disadvantage that the image brightness depends very much on the viewing angle.

The projector is best set up behind the viewers in order to avoid disturbing stray light. Consult the table on p.318 about the focal length necessary for a given distance and a given screen size. The maximum viewing distance should not exceed six times the width of the image on the screen. There is also a minimum distance for the viewers in the front row (about $1^1/_2$ times the width of the image). The screen should be fixed high enough for projection to be over the viewers' heads. The image should be projected at right angles to the screen. If the projector has to be tilted, the screen should also be tilted, if possible. Care should be taken to place the projector on a firm support.

The cables should be arranged to prevent the danger of accidentally pulling the projector off its base. Never pick the projector up when the lamp is switched on (e.g. to change the projection distance), because the lamp filaments may touch each other owing to vibration, and the lamp will become overloaded and may burn out. Before switching on check whether lamp- and mains voltage are the same. Projection lamps have only a limited life. For important lectures it is essential to have a spare lamp available.

Brilliant projection is possible only when the room is completely blacked out. Stray light is very disturbing. Should projection for some reason be desired in a semi-darkened room, a specially powerful instrument must be used, and the image size must be much smaller than usual.

Before the start of the lecture the slides are carefully cleaned and arranged in correct order. They should be spotted for immediate identification. Cardboard- or plastic framed slides are marked with corner spots during the first showing so that they will be projected right-way-round at all times. The Leitz magazines take 30, 36 or 50 slides. Their individual compartments are numbered. The slides are inserted upside down, and will be projected right-way-round when their front faces the consecutively numbered slide. Before beginning a lecture test the whole set-up, and project a few slides just to make sure.

APPENDIX

List of Leica models without bayonet mount

LEICA I

COMPUR LEICA

STANDARD LEICA

LEICA I (without changing mount)

First model of the Leica, black finish, non-interchangeable lens. 50mm Elmar f/3.5 (the first series of this lens was called Elmax), push-on rangefinder, focal-plane shutter $1/20$ to $1/500$ sec and Time.

First commercial Leica; black finish; focal-plane shutter $1/20$ to $1/500$ sec and Time; attachable vertical (later horizontal) rangefinders.

Compur LEICA,
from 1926

Black finish; non-interchangeable 50mm Elmar f/3.5 with Compur between-lens shutter, speeds from 1 to $1/300$ sec. Shutter and film transport not coupled.

LEICA I, from 1930

First Leica with interchangeable threaded lens mount, but ring not standardized. From 1931 lens mount standardized with "0" (starting with No. 60 500).

Standard LEICA,
from 1932

Black or chromium finish; lens changing thread, push-on rangefinder, focal-plane shutter $1/20$ to $1/500$ sec, pull-out rewind knob. Serial No. from 100 000.

LEICA II

LEICA IIIa

LEICA 250

LEICA II, from 1932

Black or chromium finish, with built-in, coupled range-finder, focal-plane shutter $1/20$ to $1/500$ sec and Time. Serial No. from 71 500.

LEICA III, from 1933

As Model II, but with extended shutter speed range from 1 to $1/500$ sec, rangefinder with focusing telescope (1.5 × magnification); with carrying eyelets. Serial No. from 109 000.

LEICA IIIa, from 1935

As Model III, but with addition of $1/1000$ sec speed. Serial No. from 156 201.

LEICA IIIb, from 1938

As Model IIIa, except that eyepieces for rangefinder and viewfinder are brought close together. Rangefinder eyepiece adjustment lever coaxial with rewind shaft. Serial No. from 240 017.

LEICA 250, from 1934

Special Leica with enlarged body for 10 m (33 ft) spool chambers for 250 exposures. Otherwise as Leica III.

285

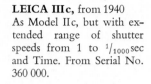

LEICA IIIc, from 1940
As Model IIc, but with extended range of shutter speeds from 1 to $^1/_{1000}$ sec and Time. From Serial No. 360 000.

LEICA IIIc

LEICA IIc, from 1948
As Model Ic, but with built-in, coupled rangefinder, shutter speeds from $^1/_{30}$ to $^1/_{500}$ sec and Time. From Serial No. 440 000.

LEICA Ic, from 1949
Shutter speeds from $^1/_{30}$ to $^1/_{500}$ sec and Bulb, attachable brilliant viewfinder and rangefinder, lens changing thread. From Serial No. 455 000.

LEICA If, from 1952
(black contact numbers)
As Model Ic, but fully synchronized, film winding knob with film indicator, from Serial No. 562 000.

LEICA Ic

LEICA If, from 1952
(red contact numbers)
As above, but with international shutter speeds $^1/_{25}$, $^1/_{50}$ sec etc. From Serial No. 564 001.

LEICA IIf, from 1951
(black contact numbers)
As Model IIc, but with built-in full synchronization, film winding knob with film indicator. From Serial No. 451 000.

LEICA IIf

LEICA IIIf

LEICA IIIg

LEICA Ig

LEICA IIf, from 1952
(red contact numbers)
As above, but with international shutter speeds $^1/_{25}$, $^1/_{50}$ to $^1/_{1000}$ sec and Time. From Serial No. 574 401.

LEICA IIIf, from 1950
(black contact numbers; without self-timer)
As Model IIIc, but with built-in full synchronization, and film winding knob with film indicator. From Serial No. 525 000.

LEICA IIIf, from 1952
(red contact numbers; without self-timer)
As above, but with international shutter speeds. From Serial No. 615 000.

LEICA IIIf, from 1954
(with self-timer)
As Model IIIf with red contact numbers, but with self-timer, about 12 sec delay. From Serial No. 685 000.

LEICA IIIg, from 1957
As Model IIIf, but large bright-line viewfinder, with automatic parallax compensation, geometric progression of shutter speeds, fully automatic synchronization (no red contact numbers), film indicator on back. From Serial No. 825 001.

LEICA Ig, from 1957
As Model IIIg, but without rangefinder, without self-timer. From Serial No. 887 001.

LEICA MODELS WITH SCREW THREAD
FOR THE INTERCHANGEABLE LENSES

From 1930 onwards Leica camera bodies were made with a threaded ring to permit the use of interchangeable lenses. It is this feature which initiated the Leica system. The great number of models differ in detail, but their basic characteristics are the same. The following description of the basic operation is based on the Model IIIf. Differences applying to the Models IIIg and Ig are dealt with on p.298. The differences of the other models are mentioned on pp.284 to 287.

Handling the Leica IIIf

Holding the Leica

Pay close attention, especially in the beginning, to holding your camera correctly and releasing the shutter smoothly. Grip the Leica firmly, but not tightly, with both hands. For horizontal pictures, the rounded ends of the base plate should rest snugly in your palms. Place your hands against your head so that the Leica, too, will receive some support. Look through the centre of the viewfinder; all four sides of the viewfinder window should be visible at the same time.

Release the shutter smoothly and steadily, not jerkily.

Two positions are possible for vertical pictures. Grip the Leica so that the tip of your right thumb rests on the release button. At the instant of release press with the thumb from one side, and with the index and middle finger from the other. In the second position, the shutter is released with the index finger as for horizontal pictures. If your Leica is in the ever-ready case, always hold the flap back during vertical exposures to prevent it from obscuring the lens.

First the position of the reverse lever is checked. It must be turned fully to A (R is the position for Rewind). Note that when this lever is in an intermediate position, the shutter may operate without opening, and no exposure will take place.

Lens changing

Lenses in collapsible mounts are gripped by the front knurled ring, pulled out as far as possible, and locked by a clockwise turn, again as far as possible.

The lenses can be detached by unscrewing them to the left. Hold the opening in the Leica body close towards your body until the other lens is in position for screwing in.

With lenses of focal lengths up to 50 mm the following method is recommended as particularly fast: Insert the lens focusing knob near the viewfinder window – place Leica flat on the left hand – give a short turn towards the left in order to feel the thread, screw home towards the right. The thread will engage at once.

The screwed-in lens should be slightly tightened; unscrewing should not require the use of any force.

Lens caps are available for the front as well as for the screw thread of the lens. Only lenses with flawless surfaces will produce brilliant pictures.

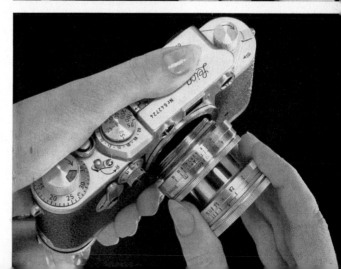

Changing lever
A = advance
R = rewind

Lug
for setting the counter
on 0.

Winding knob
rotate it in the direction
of the arrow as far
as possible.

Release button
on slight pressure
releases the shutter
(thread for cable release).

Film counter
advances through
1 division after
each film transport.

Film type indicator
lift and rotate it for setting
the film speed and type.

The winding knob is turned in the direction of the arrow in order to cock the shutter. Here, too, take care to wind the knob as far as possible. The shutter-winding action also transports the film through one frame.

The film type indicator in the winding knob can be set to show the type and speed of the film in the camera. Lift and rotate the knurled knob in the direction of the arrow for black-and-white films, against for colour (here the DIN and ASA mark will be red). The film counter is located below the film winding knob, which should be set at 0 after the film has been inserted. (Turn the little projections against the direction of the arrow.) After each film transport the film counter advances through one division.

Slight pressure on the release button actuates the shutter. Hasty or jerky release leads to camera shake. A special cable release with screw thread is used for exposures from a tripod. It is screwed over the release button.

Correct exposure is important for every picture. A very full range of shutter speeds allows the setting of the most favourable value according to the lighting conditions and the speed of the subject movement. The shutter speed range

Slow-speed dial
Set high-speed dial at 25-1 (earlier models 30-1 or 20-1).

*Push **spring catch** back and set the desired speed by rotating the dial.*

Delayed-action mechanism
built-in self timer
Cock lever, release shutter with the flat button instead of the normal release button

High-speed dial
Wind the film, lift the dial, set it at the arrow and let it engage. The slow-speed dial should be set at 25 (in earlier models 30 or 20).

differs in the various models. The engraved numbers indicate fractions of seconds. The exposure time is always read and set with the shutter cocked. The high-speed dial is raised and allowed to engage at the desired speed opposite the arrow. Intermediate values cannot be set. Since the high-speed dial rotates during the shutter release, it must not be touched while it does so, as this would alter the exposure time. This danger really exists only if you work with gloves.

At the B (formerly Z) setting the shutter remains open as long as the shutter button is depressed. The shutter speeds from $^1/_{25}$ sec★ to 1 sec are set on the slow-speed dial. The high-speed dial must be set at $^1/_{25}$ sec.★

The slow-speed dial engages at $^1/_{25}$ sec. For adjustment the small locking catch is pushed against the camera body with the thumb nail. When set on T before release the shutter opens and remains open. It closes only when the slow-speed dial is turned back to the 1 sec position (important for photomicrography and other specialized purposes).

★ Earlier models: $^1/_{20}$ or $^1/_{30}$ sec.

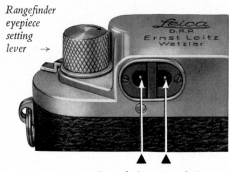

Rangefinder
eyepiece
setting
lever →

▲   ▲

Rangefinder   Viewfinder
eyepiece   eyepiece

Viewfinder and rangefinder

The *built-in viewfinder* (right-hand window) of the Leica outlines the field for the 50 mm standard focal length. The eye should be brought as close as possible to the eyepiece so that the entire viewfinder field can be surveyed at once. The sides of the field window must form a regular frame. Correct viewing can be checked by mounting the Leica on a tripod. When you look obliquely through the viewfinder, small displacements occur – to the left or right, top or bottom. The correct way is to view through the centre. In long-distance subjects slightly more appears on the film than is shown by the viewfinder, whose field applies to a subject distance of approx. 3 m (10 ft). Slight parallax is present with close-ups down to 1 m (3'4''), because of the viewfinder position above the lens. Special viewfinders must be used with lenses of other focal lengths (see p. 300). All II- and III-series Leica cameras have coupled rangefinder focusing. When the lens is focused on ∞ an object nearer the camera appears as a double image in the rangefinder. The focusing lever or ring is rotated until the double contours merge into a single sharp image; this automatically sets the cor-

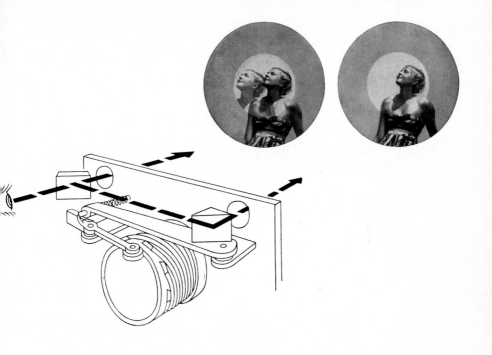

rect focusing distance for this object. The distance can be read off the feet/metre scale. The eyepiece of the rangefinder can be adjusted with the small lever located beneath the rewind knob on the left. It compensates minor visual defects, or further increases focusing accuracy in the close-up range. Owing to its 1.5× magnification the precision of the rangefinder is very high in spite of its short base. The following method is recommended for quickly and easily learning to use the rangefinder. An object with prominent outlines, e.g. a page from a calendar, is viewed through the left-hand eyepiece. The direct vision is now blocked with a finger held in front of the left-hand rangefinder field window.

Only a small circle in the centre remains visible. The eyepiece lever is now set for optimum focusing. When the finger is removed, the double image will appear. When the focusing lever is rotated the two double images approach each other until they merge completely. The most accurate measurement is obtained in the centre of the field, which remains visible when the left-hand window is blocked. Direct vision is blocked at first only in order to find the double image more easily. As soon as you have mastered this procedure you can dispense with this aid.

Loading the Leica

First make sure that the Leica is empty (test the rewind knob), and set the reversing lever at A = advance. Wind and release the shutter. Turn the toggle in the baseplate to the left and remove the baseplate. Place the Leica in front of you so that the open base faces upward.

Pull out the take-up spool and push the beginning of the film, emulsion side out, under its clamp, with the perforated edge flush alongside the spool flange. Pull the film lead out of the cassette or cartridge far enough (no more than two perforation holes of the trimmed film edge should be visible) for the cassette and take-up spool to slip readily into their respective chambers in the Leica. How to trim the film lead is shown on p.311. Length and shape of the lead are important; faulty trims should be corrected. If the cassette cannot be pushed in completely, turn the rewind knob slightly. Ascertain that the sprockets of the transport drum engage in the perforations of the film.

Replace the baseplate, wind the shutter, and gently turn the rewind knob back in the direction of the arrow, until you feel a slight resistance.

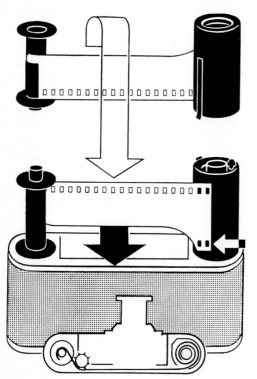

Hold the rewind knob in position without applying force. Release and wind the shutter. The winding action should be accompanied by an appropriate rotation of the rewind knob against the direction of the arrow.

Turn the film counter disc to the left to 0 by its little projection, release the shutter once more and wind it for the first exposure. The test for correct film transport is important and should always be carried out. If the rewind knob does not turn, the film is not transported, it must be rewound, and once more inserted according to the instructions. (Rewinding see "Unloading".) Before reinserting the film, check the length of the lead, and that the lead is undamaged.

294

Unloading

Once the whole film has been exposed the winding knob cannot be turned further (do not use force, or the film will tear). The film must now be rewound into the cassette. First switch the reversing lever from A to R.

Make sure that the slow-speed dial is not set at T, because here the shutter may be open during rewinding which would fog the film. If your Leica number is below 360 000, release the shutter first or rewind it with the lens cap in position.

While the film is being rewound, the outer shaft of the release button rotates in the earlier models, and the release button itself in the c- and f-models (the black dot rotates once for every exposure). After a slight resistance has been overcome the film lead has been pulled from under the clamping spring. Do not wind on if you want to reinsert the film in the camera.

You may now remove the baseplate and pull out the cassette or cartridge. The film lead still protrudes and should not be wound back completely on partly exposed and on colour films. Mark all exposed films, and note any important details of special films on this film lead. Protect all films, exposed or unexposed, from prolonged exposure to light (leaving them lying about openly in daylight) by keeping them in their metal containers. Loading and unloading should not be done in direct sunlight, but the shadow of your own body is quite adequate for this procedure.

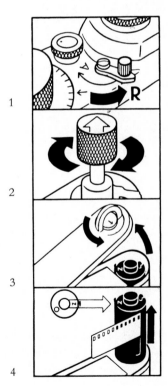

1

2

3

4

1. Move lever from A to R.

2. Pull up rewind knob, rotate it in the direction of the arrow.

3. Unlock and remove baseplate.

4. Take out cassette (at Z the cassette engages).
Store away from the light.

Flash synchronization

The synchronization built into the Leica causes the flash to be fired automatically at the right moment of the shutter action.

The high-speed dial with an adjustable contact disc below it differs in various Leica Models.

Please note:

Leicas with high-speed dial engraved 25-1
Contact numbers RED

Leicas above No. 360 000
High-speed dial engraved 30-1
Contact numbers BLACK

Leicas below No. 360 000
High-speed dial engraved 20-1
Contact numbers BLACK, or,
with black finish, WHITE.

Synchronization has been changed in the Model IIIg (further details see p. 298). For synchronized flash photography we use:

1. expendable flashbulbs (can be used only once);

2. electronic flash units; the flash tube yields many thousands of flashes.

Flashbulbs and electronic flash tubes differ widely in their flash duration and synchronization. You will find further details on flash and flash techniques in the chapter "Flash Photography" on p. 167.

The cable is secured in a contact bush next to the eyelenses of the viewfinder and rangefinder. In the Model If the bush is situated in the front of the Leica.

The contact plug is inserted so that the arrow engraved on it points at the viewfinder window, and turned to the right under slight pressure.

Flash setting values

You will find the adjustable contact disc below the dial for the high shutter speeds. The table below tells you what number to set.

	Leica If, IIf, IIIf		Leica from No. 360001		Leica up to No. 360000	
	time	red contact number	time	black contact number	time	contact number
⚡ electronic flash	$1/50$	20	$1/30$	2	$1/30$	0
	$T, 1 \rightarrow 1/25$	0	$T, 1 \rightarrow 1/20$	2	$T, 1 \rightarrow 1/20$	4
	B	2	B	6	B	6,5
💡 XM 1 PF 1	$1/15$	2	$1/15 - 1/20$	9	$1/20$	14
	$1/25$	5	$1/30$	16	$1/30$	13
	$1/50$	10				
💡 PF 5	$1/15$	2	$1/15 - 1/30$	16	$1/20 - 1/30$	14
	$1/25$	14	$1/40$	11	$1/40$	11
	$1/50$	11				
	$1/75$	5				
💡 AG 1, AG 3 flash cubes	$1/15$	2	$1/15 - 1/20$	8	$1/20$	10
	$1/25$	9	$1/30$	11	$1/30$	12
	$1/50$	8	$1/40$	8	$1/40$	8
	$1/75$	3	$1/60$	5	$1/60$	5
💡 GE 5 25	$1/15$	2	$1/15 - 1/30$	16	$1/20 - 1/30$	14
	$1/25$	14	$1/40$	11	$1/40$	11
	$1/50$	11	$1/60$	8	$1/60$	9
	$1/75$	6	$1/100$	5,5	$1/100$	7
	$1/100$	4	$1/200$	4		
	$1/200$	2				
	$1/500$	1				
💡 M 3	$1/15$	2	$1/15 - 1/20$	9	$1/20$	14
	$1/25$	7	$1/30$	15	$1/30$	13
	$1/50$	10	$1/40$	11	$1/40$	12
	$1/75$	6	$1/60$	8	$1/60$	10
💡 all	B, T		B, T		$T, 1 \rightarrow 1/8$	6
	$1 \rightarrow 1/10$	2	$1 \rightarrow 1/10$	6	B	9

LEICA Ig

The Leica Ig is a simple model without coupled rangefinder and without self-timer, but otherwise corresponds to the Leica IIIg (see below). The brilliant finder can be detached.

LEICA IIIg

Compared with the model IIIf some modifications have been introduced in this model.

Bright-line viewfinder with automatic parallax compensation

The subject is focused through the left of the twin windows. A magnifying eyepiece reproduces the object larger than it is seen with the naked eye.

The right-hand window is that of the bright-line viewfinder, whose bright, sharply outlined frame is reflected into the viewfinder image through a special window. It demarcates the field of the standard 50 mm focal length lens, and small arrows show the 90 mm lens field.

By an automatic transmission of the focusing movement to the bright frame the parallax (difference between the centre of the lens and that of the viewfinder) is compensated automatically. Important with close-ups!

New shutter speeds

The Leica IIIg has a setting dial (A) for the fast shutter speeds on the top of the camera, and a dial (B) for the slow speeds in the front. The speeds on dial (A) are: $^1/_{1000}$ - $^1/_{500}$ - $^1/_{250}$ - $^1/_{125}$ - $^1/_{60}$ - $^1/_{30}$ - B. In addition a red and a black flash symbol can be set. The dial (B) is engraved $^1/_{30}$ - $^1/_{15}$ - $^1/_8$ - $^1/_4$ - $^1/_2$ - 1 - T.

Simplified flash synchronization

All flashbulbs and electronic flash units can be synchronized. You will find the possible shutter speeds in the table opposite.

The provision of the red and black flash symbols for the synchronization of electronic flash units is new and noteworthy. The black symbol represents $^1/_{50}$ sec (fastest focal-plane shutter speed for electronic flash). The red symbol represents a $^1/_{30}$ sec shutter speed when the slow-speed dial (B) is also set at 30. If a slower speed is required, the dial (A) must remain at the red flash symbol, and only the slow-speed dial is set at the desired speed. For time exposures from a tripod the B setting of the high-speed dial (A) can be used for flashbulbs and for electronic flash.

298

Electronic flash	AG 1 AG 3 flash cubes M 2	XM 1 PF 1 PF 5	GE 5 25	M 3
B red ↯ ($= {}^1/_{30}$) ↯ ($= {}^1/_{50}$)	B red ↯ ($= {}^1/_{30}$)	B → ${}^1/_{60}$*	B → ${}^1/_{500}$*	B → ${}^1/_{125}$*
		* do not use red or black ↯ arrow setting		

For T, $1-{}^1/_{15}$ set high-speed dial at red ↯ (next to 30–1). These slow shutter speeds have a uniform setting.

  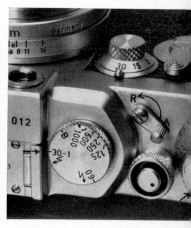

${}^1/_{125}$ sec for flashbulbs   *${}^1/_{50}$ sec for electronic flash*   *${}^1/_{30}$ sec for flash lamps*

VIEWFINDERS FOR THE LEICA

The built-in viewfinder for the Leica IIIf is matched with the 50mm focal length and can be used with all standard lenses. Its image is sharply outlined, bright, and reduced.

For exposures with lenses of other focal lengths the built-in viewfinder is unsuitable because its field is too small for shorter, and too large for longer focal lengths.

The universal viewfinder shown above can be adjusted for all focal lengths between 35 and 135mm. A screw-in attachment lens must be used with the 28mm wide-angle lens. The universal viewfinder, like all the other viewfinders described here, is inserted in the accessory shoe of the Leica. By rotation of a knurled lever it can be tilted to compensate for parallax. This screw has engraved settings from 1 m (3½ft) to ∞.

Parallax is the viewing error caused in every viewfinder by the slight displacement between the viewfinder axis and that of the lens. It is most noticeable in close-up views with long-focal-length lenses. Here, the image field will be slightly reduced. For distances below 2m (6ft 8 in) it is therefore necessary to adjust on the small division line of the rotating viewfinder ring. Once you have become accustomed to the universal viewfinder, you will want to use it even for exposures with standard lenses.

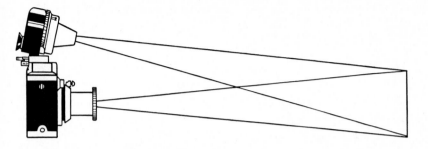

Sports- and press photographers must be able to observe what goes on outside the picture area when they look through their viewfinder. They find the frame finder which indicates the fields of view from 50 to 135 mm very useful. Parallax is compensated by means of raising the sighting frame. The frame finder can be folded flat, survives somewhat rough treatment and bad weather will not harm it. The other eye need not be closed when you look through this finder. The pinhole stop, which can be swung in, facilitates accurate sighting with 135 mm lenses.

In addition to these two universal viewfinders brilliant viewfinders are available for some focal lengths. They show the picture area outlined by a bright frame in the viewfinder field. These brilliant viewfinders, too, allow observation with both eyes. The versions for 85 mm, 90 mm, and 135 mm have adjustable parallax compensation.

Special viewfinders are available for the 200 mm and 400 mm Telyt lenses, to be used in combination with the Visoflex attachment (illustration on the right).

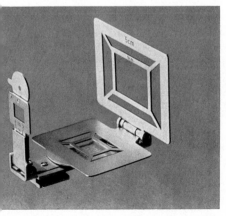

301

CLOSE-UP FOCUSING DEVICES

Special versions of the Visoflex I, the Visoflex II, and the quarto, octavo and post-card-size copying gauge were available for Leicas with screw thread. These accessories, of course, have a screw thread instead of a bayonet mount.

The new 1:1, 1:1.5, 1:2, 1:3 copying gauge can be used both with the M-models and with the screw-thread Leica (p. 192). This alternative use is possible because the bayonet adapter for the M-models is mounted on the top of the device; with the screw-thread Leicas it is locked in ring A.

The focusing slide for screw-thread Leicas

(a different version was supplied for the Models I g and III g)

The focusing slide is designed primarily for still objects in the close-up range, since it is necessary after focusing to replace the groundglass screen with the Leica body before the picture can be taken.

For a great number of subjects such as copying, object photography, advertising, botanical and zoological subjects, architectural details, medical specimens, and photomicrography exact focusing on the groundglass screen is desirable. The focusing slide is also eminently suited for work involving special difficulties such as the reduction of large-format negatives or X-ray pictures, as well as duplicating black-and-white or colour transparencies.

The focusing slide is simple to operate: The lens is unscrewed from the Leica and its mount locked in the focusing mount. A stop setting ring (VALOO) can be used to simplify setting the lens stop of the 50mm Elmar. The Leica body is clamped to the focusing slide. Picture sharpness and area are determined on the groundglass screen through a 5× magnifier. It is important first to focus the magnifier on the grain of the groundglass screen for your own eyesight. The focusing slide is moved to the right and the Leica body made to occupy the place of the groundglass screen; the film plane corresponds exactly to that of the groundglass screen. The Leica shutter is used for the exposure.

Use of the focusing slide

1. Focusing slide with magnifier and helical focusing mount in position. The Leica body is placed on the focusing slide with the lens changing ring and secured in position by means of the bracket.

2. The 50mm Elmar is locked in the focusing mount by means of the bayonet fitting.

3. The stop device, adjustable in two directions, makes it possible to align the Leica body parallel to the slide guide. The correct adjustment is carried out once and for all by means of tightening or loosening screw B. In order to attach the Leica body screw A is loosened, the body placed in position and screw A tightened, and the end of the stop device simultaneously depressed.

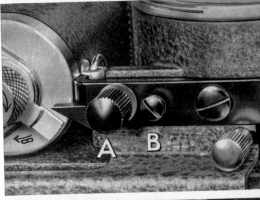

4. The stop, which has a knurled screw, is lifted for adjustment. When the stop is completely withdrawn (1) the slide can be pulled out of the guide grooves towards the left for cleaning; the intermediate position of the stop (2) limits the movement of the focusing slide towards the left during normal use; when the stop is pushed in completely (3) the focusing slide is arrested. A 90° rotation of the lever (4) also arrests the focusing slide.

303

Close-up device 1:1.5 – 1:2 – 1:3
(for all Leicas with screw thread)

These "spider's legs" make it simple to work with the camera hand held; they are practical for certain purposes, and easily carried about. If you have to change the reproduction scale frequently and like to check what you have focused on you will prefer the focusing slide and mirror housing for close-up work. But if a certain range occurs again and again, this method of fixed settings is superior to all others.

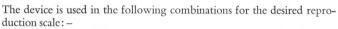

The device is used in the following combinations for the desired reproduction scale: –

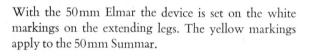

Ring designation	Leg marking	Clamping ring marking	Format	Exposure factor
M 1:1.5	lower	1.5	36×54 mm	2.8×
M 1:2	middle	2	48×72 mm	2.3×
			(appr. 2×3″)	
M 1:3	upper	3	72×108 mm	1.7×
			(appr. 3×4¹/₄″)	

With the 50 mm Elmar the device is set on the white markings on the extending legs. The yellow markings apply to the 50 mm Summar.

The appropriate extension tube is introduced between camera and lens. The four legs are screwed into the appropriate bushes in the attachable clamping ring and extended to the correct length. The tips of the legs are sighted over the edge of the camera baseplate for accurate alignment. A bush on earlier clamping rings marked V indicated the use of supplementary front lenses.

The exposure technique has been described in the chapter "Quarto, Octavo, Postcard size Copying Gauge". But the reduced size of the picture fields makes the extension factors already appreciable. The depth of field, too, is shallower, and the lens should be stopped down to f/11, if possible.

Optical near-focusing device

For Leica models with screw thread and coupled rangefinder (except Leica Model III g).

Available in three versions for

50 mm Elmar   NOOKY
50 mm Summitar   NOOKY-HESUM
(suitable also for 50 mm Summar and Hektor)
50 mm Summicron SOOKY
(focusing range from 1 m to 50 cm [40 to 20"])

It is possible with this near-focusing device to work with the camera handheld, as it is rangefinder-coupled. The focusing range is changed to 1 m to 44 cm (40 to $17^3/_4$") by a built-in glass wedge (distances measured from the film plane). During focusing a mask is adjusted in front of the viewfinder, compensating the parallax and allowing for the reduction of the image field. The engraved numbers 1:17.5 to 1:6.5 indicate the reproduction scale set opposite the index line.

The device is screwed into the Leica, the lens locked in it with its bayonet (the lens thread remains unused).

Close-up device 1:1

(for all screw thread Leicas)
for the 50 mm Elmar f/3.5 BELUN – for the 50 mm Summitar f/2 BELUN-HESUM

24×36 mm objects are reproduced on the film at natural size with the closeup device 1:1. The extension is obtained with an extension tube screwed between the Leica and the lens (which should be pulled out and locked in the ∞ position). The three-legged support with the baseplate which demarcates the picture area is attached to the lens and aligned parallel to the camera field of view. Since the depth of field is negligible, the lens should be stopped down to f/8 or f/11. Please note that the exposure time must be increased by a factor of 4.

Operation is very simple. The baseplate is placed on the object; in this position it also serves as tripod. With a flash unit, handheld exposures are possible provided the object is brought into the plane of the baseplate.

Visoflex II

The Visoflex II was supplied in two versions: screw-thread and bayonet. It has the same length as the Visoflex III, so that the same accessories are used.

Before you attach the Visoflex, press the arresting button and pull off the observation magnifier to the rear. Grip the shaft of the release lever, pull it out and turn it to the right. For attachment to the Leica red dot must face red dot; rotate the Visoflex to the right until it engages. If with a screw-thread Leica the Visoflex is not lined up parallel, unscrew the screws at the side of the screw thread; the Visoflex can now be lined up. Firmly tighten the screws.

Grip the shaft of the release lever, pull it out and swing it back. The distance to the camera release button should be about 1 mm; it can be changed with the adjustment screw. When the small chromium-plated lever is depressed the mirror will be wound up.

The prism magnifier has a focusing eyelens. The little black circle on the ground-glass screen must appear in sharp focus when the Visoflex is pointed at a bright area.

Visoflex I

(Special versions for screw-thread Leicas)

The larger size of the Visoflex I makes it most suitable for use on a tripod. Its substantial, bright groundglass screen image is unequalled in quality. Since its housing measures 63.5 mm (appr. $2^1/_2''$) in depth it can be focused on infinity only from focal lengths of 125 mm and upwards.

The mirror must be swung out of the beam path before the exposure can take place. For this a twin cable release is used. It employs two different cables to ensure that the correct sequence – removal of mirror followed by the shutter release – is maintained. With time exposures and slow instantaneous speeds the cable must remain pressed until the shutter action is complete, otherwise the mirror will return into, and block, the beam path prematurely with the result of underexposure. The button for swinging out the mirror has a knurled ring, which is slightly rotated to arrest the mirror in its swung-out position. This arrest is necessary if the sports finders for the 200 mm or the 400 mm Telyt are to be used. A special bracket for these viewfinders is mounted on the side of the Visoflex I.

The 5× magnifier (16,486) with vertical viewing can, if required, be interchanged with the 4× magnifier. This allows oblique viewing at an angle of 45°. The image is upright in both magnifiers. It is, however, side-reversed in the straight magnifier.

The Visoflex attachment is used with the groundglass screen on top. In order to change between upright and horizontal pictures the Leica is rotated around the lens axis. By means of a gear mechanism a picture mask below the groundglass screen is rotated through 90° at the same time. The mechanism locking the camera in the upright and horizontal positions can be released by means of pressing a button.

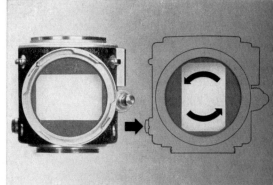

The 135mm lens can be unscrewed from its long mount for use in the short mount (14,071) or in the universal focusing bellows. When a short mount is ordered at a later date, the number of the lens should be stated.

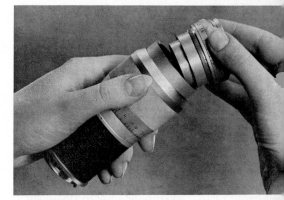

Special viewfinders for the 200mm and 400mm Telyts are pushed into a shoe on the side of the Visoflex (upright camera position). They are used for direct viewing after focusing on the groundglass screen. (The mirror must be locked during use.)

307

Assembling the equipment

The Leica is first attached to the Visoflex, and the resulting combination to the baseplate of the focusing bellows, with the front of the Visoflex I pressed against the rear plate of the focusing bellows.

The lens head of the 135 mm Elmar or Hektor is unscrewed from its range-finder focusing mount and screwed into the intermediate ring 16 580. This ring has a standard Leica thread at the other end, so that it fits the larger ring 16 590 which is screwed into the front plate of the focusing bellows.

The lens is focused with the knobs of the fine-adjustment mechanism. The reproduction scale set can be read off the left of the slide guide in white decimal figures. The extension factors for the exposure are indicated in red on the same scale. The reproduction scale for the 125 mm Hektor is engraved on the right of the slide guide. Of this lens also, only the head is screwed into the adapter ring 16 572. The following adapter rings are required for other lens combinations:

16 596	*16 598*	*16 585*	*16 572*
for lenses in	*for 90 mm*	*for 90 mm*	*for 125 mm*
bayonet	*Summicron*	*Elmar and*	*Hektor*
mount	*f/2*	*Elmarit*	*without*
			mount

Leica M 1

Its construction is the same as that of the Leica M2, but without the rangefinder and the field-of-view selector. The field-of-view frames for 35 and 50mm are faded into the viewfinder field. The brightline frames are always visible; their parallax compensation is automatic. With the Visoflex and Reprovit the use of the Leica M1 is unrestricted. The Leicameter, all lenses, and all accessories of the Leica-M system can be attached.

Leica MD

The construction of the Leica MD corresponds to that of the Leica M1, except that it is without the brightline viewfinder. This model can therefore be used only with push-on finders or combined with the Visoflex or the Reprovit. The Model MD has now been replaced by the Model MDa.

Leica MP

The Leica MP is a special model for press photographers which was briefly available before the M2 appeared on the market. The viewfinder corresponds to that of the Leica M3; but the film counter is not automatic; the film counting disc is the same as that of the Leica M2, and must be manually adjusted. This model was originally supplied with the Leicavit MP rapid winder.

Leicavit MP

The Leicavit is attached to the bottom of the Leica body in place of the base-plate. Before pressing the release button fully cock the winding lever, and allow it to spring back to its starting position. When re-cocking remove index finger from the release button. During the exposures the camera remains in front of the eye. When not in use the winding lever can be parked.

Leica M3 (up to No. 854000)

In the first version of this model the film transport lever had to be moved twice in two short strokes. The shutter speeds were engraved according to the old international scale of $^1/_5$, $^1/_{10}$, $^1/_{25}$, $^1/_{50}$, $^1/_{100}$ sec. The other speeds are the same as those of the current version.

THE ORIGINAL LEICA CASSETTE

The film manufacturers supply Leica films ready for use in daylight cartridges. Ready-cut and trimmed 35mm films are also available as daylight- and as darkroom refills; finally, large consumers can buy bulk quantities in tins containing up to 100 ft of film. These films must be loaded in suitable cassettes.

The original Leica cassette accepts 1.6 m (5 ft) of perforated 35mm film for 36 exposures. The new "N" version fits all Leica models, the "B" version only models up to III g. Both consist of an outer and an inner shell, and a cassette spool.

For loading, the cassette spring on the outer shell is lifted slightly, when it will be possible to rotate the inner shell. When the cassette mouth is fully open, the inner shell and cassette spool can be taken out of the outer shell. The spool is taken in the right hand (see illustration), the trimmed film end is pushed into the slot, and pulled slightly to make certain it has been gripped, it is then wound up, emulsion side in, by clockwise rotation of the spool (on old spools the film end is pushed under a clamping spring and doubled over).

Avoid touching the emulsion side of the film. Here, the hand-loader is very useful; it is pushed into the underside of the cassette spool and the film wound taut enough to avoid the risk of scratching by pulling it tight after winding. Finally the end of the film is curled outward in order to make it protrude more readily from the cassette mouth, and to get hold of it more easily.

The three parts of the cassette are reassembled as follows: insert the spool, knurled knob first, into the inner shell (the wound film must be held firmly) and push the outer over the inner shell; both slots must be in line. The end of the film will now curl out of the open slot. Pull it out an inch or two, and close the cassette by turning the projecting lug on the inner shell to the left until the cassette spring is engaged.

For the Leica M models the film need not be trimmed; this is, however, essential for screw-thread Leicas. The shape and length of the trim are also important for correct film insertion and trouble-free film transport. Further hints on the insertion of short lengths of film are given on p. 56.

The Leica N metal cassette is suitable for all Leica models; the earlier version B can be used for models up to III g only.

The distinctive features of the N cassette are:

1. Shorter outer shell.

2. Knob of the inner shell chromium-plated. (The cassette spool is identical in both versions.)

outer shell   inner shell   cassette spool

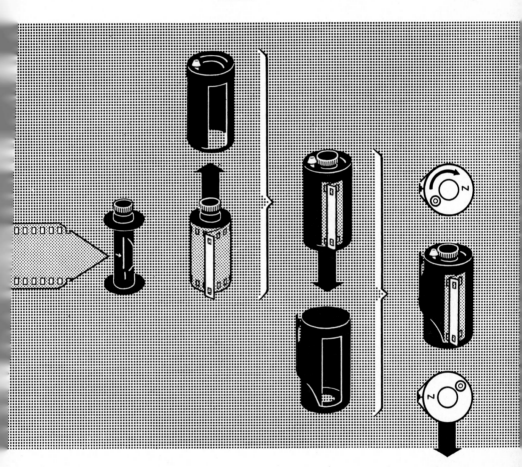

Insert the film in the darkroom or in complete darkness.

The line shows the correct trim. Do not cut any perforation holes. Use a pair of scissors for trimming. Total length 12 cm (4⁷/₈") trim and 2 perforation holes.

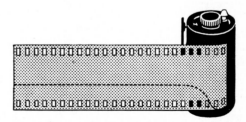

Technical data of the Leica lenses with screw thread (discontinued)

Lens	Speed f/	Focal length (mm)	Angle of field	Number of elements	Filter	Focusing range (mm) from ∞ to	Remarks
Super-Angulon	4	21	92°	9	E 39	0.40	
Hektor	6.3	28	76°	5	A 36	1	
Summaron	5.6	28	76°	6	A 36	1	
Elmar	3.5	35	64°	4	A 36	1	
Summaron	3.5	35	64°	6	A 36	1	from No. 1423141 filter E 39
Summicron	2	35	64°	8	E 39	0.7	
Elmar	3.5	50	45°	4	A 36	1	
Elmar	2.8	50	45°	4	E 39	1	
Hektor	2.5	50	45°	6	A 36	1	
Summar	2	50	45°	6	A 36	1	first version rigid tube
Summitar	2	50	45°	7	E 36,5	1	
Xenon	1.5	50	45°	7	E 41	1	
Summarit	1.5	50	45°	7	E 41	1	
Summicron	2	50	45°	7	E 39	1	
Hektor	1.9	73	34°	6	(39 × 55)	1.50	version with non-rotating focusing mount for Agfa lenticular screen film
Summarex	1.5	85	28°	7	E 58	1.50	
Elmar	4	90	27°	4	A 36	1	from No. 1573001 filter E 39
Thambar	2	90	27°	6	E 48	1	soft-focus lens with central stop
Summicron	2	90	27°	6	E 48	1	
Elmarit	2.8	90	27°	5	E 39	1	
Elmar	6.3	105	24°	4	(23 × 0,5)	2.60	
Hektor	2.5	125	20°	4	E 58	1.20	focusing via Visoflex
Elmar	4.5	135	18°	4	A 36	1.50	
Hektor	4.5	135	18°	4	A 36	1.50	from No. 1416001 filter E 39
Telyt	4.5	200	12°	5	E 48	3	focusing via Visoflex
Telyt	5	400	6°	5	E 85	8	focusing via Visoflex
Telyt	5	400	6°	4	E 85	8	focusing via Visoflex

If the helical focusing mount covers distances below 1 m (40 in), rangefinder coupling is no longer in operation.

Hints for flash tables

1. Flashbulbs can be used up to the indicated shutter speeds. With speeds higher than $^1/_{60}$ sec it must be borne in mind that the guide number given by the manufacturer becomes lower according to the shutter speed. You will find more detailed information by the manufacturers enclosed with the flash-bulbs.

2. *Electronic flash units* can be used up to the ⚡ setting (= $^1/_{50}$ sec) according to the table.

3. The manufacturer's *guide numbers* are no more than yardsticks. They are considerably lower in large rooms and outdoors where there are no reflecting walls.

4. *Colour film.* Blue-tinted flashbulbs or electronic flash are suitable for daylight emulsions as well as for colour negative film.

   Artificial-light colour film can be used with the daylight conversion filters.

LEICA		MD, MDa, M1, M2, M3, M4 from No.854001		M 3 up to No. 854000
Electronic flash	⚡	B→⚡(=$^1/_{50}$)	⚡	B→$^1/_{50}$
Flashbulbs AG1 AG3 Flash cubes M2	⚡	B→$^1/_{30}$	⚡	B→$^1/_{25}$
XM1 PF1 PF5	⍾	B→$^1/_{60}$	⍾	B→$^1/_{50}$
GE5 25	⍾	B→$^1/_{500}$	⍾	B→$^1/_{500}$
M3	⍾	B→$^1/_{125}$	⍾	B→$^1/_{100}$

⚡ = contact bush for electronic flash   ⍾ = contact bush for flashbulbs

Comparison of film speeds

In the table below the various speed rating systems are compared. The individual values correspond only approximately, as the various rating systems are based on different principles.

DIN	ASA		General Electric	Weston	American Scheiner	European Scheiner
	Arith-metic	Log-arithmic				
9	6	1	8	5	16	20
10	8		10	6	17	21
11	10	1.5	12	8	18	22
12	12	2	16	10	19	23
13	16		20	12	20	24
14	20	2.5	25	16	21	25
15	25	3	32	20	22	26
16	32		40	25	23	27
17	40	3.5	50	32	24	28
18	50	4	64	40	25	29
19	64		80	50	26	30
20	80	4.5	100	64	27	31
21	100	5	125	80	28	32
22	125		160	100	29	33
23	160	5.5	200	125	30	34
24	200	6	250	160	31	35
25	250		320	200	32	36
26	320	6.5	400	250	33	37
27	400	7	500	320	34	38
28	500		640	400	35	39
29	640	7.5	800	500	36	40
30	800	8	1000	640	37	41
31	1000		1250	800	38	42
32	1250	8.5	1600	1000	39	43

Reproduction scale
Object size and depth of field zone in close-up photography

With close-up subjects it is often useful to know the distance the subject must have from the Leica in order to utilize the film format.

The extension of the lens and the exposure factor resulting from it are also interesting data.

This information is usually supplied in the form of tables. But their calculation is quite simple; it is based on the reproduction scale, i.e. the ratio between the dimensions of the object and the 24×36 mm Leica format, which may be expressed in whole numbers, fractions, or decimals. A picture, size 96×144 mm reproduced on 24×36 mm is reduced to $^1/_4$ of its original size; the reproduction scale is $1:4$, and the decimal reduction is 0.25.

The distance between the film and the rear principal point of the lens is now $1\,f+^1/_4\,f$ (f = focal length, $^1/_4\,f$ = extension, which always corresponds to the value of the magnification or reduction) and the distance between the principal point and the original $1\,f+4\,f$ (4 is the reciprocal value of the reproduction scale), i.e. the total distance is $6^1/_4 f = 6.25f$.

If a 50 mm Elmar is used, the value of the focal length is inserted in the equation 6.25×5 cm $= 31.25$ cm ≈ 32 cm. The total distance between the film plane (camera back) and the photographic object is therefore approx. 32 cm (13″). The extension factor for the exposure time is calculated from the square of $(1+\text{extension value})$, in our case $(1+^1/_4)^2 = 1.25^2 = 1.56 \approx 1.6$.

With close-up subjects half of the depth-of-field zone extends in front, and half to the rear of the focused subject (with longer exposure distances the values are $^1/_3$ in front, $^2/_3$ in the rear). – For copying as well as for close-ups with direct magnification f/11 is preferred, since experience has shown that it produces the best results.

The table on the facing page is based on a $^1/_{30}$ mm circle of confusion. In the close-up range the depth of field depends on the reproduction scale, so that the table applies to all focal lengths.

Depth of field range at reproduction ratios from 1:20 to 6:1

Repro-duction ratio	Decimal	Object area	Depth of field at f/				Approximate exposure factor
			5,6	8	11	16	
		cm	mm	mm	mm	mm	
1/20	0.050	48.0 x 72.0	156.8	224.0	308.0	448.0	1.1
1/18	0.055	43.2 x 64.8	127.7	182.4	250.8	364.8	1.1
1/17	0.059	40.8 x 61.2	114.2	163.2	224.4	326.4	1.1
1/16	0.062	38.4 x 57.6	101.5	145.1	199.5	290.1	1.1
1/15	0.066	36.0 x 54.0	89.6	128.0	176.0	256.0	1.1
1/14	0.071	33.6 x 50.4	78.4	112.0	154.0	224.0	1.1
1/13	0.077	31.2 x 46.8	68.0	97.1	133.5	194.1	1.2
1/12	0.083	28.8 x 43.2	58.2	83.2	114.4	166.4	1.2
1/11	0.091	26.4 x 39.6	49.3	70.4	96.8	140.8	1.2
1/10	0.100	24.0 x 36.0	41.1	58.7	80.7	117.3	1.2
1/9	0.111	21.6 x 32.4	33.6	48.0	66.0	96.0	1.2
1/8	0.125	19.2 x 28.8	26.9	38.4	52.8	76.8	1.3
1/7	0.143	16.8 x 25.2	20.9	29.9	41.1	59.7	1.3
1/6	0.167	14.4 x 21.6	15.7	22.4	30.8	44.8	1.4
1/5	0.20	12.0 x 18.0	11.2	16.0	22.0	32.0	1.4
1/4	0.25	9.6 x 14.4	7.5	10.7	14,7	21.3	1.6
1/3	0.33	7.2 x 10.8	4.5	6.4	8.8	12.8	1.8
1/2	0.50	4.8 x 7.2	2.2	3.2	4.4	6.4	2.3
2/3	0.67	3.6 x 5.4	1.4	2.0	2.8	4.0	2.8
3/4	0.75	3.2 x 4.8	1.2	1.7	2.3	3.3	3.1
1	1.0	2.4 x 3.6	0.75	1.1	1.5	2.1	4
1.5:1	1.5	1.6 x 2.4	0.41	0.59	0.81	1.19	6.3
2:1	2.0	1.2 x 1.8	0.28	0.40	0.55	0.80	9
3:1	3.0	0.8 x 1.2	0.17	0.24	0.33	0.47	16
4:1	4.0	0.6 x 0.9	0.12	0.17	0.23	0.33	25
5:1	5.0	0.48 x 0.72	0.09	0.13	0.18	0.26	36
6:1	6.0	0.4 x 0.6	0.07	0.10	0.14	0.21	49

Depth of field and subject area for the near-focusing devices NOOKY, NOOKY-HESUM, SOOKY and SOOKY-M

Circle of confusion $1/30$ mm

Reproduction ratio	Depth of field in inches						Subject area in inches
	f/ 4	5.6	8	11	16	22	
1:17.5	3.44"	4.8"	6.88"	9.52"	13.76"	19.04"	16.8×25.2"
1:16	2.88"	4.08"	5.8"	8.0"	11.6"	16.0"	15.4×23"
1:14	2.24"	3.12"	4.48"	6.16"	8.96"	12.32"	13.4×20.2"
1:12	1.68"	2.32"	3.32"	4.56"	6.64"	9.12"	11.5×17.3"
1:10	1.16"	1.64"	2.36"	3.24"	4.68"	6.48"	9.6×14.4"
1:9	0.96"	1.36"	1.92"	2.64"	3.84"	5.28"	8.6×13"
1:8	0.76"	1.08"	1.52"	2.12"	3.08"	4.24"	7.7×11.5"
1:7.5	0.68"	0.96"	1.36"	1.88"	2.72"	3.76"	7.2×10.8"
1:7	0.6"	0.84"	1.2"	1.64"	2.4"	3.28"	6.7×10.1"
1:6.5	0.52"	0.72"	1.04"	1.44"	2.08"	2.88"	6.2×9.4"

Depth of field with the copying gauge for quarto, octavo, and postcard size based on a $1/30$ mm circle of confusion

Format	DIN A6	DIN A5	DIN A4
in inches	4.2×5.9"	5.9×8.4"	8.4×11.9"
approx. ratio	1:4	1:6	1:9
Exposure factor	1.6	1.4	1.25

f/stop	Depth of field		
4	0.25"	0.5"	0.9"
5.6	0.3"	0.6"	1.3"
8	0.5"	1.0"	1.8"
11	0.7"	1.3"	2.5"
16	1.0"	1.9"	3.7"

For copying originals under glass, the legs must be shortened by the thickness of the glass plate. On the other hand, they have to be extended if the objects (coins, crystals, etc.) to be photographed stand out in bold relief. Objects smaller than quarto, octavo, or postcard size can of course also be photographed, but the film format will then not be fully utilized.

Projection distances and screen dimensions

Projection distance in ft	Leica-Format 24 × 36 mm					
	focal length of the projection lens					
	9 cm	12 cm	15 cm	17.5 cm	20 cm	25 cm
10'	3'10"					
13'4"	5'2"	4'				
16'8"	6'8"	5'	4'			
20'	7'10"	6'	4'8"	4'4"		
23"	9'2"	7'	5'6"	4'10"		
27'	10'6"	7'10"	6'4"	5'6"	4'8"	
33'	13"	10'	8'	7'	5'10"	4'8"
40'		12'	9'6"	8'4"	7'	5'8"
47'		14'	11'2"	9'8"	8'4"	6'8"
54'			12'4"	11'10"	9'6"	7'6"
60'	A square screen is necessary for projecting both upright and horizontal pictures. Its dimensions are given in the table.		14'4"	12'6"	10'8"	8'6"
67'				14'	12'	9'6"
83'					15'	12'
100'						14'4"

The impact of projected images depends on size and viewing distance. Because the viewers in a large room sit at varying distances from the screen, the following points should be noted:

The height of the screen should be at least $1/5$ to $1/6$ the length of the room; for instance, it should not be less than 3m (10ft) square for a room 18m (60ft) long. The minimum viewing distance should not be less than $1^{1}/_{2} \times$ the height of the screen. The most favourable viewing distances are between 2 and 3 times the height of the screen. In home projection, these conditions are usually easy to meet.

INDEX

320

321

Standard Books on Photography

Kisselbach / Windisch

The Manual of Modern Photography

204 pp. with many four-colour and black-and-white pictures, drawings, and tables.

Besides being one of the world's most successful books on photography, it is the classical textbook on this fascinating subject. It offers all the important ingredients for successful picture making from the rule of thumb for the beginner to the most cunning trick for the advanced enthusiast.

Dr. Gareis / Scheerer

Creative Colour Photography

Exposure · Darkroom · Experiments · Presentation

202 pp. All pictures in colour; many drawings and tables.

A handbook of modern colour photography with remarkable pictures and instructive text and tables. Written in a "with it" style, easy to read, full of interest, to the point yet comprehensive, and completely up to date. A book that will give any budding colour photographer the essential stimulus for creative work.

Heering-Verlag · Munich